# SYSTEMATIC TRAINING FOR CIVIL SERVICES

# SYSTEMATIC TRAINING FOR CIVIL SERVICES

Dr. A.N. Chakravarty

GYAN PUBLISHING HOUSE
NEW DELHI-110 002

**SYSTEMATIC TRAINING FOR CIVIL SERVICES**

ISBN: 81-212-0710-X



Published in 2000 in India by
Gyan Publishing House
5, Ansari Road,
New Delhi-110 002
Phone : 3282060, 3261060
Fax : 3285914
E-mail: gyanbook@del2.vsnl.del.in

*Laser Typesetting at:* Power Photocomposers, New Delhi-110 002
*Printed at:* Mehra Offset Printers, Delhi-110 002.

# Contents

**PART - B**

**APPENDICES**

# Preface

Since Independence, the role of the government in the socio-economic development of the country has undergone a gradual change. The state is now playing an increasingly dynamic role in the management of human and material resources for promoting the well-being of the people. The basic tasks of development administration flow directly from the national goals and objectives, as enshrined in the Constitution. In a democratic set up, it is the prerogative of the people's representatives who constitute the government, to lay down the policy and it is the privilege of the administration to implement and execute such policies. The administration not only assists and advises the government in the formulation of the policy, but also executes it, translates it into action plan and achieves the predetermined goals and objectives.

Closely linked is the quality of administrative personnel—in terms of their technical competence, values attitudes and motivations. This calls for regular training of administrative personnel for self-development; to enable them not only to perform their jobs better, but also to competently handle greater responsibilities on promotion to higher positions, and new jobs and responsibilities to be created in future in response to organisational, functional or technical changes.

Being a practicing trainer in public administration for a considerable period, I picked up an Action Research on systematic training with the particular case of the Central Secretariat Service (CSS) for my doctorate thesis. The topic for the study originated as a sequel to my participation in the Design of Training Workshop under the tutorship of Mr Brian Sheardown of the Thames Valley University, UK. During the proceedings of the 'design workshop', the members deliberated in depth on various aspects of the systematic training, and divergent views were aired on adaptability and validity of various features of an effective design in the context of the Indian scenario in general, and its civil services in particular. With a view to get an acceptable answer to the basic question, can't we put into practice the principles that we accept and teach as trainers, with reference to design of systematic training model for an organised civil service—it was considered worthwhile to undertake an Action Research study on systematic training for the CSS officers. The study, attempted to analyse various steps and factors involved in the systematic training and development of the members of civil services with particular reference to CSS. It also included analysis and evaluation of the structure and organisation of a training institution with a view to identifying the factors which influence the functioning of such institutes as training institutions of public administration.

I would like to pay my tributes and express my profound gratitude to Prof. K D Trivedi, Professor, Department of Public Administation, University of Rajasthan, and my first supervisor for the research project, who passed away suddenly leaving us in distress. His astute guidance, precise and thoughtful ideas helped me complete my basic research work by February 1995, and the final thesis was submitted under the valuable supei vision of Dr. (Mrs) Kamala Trivedi, Associate Professor, Department of Public Administration, University of Rajasthan. I am also grateful to Mr. P S Bhatnagar, the then Head, Department of Public Administration, University of Rajasthan, for his encouragement and support at the final and crucial stage of the project. I am also deeply indebted to my senior colleague Dr. C Chandra Sekharan, Joint Director, Institute of Secretariat Training and Management (ISTM) for his constant guidance with his valuable professional expertise in writing the thesis. I am also grateful to Mr. A K Chaudhuri, Director, ISTM, for the organisational and personal support he extended to my work.

Thanks are due to the participants of the various foundational and refreshers courses for CSS officers conducted at ISTM, and those CSS officers in ministries/departments, who responded to my questionnaires. I gratefully acknowledge the library and reference services extended by Ms. M Bose, Chief Librarian, Ministry of Home Affairs Library, Mrs. Sachdeva, Librarian, Training Division Library,

Mrs. Bakshi, Assistant Librarian, Indian Institute of Public Administration (IIPA) Library, Mr. P K Roy and Ms. Jaya Ravindran, Archivists and Mr. Sabiuddin Khan, Assistant Archivist, National Archives of India, and Mr. A P Srivastava, Central Reference Library, University of Delhi.

Training has acquired an added relevance for building up the necessary leadership and confidence among civi servants to measure public expectation in the context of rapid technological changes, as also the economic and political transformation taking place in the country. National Training Policy has been formulated by the Government of India, spelling out the objectives, strategies, content and modalities to be followed in the field of training. It stresses the systematic approach to training (SAT) as an integrated effort, based on a cycle that starts with training needs analysis, on the basis of which training can be designed and delivered appropriately, and feeds in to monitoring and review/feedback to improve the training intervention.

Though the thesis was completed in 1996, in the present scenario, it is felt that the deliberations and findings of the study would have ample relevance to the implementation of the National Training Policy. Hence, the book, with its present title, based on the research study carried out by the author, is brought out with a view to sharing the experience with the training managers and training professionals. Though the study, an Action Research, was based on application of systematic approach to training on one specific case of CSS, the strategy, model and methodology would hold good in cases of the most civil services in India.

The book has been divided into two parts—A and B. Part A, the main body of the book is in six broad chapters with sub-chapters as described below, while Part B contains in the form of Appendices, the Service Rules extracts, Cadre Training Plan, training syllabi, data tables and questionnaires used. The first chapter entitled 'The Civil Services and Training', has started with (a) an overview of the role of civil services, followed by a, (b) theoretical framework of the various concepts of systematic training, (c) review of literatures and reports on the subject. In the sub-section (d) thereof, object and scope of the study have been defined followed by the questions studied. Chapter 2 described the chronological facts on the evolution of the civil services in India, and structure and organization of the CSS and the existing provision on training of the members of the service. Chapter 3 has covered the organization and functioning of institutes for civil services in general and for the CSS in particular viz. Institute of Secretariat Training and Management, including analyses of factors which influence the functioning of the institute. Chapter 4 titled 'Providing Training Opportunities' deals with the existing courses of training at ISTM and outside, the need and feasibility of systematic training model, role of organisation therein. Chapter 5 has been devoted on the action research on assessment of effectiveness or impact of training courses on the efficiency of the trainees and the organisation, and the conclusions have been summarized in Chapter 6.

I wish to convey my gratitude and thanks to Prof. O P Minocha, who approved my work and extended valuable suggestions, and Dr Jayatilak Guha Roy of Indian Institute of Public Administration for encouraging me and helping in publication of this book.

**—A.N. Chakravarty**

# PART—A

# 1

# Civil Services and Training—An Overview

## Role of Civil Servants in India

1.1 In many developing societies, there exists a gap between the fast changing politico-administrative environment and the traditional administrative behaviour. This gap obstructs realization of the goal of nation-building and modernization. The developing countries with structural differences are in the process of a social change, which is critical and disruptive. In these countries, political parties with different ideologies, orientation, strategy and origin agree on the need for social changes and modernization. In the post-Independent era of Indian administrative system, policy-making is done by the elected leaders of the people, and the role of civil servants is to implement the schemes for modernization and economic development. The activities of the state have increased manifold, and the involvement of the people have become essential. But the task of implementing the policies rests with the civil servants. To implement the programmes and policies of the political leadership effectively, the civil servants have to adjust themselves to the new regime, and prepare themselves to face the new challenges by mobilising whatever manpower and resources they have at their disposal. The dominance of the popular leadership in decision-making persists a change in the behaviour patterns of the bureaucrats and greater responsiveness on their part to the needs of the people. But it is easier said than done, for the bureaucracy in developing countries in general and India in particular, enjoy a monopoly of expertise and knowledge of rules and procedure, and the political executives have to depend on them.

1.2 The world is passing through far-reaching economic, social and political changes, and these changes are evident in India too. The Government of India has taken major economic policy decisions with a view to augmenting economic resources and national wealth, and major social changes are being made through legislation and executive orders. The task before the state is, therefore stupendous.

The nature of an administrative system depends upon the situation prevailing in the society. Since an administrative system is largely determined by its environment, the social value, culture, norms and customs of the country are its main determinants. For an administrative structure to be meaningful in India, it is necessary that the structure take cognizance of this diversity and be responsive to it.

The task of nation-building requires value-orientation of the administration. In India, the dominant traditional values are characterized by hierarchy, holism, continuity and transcendence. After Independence, the cultural penetration of the West has led to the contemporary crises in our cultural values. For administration to be meaningful, it has to be based on the age-old values of India rather than the Western values, which have crept into the Indian society.

1.3 The initial problem of developing administration is how to utilize the new initiative and loyalty to evolve new patterns of organization and action. The transformation and development of the Indian society involves political and administrative modernization linked with massive changes in the field of technology and economics. Unfortunately, there is a lot of administrative centralisation in India and confusion about the functions and responsibilities of different units. This results in duplication and overlapping of functions and wastage of time and energy. Quite often, the organization of administration for various functions is inadequate. Implementation of the programmes for social and economic development require the administrative personnel to be well-trained for tasks allotted to them.[1]

## The Problem

1.4 In a developing society and one which is aiming at change, professionalization of public services must be of a dynamic character, capable of absorbing new managerial concepts, new ways of doing things more effectively and a constant learning approach. As Fulton Report puts it "...as a body, civil servants today have to be equipped to tackle the political, scientific, social, economic and technical problems of our time. They have to be aware of the interests and opinions throughout the country and of developments abroad. In short, the civil service is no place for the amateur. It must involve men and women who are truly professional."[2]

1.5 The Institute of Secretarial Training and Management (ISTM) has played an important role in providing training in the areas of public administration to all level of civil servants, particularly to the officers of the Central Secretariat Service for the last four decades. However, with the growing awareness about the role and importance of effective training in public administration during the recent years, the efficacy of the system of training in most of the services including the officers of the Central Secretariat have been matters of discussion and debate.

1.6 Volumes of books have been written and series of training courses have been conducted on Systems and Systematic Approaches to Training and Development in the country. However, very little have been adopted by the training institutes in their own training programmes. As a result, there has been hardly any visible impact of these training courses on the performance and efficiency of the Secretariat. The ministries and government departments hardly give credence to the effect and utility of training, and therefore, the officers are not released for training courses in time nor is there any system of post-training follow up of the trained officers.

1.7 With the diversion of a sizable economic and human resources into this strategic area of national development, there should be a simultaneous endeavour to explore and study the various factors that affect the training and development of the civil servants, starting from the organization and structure of the respective service cadre, their roles and functions in the broader system of public administration, organization and structure of the training institutions, their contributions, the training policy of the organization, the identification of training needs, proper designing of training, intervention strategies, the supportive climate provided to the trainees in the organization, the subsequent impact of the course on the trainees in their efficiency, and its effect on the organization. Study of such aspects of the training system would help in proper understanding and appreciation of various underlying factors and specifications of the variables that affect outcomes.

1.8 In spite of the huge investments in 'training' as an activity of the public personnel administration, very little has been done to systematically studying and evaluating its impact and in trying to improve the functional efficiency of the organizations. Hardly any research has so far been done to show whether and to what extent the training institutes have succeeded in their task of preparing professionals for coping with their responsibilities so that it may yield beneficial results to the ministries/departments. It may perhaps be worthwhile to study the whole process in depth to find out whether the total training provisions for the civil servants, with particular reference to one Service viz., Central Secretariat Service, resulted in the acquisition of knowledge, skills and attitude and whether they in turn result in organizational improvement through changed behaviour.

## SYSTEMATIC TRAINING—A CONCEPTUAL FRAMEWORK

### What is Training?

1.9 Training can be defined as that process which attempts to fill the gap between what an employee has to offer by way of accumulated skill, experience and aptitude, and what is demanded by the job. It can be distinguished from education in that it is job related in purpose, while education is concerned with the broader development of the individual with no specific job related objective in mind. Its objective is to help employees acquire the knowledge, skill and capacity necessary to do their work well. Davies suggests that it is about bridging what he describes as "the ability gap between what knowledge, skill and attitudes the employee already possesses and those which he is required to learn in order to perform the job". The answer, he suggests, may lie with selection and training, or may involve a fundamental redesigning of the job.

1.10 The objectives are only likely to be achieved if a systematic approach to training is adopted. The advantages of such an approach are as follows:

1. Training will be more effective because it is based on analysis and evaluation of individual and organizational needs which are regularly kept up to date.
2. Employees will concentrate more on the results they are trying to achieve rather than simply on their immediate activities. Organizational structure of the department for introducing new ideas and methods will be more apparent.

1.11 Yet no trainer can hope to be truly effective without an appreciation of the basics of the learning theory. He must understand that in order to complete the process of teaching a task or skill, indeed of developing a required positive attitude, it is essential that the process of training involved should be based on the four concepts; motivation (or drive), stimulus, response and reinforcer.[3]

*Motivation* is essential for any behaviour to occur at all. We must appreciate the fact that *drives* play a significant role in training, in that they are what pushes the trainee to train.

*Stimulus* is the factor which brings out the desired response. It may be the tone of a machine's engine, the tightness in placing one component into the other, or something as subtle as tone of voice or facial expression.

*Response* is the behavioural result of the stimulation. The desired response is what the training is all about. It may be in slowing the engine or to modifying one's approach to another person.

*Reinforcer* has been described by Lewis as "...any object or event that serves to increase or maintain the strength of a response". Having produced the required response, the trainee may have that achievement reinforced, driven home by a friendly pat on the back, a word of encouragement, a reward of some kind, etc.

Awareness of the variations in the rate of learning is also fundamental to good training. Some tasks are so complex that learning may be a slow process until the trainee has acquired the basic principles, when the speed of learning may increase. Some jobs are simple that varies initial Acquisition of knowledge and skill may be pursued by a toning down in the rate of learning.

## Training System

1.12 To put training into perspective and to allow us to identify the constituent elements of the total training process, it is useful to adopt a systematic approach to training. This is sometimes referred to as 'instructional technology'.

Goldstein puts forward a simple model of an instructional system[4], in which he identifies the three main phases as the assessment, training and development and evaluation phases see fig.1.

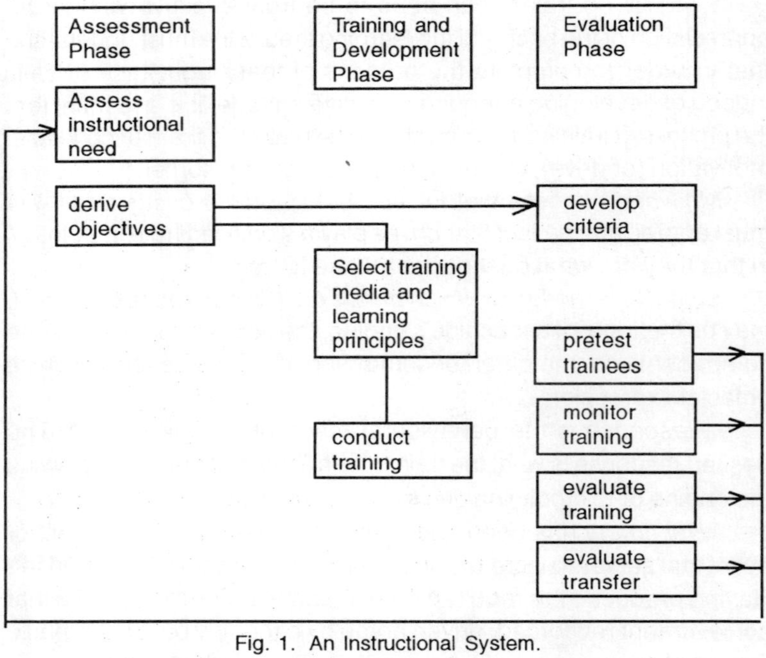


Fig. 1. An Instructional System.

1.13 The diagrammatic representation of a systematic approach is a working tool and as such it should be expected that trainers will draw up a model which is comfortable for them to use as individuals or as member of a training department who needs to monitor the progress of their training project. A close study of such models will show that they all contain the same activities even though they may be presented in different formats. Whatever be the format, all models are likely to have individual variations around four main activities Fig. 2.

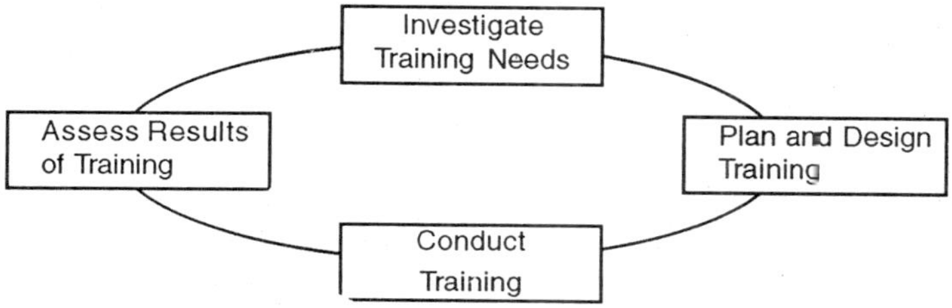


Fig. 2. Stages of Systematic Training.

## Identification of Training Need

1.14 When deciding whether or not to train, the first matter of importance is to define what constitutes a training need. Buckley and Caple[5] have suggested that a training need can be assumed to exist when the following two conditions are present:

*Condition 1* : Training, in some form, is the most effective mean of overcoming a current or an anticipated shortfall in performance, or all things being equal, training will result in current or future performance objectives being achieved more economically, thus allowing resources to be freed for alternative organizational objectives to be pursued.

The first part of *condition 1* implies that performance problems may be caused by one or several of a variety of factors other than the lack of ability of the job holder(s), and that training may not be a viable solution to such a problem. The second part of *condition 1* points to the role training can play in performance improvement and personal development. In some circumstances, the failure to address training needs associated with the second part of this condition may eventually lead to those needs emerging which were included in the first part.

*Condition 2 :* Present or future job objectives are clearly linked to the organization's objectives. This condition or pre-condition underlines the fact that if a job is redundant or is a 'non-job' in respect of current or future organizational requirements, then it is quite inappropriate to regard a performance deficiency on such a job as indicating a training need.

1.15 Apart from this present-future dichotomy another valid way of clarifying training needs is by the level at which the needs occur within the organization. A number of writers have suggested a tripartite classification:

*At the organizational level*—when general performance weaknesses have been observed or are anticipated in functions at or across divisional boundaries.

*At job or occupational level*—when distinct groups of employees have been identified as having a common need for training.

*At the individual level*—when performance weaknesses have been found in individual members in the organization. Training needs are to be identified by the concerned organization in consultation with training institutions. The organization level needs should be identified by considering discrepancies in the working of the organization as a whole which can be removed through training. At this stage, needs of training arising out of the change in organizational objectives, technology and environment as also emerging features in organizational work should be considered by the organization at the top level.

At the occupational level, needs of specific groups working at that level should be identified. This identification can be better done at the senior management level, supervising the occupational level considered for training.

The individual level needs for those having a specific discrepancy should be obtained by seeking information from individuals as also from their immediate supervisors.

## Objectives

1.16 The first task of any training modeller is to establish what the objectives are. One of the greatest mistakes still all too frequently made is to decide what we are going to put into our training programme before identifying the ultimate objective, the situation we want to end up with. Quite apart from the effects of objectives setting upon the production of a systematic and relevant training programme, it also makes it less difficult to sell training to sceptical senior management, where the latter can see at a glance what the end result of the training is expected to be.

## Training Classification

1.17 The success or otherwise of training depends to a large part upon the identification of the correct training needs. There will be a natural correlation between the training need and the type of training as well as the recipients and duration of the training. Most training may be described as fitting into one of the following categories:

(a) *Entry training*—to the organization or a new job;
(b) *Problem-resolution training*—rectification of personal knowledge or skill deficiencies;
(c) *Development training*—to prepare an individual for increased responsibility in an unspecified future role;
(d) *Change training*—to enable an individual to cope more effectively with anticipated technological or socio-organizational—organizational change.

## Training Methods

1.18 The choice of training method must be based upon what Mumford (1971) described as "...the analytical stages of defining needs and determining the programme..." and this should be followed by "...an equally stringent examination of possible methods". So to choose what method to use, we should first examine the particular nature of each training need and secondly, scrutinize internally available and affordable external training resources. The method to use will be the one which most cost effectively meets the need.

## Internal (organizational) training

1.19 Training within the organization generally has the advantage of immediacy and of opportunity for maximizing relevance, in that departmental facilities, services and personnel can be employed. This ought to lessen the problems of transferring the individual from the training environment to the full-time working situation. Training within the organization may be either *on* or *off* the job.

*On-the-job* training is unquestionably the most common form of training in use. Everyone who has ever been in employment would have undergone some form of on-the-job training. This may have been merely that period of time, whether long or short, when the newly appointed job holder has had to 'muddle along', attempting to avoid or to correct mistakes by seeking the advice of a more experienced colleague. On the other hand, it may have been a highly systematic period of planned job exposure, following well-defined steps, key points and other important features of the job being pointed out by an experienced co-worker, who has himself been trained in job instructional techniques. This approach may virtually eliminate transfer problems. One of the difficulties, however, is that because on-the-job trainers have also got their own normal job to do, they are potentially less effective than a full-time professional instructor.

*Off-the-job* training may occur either within the organization or at an outside centre. Most large organizations have their own training schools or centres, to which trainees can be sent to acquire relevant job knowledge and skills at the hands of professional instructors. Where an organization has large numbers of trainees following the same programme of training, they can afford to employ professional instructors in that area. The larger organizations sometimes have residential training centres staffed by full-time training staff. The latter may direct 'management development' type course but buy in specialists from outside. This pattern is normal with organizations like banks, large public sector undertakings, railways, income-tax department, police and so on. Smaller organizations cannot afford such luxuries, however, and will be forced to use external training sources.

**External (institutional) training**

1.20 The function of a trainer is to help establish an atmosphere conducive to the learning process (Donaldson and Scannel, 1978). An institutionalised training has the advantage of creating such a climate more easily. It can provide a degree of independence both from the distraction of the work situation and from the dangers of absorbing too many old-fashioned methods of working. In a developing country where public officers are frequently transferred, where experience in departments is often limited, with a consequent shortfall in expertise, and where even jobs are continually changing, it is difficult to organize systematic training on the job. It is far easier to organize and control training on an institutional basis. Attitudes of mind, standards of conduct, and approach to work are more easily impressed upon trainees on a uniform, service-wise basis at a national, state or district level institute than when training is left to each individual's supervisor in the work situation (Wyn Reilly, 1979).

1.21 Training programmes conducted at the institutional level can be broadly divided into two categories, i.e., *induction* and *in-service* training programmes. *Induction* training programmes are meant for newly recruited persons for equipping them with conceptual, technical and human relations skills so as to prepare them for their future jobs. On the other hand, the main objective of *in-service* training is to replace old unproductive habits by productive ones.

## Assessing effectiveness of training

1.22 Assessment of impact of training must be distinguished from the assessment of trainer. Many organizations, when seeking to measure the effectiveness of a training course will apply measures of the trainer's personality, delivery, use of humour, audio-visual aids etc. If we are to assess the effectiveness of training itself, then we must make sure that we do not confuse the process with the person administering that process.

## What is 'evaluation' in training?

1.23 Hamblin (1974) says that it is an attempt to obtain information on the effects of training programmes and to assess the value of training in the light of that information[6]. The Department of Employment's Glossary of Training Terms (1971), however, establishes a useful distinction between evaluation and validation in stating that evaluation is "...the assessment of a total value of training system, training course or programme, in social as well as in financial terms. Evaluation differs from validation in that it attempts to measure the overall cash benefit of the course or programme, and not just the achievement of its laid down objectives". In other words, when most people talk of evaluation what they are really referring to is the degree to which the training undertaken has successfully achieved its objectives, or more properly, validation. The term validation is a process carried out to see that the training given has been successful in achieving its aim. What we may assume is that the total process of evaluation includes the validation of training. Assessment has been used here as a common or general term to measure both effectiveness as well as effeciency of training.

**How do we validate our training?**

1.24 Hamblin (1974) puts forward a four-level approach.[7]

(a) *Reactions level*: This is defined in terms of the processes of collecting and using information about trainees' expressed reaction in order to improve training. It usually takes the form of an assessment sheet which is completed by the trainee immediately on completing the training programme, or sometimes a definable section of it. In it, he judges, through reporting on or just rating, various aspects of the training he has just undergone. It is inevitably very subjective, but has the advantage of going directly to the subject himself and letting him know that his views are of importance to those responsible for the investment in his training.

(b) *Immediate outcome level :* Here, the terminal behaviour of the trainee is measured objectively so that quantified results can be obtained. These are then compared to the trainee's behaviour at the commencement of the programme to judge exactly what change has occurred as a direct result of the training. This measurement is made before the trainee returns to the actual job situation so as to reduce the chances of any contamination of the results of the measurement by job-related factors.

(c) *Intermediate outcome level :* This occurs some time after the trainee's return to the job situation as a result of systematic appraisal of on-the-job performance.

(d) *Ultimate outcome level :* This is an attempt to measure the effects of the changed job behaviour upon the organization itself. Such changes might be assessed in terms of impact on cost, improved productivity, reduced arrears, better motivated subordinates, and so on. As may be imagined, this level of evaluation is highly desirable but is generally regarded as extremely difficult in practise because of the near impossibility of isolating the training effect from all other factors.

## Review of Literature

1.25 The history of training in the public service goes back not more than half a century from now. While many of the economically advanced countries now have broad programmes of training in their civil services, there is usually some segment of the public service particularly local government services in which little training is offered. "[Thus, training in the public service presents many problems which are common to practically all countries, irrespective of their stage of economic development][8].

1.26 According to Shri P.R. Dubhasi[9], "it is a truth universally acknowledged that no organization can do more than what the persons working in the organizations are capable of accomplishing and the level of accomplishment depends, among other things, on the training imparted to the personnel. At a comparative underdeveloped stage of public administration, the importance of training is not adequately recognised but as the responsibilities of public administration expand and diversify and the jobs to be performed become more complex and complicated, the need for intensive and systematic training becomes more and more relevant and important. It is only through such a systematic programme of training that necessary professional knowledge is imparted, skills developed and attitudes attuned to work situations".

1.27 During the last fifteen years, two important issue based training conferences were conducted by the Government of India, Department of Personnel and Administrative Reforms, the one on the theme—*Issues in-service training* "in May 1981[10] and the other on *Training in Government - Objectives, Challenges and Opportunities*" in 1984[11]. The recommendations of the Working Groups *inter alia* included the following:

"A training policy should be evolved indicating the need for training, training for whom, and priorities in training, etc. A strategy for in-service training should be adopted. It should be a realistic strategy which could be trained into action.

"With a view to making training worthwhile and effective, the departmental authorities should adopt an aptitude of positive concern for training of personnel in their respective organizations. The existing training opportunities should be properly utilized. The top brass of an organization should also be trained in suitably designed programmes for creating an awareness and faith in training.

"Training needs should be identified before planning for in-service training programmes. There is an urgent need for undertaking a survey of the training needs both in the states and the centre. The training institutions/organizations must take a lead in consulting the departments in identifying their training needs. There should be a greater effort to identify the training needs of various groups of government employees. For identifying the training needs it would be essential to consult the client departments who alone are in the best position to advise on the existing job requirements and future career prospects of their employees. The individual training needs and the group training needs are distinct and have to be separately identified.

"Identification of the function-oriented needs of the user departments should determine the basic training input requirement for the core cadre to discharge their duties in the initial years of service. This should also determine the course content and design of the induction training. The professional in-service programmes should cover management subjects as one of their key inputs.

"With a view to meeting the training needs of a very large number of employees, the training institutions should undertake the preparation of training materials/manuals which should be distributed to various employees who could with the help of that material train themselves. The training institute's research programme should focus on identification of training needs, development of training materials and evaluation, etc.

" Training should be planned for equipping an official to do his present assignment better as well as be able to develop his potential for taking greater responsibility and higher jobs. After induction training, an employee should be provided opportunities of at least two in-service training programmes during his service.

"The training in government should continue to remain job oriented and within this framework, attempts must be made to explore the possibilities of visualising and implementing innovations with programme design, aimed to develop conceptual, technical and attitudinal skills.

"On account of rapid changes in the field of technology, organization of work and systems in the public administration, there is need to give opportunities to public officials, so that they may be exposed to new ideas, have an opportunity to refresh themselves and become aware of the new challenges facing them. Such an exposure may be given at least three to four times during their service career.

"The target group of training is often at present There is need for greater homogeneity in the target group. With proper identification of training needs and organization of training programmes on the basis of occupational level and organizational level training requirements, it would be possible to get greater homogeneity. Often one experiences reluctance on the part of the trainees to attend a course partly due to their lack of participation and partly due to the organization not realizing the importance of training. Since low nomination in training programmes results in wastage of scarce training resources, efforts should be made to bring in some degree of compulsion on the part of organization to ensure that those nominated for training courses necessarily attend training programmes. Simultaneously, it would be necessary for the training institutes to make training programmes more attractive by making training more compact, participative and by making training more relevant to job needs of the target group.

" While induction training programmes should focus on giving information built skills and drilling new entrants into the government work and processes, in-service training programmes should aim at developing conceptual skills, participative culture and proper attitudes in behavioral skills. If courses are properly designed and needs are properly identified, the training institute would also be able to function as a generator of ideas for system improvements."

1.28 The proceedings of the conference and the reports of the Working Groups were published by IIPA and are being stacked in the libraries of most of the Central and state training institutes. Since then there has not been many such Annual Conferences organized by the Training Division. In July 1993, a Working Group was, however, set up on National Training Policy to recommend a document on training policy, apart from identifying the objectives which training should meet in the context of the economic liberalisation under way. It is not known whether the Working Group have taken into consideration the outcome of the earlier conferences attended by a band of eminent training experts. However, the government will no doubt elicit their views on the subject before finalising the policy.

1.29 The UN Handbook of Training in the Public Service published in 1966 by the Department of Economic and Social Affairs (Public Administration Branch) present a review of experience under widely differing conditions and much advice, which can be useful to policy forming officers, heads of agencies and highest administrators. The principal kinds of training institutions, their missions and functions, their internal organization and operational problems are all discussed and explained in this publication, and are found to be relevant to the public service training in this country as on date. Therefore, the guidelines and models provided therein can be heavily relied upon for the purpose of critical study of the training systems in a particular clan or category of civil services in India. In the Preface it is stated, " all phases of public administration have an intensely national application. Administrative organization and practises can be said to be successful only in the national setting in which they are found. In no phase of public administration is this often-repeated observation more true than in training. Training in the public service must somehow fit into the national culture, and it must be full of practical applications to the work situation prevailing in the country where the training is being offered."

1.30 A useful research study had, however, been conducted by Prof B.R. Virmani of ASCI (1985) on evaluation of management training and development in the country.[12] It focuses on the methods of determining both the efficiency and effectiveness of such programmes. The researcher emphasised on the fact that any learning from training must also contribute to the transfer of learning on the job. The approach to evaluation of management training and development has to be based on action research where the researcher themselves can play a leading role improving the training and development process and contribute to implementation of learning to the job. In their book "Evaluating Management Training and Development," the authors Prof Virmani and Ms Promilla Seth offer a great deal of guidance about the various factors which determine the effectiveness of training, the procedure for selecting trainer, clear goal setting in relation to results sought, post-training follow-up, etc. and developed an evaluation model which in general with necessary changes could be adopted in all levels of institutional training. Attempts have no doubt been made in the past to study the impact of training imparted by various training institutions but none of the studies in India so far conducted has been done on the basis of the integrated approach to total training system and its effect with reference to a specific organized service of the Indian civil services.

## Aims and Objectives of the Study

1.31 The research study was aimed at studying the various steps and factors involved in the systematic training and development of the members at different levels of an organised civil services with particular reference to the Central Secretariat Service.

ISTM is primarily responsible for imparting foundational and in-service training to the officers of the levels of Assistant, Section Officer and Under Secretary of Central Secretariat Service. The aims of the study also included analysis and evaluation of the structure and organization of ISTM with a view to identifying the factors which influenced the functioning of ISTM as a training institute of public administration.

In the context of systematic approach to training, even when they are conducted at the institute, the client organizations play important roles in identifying the training needs, transfer of learning to their jobs and post-training evaluation of training imparted by ISTM with reference to the functional need of the officers of CSS. Therefore, the study also aimed to investigate and understand the policies and practises of selecting/nominating trainers, follow-up of trained officers and other training activities practised in the Ministries/ Departments.

1.32 In order to achieve the broad aims discussed above, the main objective set out for the study was to explore the facts, analyse them and suggest corrective measures in a given situation, in the context of the following:

(1) The training policy, strategies and opportunities provided at all levels of the Central Secretariat Service.

(2) The role of client organization in management of systematic training.

(3) The need, content and methods of foundational and in-service training programmes.

(4) The objective, function, structure and organization of ISTM and their impact on training courses conducted by it.

(5) The impact of the foundational and in-service training for Assistants, Section Officers and Under Secretaries on the functional efficiency of the officers.

(6) The factors—individual, psychological and organizational influencing the learning derived through training.

**Hypotheses and Major Questions Studied**

1.33 The training and development of the officers of the Central Secretariat Service ever-since its creation and subsequent re-organization, have been regulated by general executive instructions issued from time to time by the CS Division of the Department of Personnel and Training. In 1988 and 1989, the Department issued a comprehensive Cadre Training Plan for the officers of the CSS upto the level of Deputy Secretary. As per the Cadre Training Plan all directly recruited Section Officers and Assistants are required to complete their foundational training course at ISTM within a period of one year of their appointment.

However, on a preliminary survey it was observed that while a large number of Assistants remained untrained long after their appointment, the courses at ISTM remained underutilized. In view of this, the major questions to be studied are:

1. Has the organization and structure of the Central Secretariat Service made adequate provisions for the training and

development of its officers as part of the cadre management of the Service?

2. Are the cadre Ministries/Department conscious about the need of systematic training to its officers and their (Ministries') role in providing opportunities for adequate and timely training to these officers?
3. Is there any declared policy on training for the civil servants in general and CSS officers in particular?
4. Is the Cadre Training Plan need-based-has any survey of training need been conducted and beneficiary Ministries consulted in the matter?
5. What are the practises in Ministries in the matter of selection and nomination of officers to various training courses, and commitment of the organisations?

ISTM has been conducting the foundational and in-service training courses for the Assistants, Section Officers and Under Secretaries of CSS for the last four decades. Besides, over all these years, the institute has grown into an eminent training resource centre for training of trainer and conducting training courses in Design of Training and Direct Trainers' Skills. However, the courses designed and conducted by the ISTM is not causing the necessary impact on the efficiency of the officers of the Secretariat, thus the credibility of these training before the client organization is lost. The questions may be studied:

6. What are the problems relating to the organization and functioning of ISTM in achieving its objectives as an institute of public administration, and the factors influencing its growth and development?
7. What role has ISTM played in providing necessary training opportunities to the members of the CSS for the last four decades?
8. Is there any systematic identification of training needs of officers of CSS before designing the courses by ISTM? There is little interaction and coordination between the Ministry and the training institute in the matter.
9. Does the training methodology deployed take note of training requirements of the target group and appropriate learning

techniques for the instructions imparted? Another major question need to be studied is the design including content and methods for various training courses for the CSS officers.

10. In the assessment of effectiveness of training, is there any linkage between the institute and organization to conduct post-training follow up.

## Research Methodology

1.34 According to Lynton and Pareek[13], "By research, we mean, in the first place, a wish for improvement followed by action... Improvement comes out of concerted effort to face squarely the questions needing to be answered, to search systematically for answers to such questions, to test the answers rigorously, and to accept the tested solutions for action that was the best now available, and as a basis for further search, if necessary. This approach requires a new kind of discipline on the part of the trainer, one to use side by side with his intuition guided by experience. It is the discipline of action research, research to improve action."

1.35 The research project aimed to—

(1) discover and establish facts regarding provisions and practises in regard to training in CSS, and its effect on the efficiency and performance of the officers in the job;
(2) analyze their sequential relationship and explanation which were derived within an appropriate theoretical frame of reference; and
(3) develop new models of effective training.

Thus, the present study is partly descriptive and partly exploratory in nature and instrumental in perspective. This has required a series of research techniques in order to find facts and suggest remedial measures for increasing effectiveness and efficacy of the present system on the basis of observations and opinions. As regards (1) and (2) the Survey Research Technique has been used. Since the study seeks to use the data generated through (1) and (2), for improving future training programmes, the study to that extent has also adopted the Action Research Approach, which would involve (i) closer collaboration with the trainees and sponsoring organization in order to ascertain what the trainers are trying to offer through a training programme and what the trainees and the sponsoring organizations are trying to achieve, (ii) formulation of some measures in the form of tests and questionnaires to assess the degree of achievement of intended objectives, (iii) Use of tools other than tests and questionnaires, such as interviews, observations, discussions and expert opinion, for the assessment of the degree of achievement of training objectives, and (iv) an intimate process of action feedback and change that has to emerge after the feedback. Action Research, according to Corey[14], is "the process by which practitioners attempt to study their problem scientifically in order to guide, correct and evaluate their decision and 'action'. Action Research as opposed to the scientific or logico-deductive approach has advantages which are ideally suited for evaluation studies. It identifies a problem, develops a solution and implements changes cooperatively with research client. The benefits of action research approach extends beyond the framework of training and evaluation. The direct influence of such research can be viewed not only as a general technique for improving training programme but research for evolving new methodologies for effective evaluation.

1.36 The information collected for the study can be divided into the following three categories:

(i) Theoretical concepts
(ii) Historical facts
(iii) Opinion surveys

The major source of historical and existing facts for the study were the Annual Reports of Ministry of Home Affairs, Secretariat Training School and ISTM, recorded files and other reports and proceedings of ARC, training conferences etc. The theoretical framework has been adopted from selected books, reports, monographs, articles, etc. For a survey of reactions, views and suggestions, a mix of questionnaire, interviews and observations have been adopted.

The questionnaires have been devised, besides as a means for collecting factual data, for conducting the survey of opinion on various aspects of the training process of the CSS officers. Except in the one to the training faculty of ISTM, which invited wide ranging replies to some open ended questions, all questionnaires have been designed so as to facilitate busy officers in formulating their thoughts and to relieve them from preparing lengthy written report, by offering a choice of short responses, to select the one which most closely accord with his opinion.

**Sample Size**

1.37 Where the number was limited to 30-40, such as the client organization i.e. cadre Ministries of CSS, and the faculty members of ISTM, the relevant questionnaires were sent to the entire population. In the case of survey of opinion on training need of individual officers of CSS, the questionnaire was circulated to about 10 per cent of the total working strength in each grade of Assistant(4615), Section Officer (2225), and Under Secretary (665) spread over all cadre units as evenly as possible.

For the purpose of pre-training and post-training feedback, questionnaires were operated on two batches of participants of each category of courses conducted by ISTM during the year 1993-94 and 1994-95. Besides these, the information collected through Immediate Reaction Questionnaire used by various course coordinators of the above courses have also been used for the study.

**National Training Policy**

1.38 A conscious policy for the development of the human resources available to the Government of India had been sought to be evolved for meeting the challenges of development—social, economical and political. In this context, the Government constituted a Working Group to formulate a National Training Policy which, apart from identifying the objectives which training should meet, would help in balancing knowledge and skills with attitudinal changes wherever required. Based on the report of the Working Group, the Government, in 1996, issued detailed guidelines on various aspects of a comprehensive strategy for implementing the National Training Policy[15]. The National Training Policy : Operational Guidelines is available at Appendix 1.1.

1.39 Though the present study was completed well before declaration of the said National Training Policy most of the strategies contemplated in the national policy are in line with the model suggested in this book. The new concept of 'Training Manager' has already been visualised by the author in his report. The policy of setting apart a percentage of its salary budget to be used solely for the purpose of training will go a long way in drawing participation of the organizations in the development of its employees, which has hitherto been confined to the training institutions.

So far, the approach to training has been mainly *supply-driven,* that is, training institutions run training courses and invited trainees. The National Training Policy contemplates a shift to *demand-led* training opportunities, which enables the departments to focus on their organizational needs match the training objectives, and ensure the training design would deliver the required output and in turn a reasonable return on the investment made in training. Departments can demand that training designed on the basis of needs-analysis, and demonstrable results of improved performance be achieved.

1.40 As the policy lays down, training for all levels should aim at continuous attitudinal reorientation in changing organizational ambience so as to help the civil servants appreciate the imperatives of a democratic society, namely, respect and concern for the citizen's right and recognition of the community as focal point of all public efforts.

## References

1. Rajput, R.S., *Nature of Administration—Role in Political and Development Process. Indian Government and Politics,* Ed. Sunder Rama, Allied Publishers.
2. *The Fulton Report—The Civil Service*, London, Her Majesty's Stationary Office (1958), p.10.
3. Leek, Chris—*Manpower Strategy and Techniques in an Organisation Context.*
4. Goldstein, I.L.—*Training Programme Development and Evaluation,* Cole Publishing, California (1974).
5. Buckley, Roger and Caple, Jim—*The Theory and Practice of Training,* Kogan Page (1992), pp. 29, 40-42.
6. Hamblin, A.C.—*Evaluation and Control of Training*, Mc Graw Hill, London (1974).
7. *Ibid.*
8. *United Nations Handbook of Training in the Public Service,* New York (1966), Preface (pp. vi-vii).
9. Dubhashi, P.R.—*Strengthening of Training Facilities*, in Mathur, Hari Mohan (ed) *Issues in In-service Training* ( IPA), p. 28.

10. Mathur, Hari Mohan (Ed.)—*Issues in In-service Training*, IIPA, 1982.
11. Saxena, A.P. (ed.)—*Training in Government: Objectives and Opportunities*, IIPA, 1985.
12. Virmani, B.R., Seth,P.—*Evaluating Management Training and Development*, Vision Books (1985).
13. Lynton, R.P., Pareek Udai—*Training for Development*, B. Taraporevala Sons & Co. 1973.
14. Corey S.M., *Action Research to Improve School Practice*, Bureau of Publication, Teacher College, Columbia University, New York, 1953, p.161.
15. Department of Personnel and Training, Training Division, *National Training Policy*, 1996.

# 2

# The Service—Its Organisation, Structure and Management

## Evolution of Civil Service in India

2.1 The service structure which developed during British rule in India primarily fed the various functional departments, especially the higher administrative positions, and came to form the basis of its personnel system. A service, denoted in the Indian context, was a group of civil servants with common recruitment conditions, prospects and careers. It was recruited on merit to hold a group of positions requiring similar skills, which might be technical, professional or administrative. Within a service itself, there might be more than one grade arranged vertically according to the level of responsibility and horizontally according to the type of skills/ specialisation required. This concept presupposed that, within a service, position at the same level were analogous and that any of its members in a particular grade or position could be posted to it. While constituting a service, care was taken not only to examine its positions or grades with reference to the skills required but also to determine whether these were equivalent and inter-changeable in terms of qualifications and pay scales.

2.2 The classification of the services into the four classes and their equivalents had been done on the basis of status and the corresponding privileges attached to them. Until the Islington Commission (1912-15), public servants used to be classified into superior, subordinate and inferior services. The Islington Commission introduced two new services or two classes of one service placed in between the subordinate service and the top Imperial Service.[1]

These were called Class I and Class II, assigned to a body of work which was not sufficiently important to be given to the Imperial Services recruited in England, but yet of a nature which could not be entrusted to the subordinate staff. The nomenclature Class I and Class II came into use in 1926. The terms Class III and Class IV as substitute for subordinate and inferior services respectively were introduced by the First Central Pay Commission known as Vardachari Commission (1946-47). In order to promote the classless culture initiated in Smt Gandhi's era, on the recommendation of the Third Pay Commission the Class was renamed as 'Group' and Roman I to IV were converted into English alphabets A,B,C and D. The distinctions, however, continued. The Services continued to be classified (in Groups) on the basis of status according to service-wise classification; by categorization into four classes, by division into gazetted and non-gazetted categories and in accordance with pay scale.

## The Secretariat Service

2.3 A Ministry was identified with the charge of a Minister, while the Department was the charge of a Secretary. The main advice agency and the channel through which the Minister must operate is the Secretariat. This is organized pyramidally, one result of that being the concept of a Chief Adviser in the person of the Secretary of the Ministry. The Chief Adviser, his immediate Lieutenants and their Assistants are all usually generalists, who are supposed to have a broad appreciation of administration and of national problems, but not necessarily any specialised or technical knowledge. The Secretariat has an apex position and is the repository of all powers. Non-Secretariat Organizations are arranged pyramidally below the Secretariat. Thus, the Ministry functions with the aid and assistance of the Secretariat. The effective decision-making level below the Minister and the Secretary is that of the subject Joint Secretaries. The Joint Secretary's responsibility is mainly in the sphere of policy making and also in scrutinising proposals made by the head of the Non-Secretariat Organisation. The whole system is thus very much secretariat-centered. The concept of a Secretariat-centered machinery was devised under British rule, but has undergone considerable development since then. An important feature of the Secretariat then was that it was small, but that is not now.[2] In addition to its supportive staff, the Secretariat consisted of 'consideration' levels and policy formulation levels. The 'consideration' level comprised of Under Secretaries and Deputy Secretaries, while the policy formulation levels included officers of the ranks of Joint Secretary and Additional Secretary.[3] At the supportive level, the office comprised of a team of Assistants under the direct supervision of a Section Officer. This category of staff actually provided the continuity and thus consistency in the decision-making process of consideration and policy formulation levels by collection and submission of rules, procedures and precedents. The former Imperial Secretariat Service in the Government of India had been designed merely to man these positions of the Central Secretariat.[4] Decision-making levels in the Secretariat then were almost wholly manned by officers of the Indian Civil Services, who belonged to the various provincial cadres and came to the Centre on limited tenures.

2.4 Today the decision-making levels are staffed principally by the Indian Administrative Service, but there are substantial contributions from the CSS and from other central services, particularly at lower levels. This is clear from the following Table 1.1.

**TABLE 1.1**
**Distribution of Officers at the Centre as on 1.12.99**

| | *IAS* | *CSS* | *Others* |
|---|---|---|---|
| Secretaries | 97 | 0 | 59 |
| Additional Secretaries | 63 | 4 | 34 |
| Joint Secretaries | 262 | 35 | 146 |
| Directors | 172 | 89 | 251 |
| Deputy Secretaries | 119 | 114 | 189 |
| Under Secretaries | 11 | 537 | 8 |
| Percentage of the Total (2197) | 32.95 | 35.46 | 31.59 |

At the senior level the CSS officers have provided the stability and continuity which was not available due to tenure rule for the All India Service officers. On the other hand, a large proportion of these (CSS) officers did not have field or executive experience necessary for policy formulation.

As the study team on 'Machinery of the Government of India

and its Procedure of Work' of the Administrative Reforms Commission (ARC) observed, "in the face of rapid expansion, the quality of Secretariat personnel has gone down. One of the requirements for the present system to work well would seem to be that the Secretariat should remain small and of high quality, for otherwise it is liable to do more harm than good."[5]

**The Central Secretariat Service**

2.5 The history and origin of the Secretariat Service goes back to the pre-war days of British imperialism. Before the outbreak of the War in 1939, the Central Secretariat upto the level of Assistant and Under Secretary was staffed by the Imperial Secretariat Service constituted in 1919. Direct recruitment used to be made at the level of Assistants through the competitive examinations held by the Federal Public Service Commission, the minimum qualification required being a university degree. The Assistants so appointed were eligible for promotion to the posts of Superintendents, which were regarded as selection posts. The next higher post was that of Assistant Secretary to be filled by selection from among the Superintendents. The post of Assistant Secretary was the highest post normally open to members of the Imperial Secretariat Service. The post of Under Secretary, on the other hand, was drawn generally from the Indian Civil Service cadre and considered to be a training post for its officers. The duties of Assistant Secretaries and Under Secretaries were not marked. Both categories of officers held charge of Secretariat branches and discharged more or less similar functions. But while Assistant Secretaries were generally entrusted with routine administrative work, that relating to matters of policy was handled by Under Secretaries.

**Reorganization and Reinforcement**

2.6 The necessity of reorganizing the erstwhile Imperial Secretariat Service arose, for the first time, in view of a gradual dilution of its quality resulting from its enormous expansion in the course of the War[6]. In pre-War days Assistants were persons who had achieved distinction in an all-India competitive examination, had to work for 12 to 15 years in that grade and prove his worth before he could look forward to promotion to the post of

Superintendent. Few Superintendents, on the other hand, could become Assistant Secretaries much before retirement. In the course of the War, however, the large expansion in the upper layers of the service led to rapid promotions from the lower levels. The clerical staff which had at the close of the War increased by nearly five times was 'made up of anyone who happened to be readily available to anyone of the numerous appointing authorities'. Promotion to higher posts from here meant that far too many inexperienced people came to hold posts for which they were not fitted. An incompetent Superintendent, for instance, could not guide and train his Assistants. The poor quality and inexperience of Assistants called for more men to do the same work, and this tendency to press for increasing staff applied also to the higher levels of the service, a tendency which led to the progressive deterioration of quality and efficiency.

Another important consequence of increase in the size of the Secretariat staff was the steady growth of temporary hands. Of the 2306 Assistants in 1948, for example, all except 95 were temporary, the others being promoted to higher grades comprising, even there, considerable numbers of temporaries. This caused a sense of insecurity and uncertainty which could not be resolved so long as the total cadre required for the Secretariat Service remained undetermined in terms of its permanent strength. In the meantime, efficiency continued to be a serious casualty[7].

2.7 The problem of reform in the post-Independence period was not only to restore efficiency and economy, but also to meet the shortage of ICS officers who earlier used to man roughly half the posts of Under Secretaries. In the course of the War itself, the former distinction between them and Assistant Secretaries had begun to be given up. Such officers as provinces were able to spare were required to man the higher layers in the Central Secretariat, especially on the retirement of Europeans. The posts of Assistant and Under Secretaries in these circumstances came to be filled almost entirely by the Central Secretariat Service, supplemented on an ad hoc basis from a variety of sources. The change so brought about during the War and its aftermath came to stay and was recognized as permanent. The reorganization of the Central Secretariat Service had to proceed not only on the basis that it should provide practically all the officers required for the grade of Assistant and Under Secretaries, but also to supply officers for the higher grade.

2.8 It was in this context that the importance of 'reinforcement' acquired much greater emphasis. This reinforcement became necessary at the level of Superintendents, not of Assistants, where it was essential to weed out poor material and provide better training facilities. The main objective of reinforcement was to provide for a new grade of Assistant Superintendents, a class of direct recruits, superior to the average category of Assistants whose quality had become too diluted to be able to supply through promotion, the personnel required for the posts of Superintendents. It was felt that great leeway would have to be made in raising the standard of Assistants to make them fit for promotion. The direct recruitment of Assistant Superintendents of a higher calibre was thus sought to be an instrument of 'reinforcement' for the grade of Superintendents, a regular system of training being provided at the same time to fit them for that grade in a relatively short period. This arrangement, however, did not exclude the selection of competent persons from among the existing incumbents.

2.9 Reorganization and reinforcement were thus interrelated. Both were designed to provide a reserve of qualified men for selection and promotion, not only for the posts of Under Secretaries but also for higher grade, including executive posts under the Central Government or even under Provincial Governments. This objective was sought to be achieved by a scheme, which was approved by the Cabinet on 22nd October, 1948 and notified as CSS (Reorganisation and Reinforcement) Scheme, 1948[8]. With this started the modern era of Central Secretariat Service, replacing the old Imperial Secretariat Service and provided the following layers upto the grade of Under Secretary:

| | | |
|---|---|---|
| Grade I | — Under Secretary Class I | (Gazetted) |
| Grade II | — Superintendent Class I | -do- |
| Grade III | — Asstt. Superintendent Class II | -do- |
| Grade IV | — Assistant Class I | (Non-gazetted) |

The scheme embraced all posts included in the Imperial Secretariat Service from Assistant upto Under Secretary, except those specially excluded with the consent of the Home Ministry. It provided for a review of permanent, quasi-permanent and purely temporary posts in the Central Secretariat and its attached offices, the objective being to determine the cadre strength of the Service based on its permanent and quasi-permanent posts which were likely to last for more than three years.

2.10 The highest grade of Under Secretary comprised not only the existing posts of Under Secretaries but also those of Assistant Secretaries, and the distinction between the two was abolished formally on reorganization. The next lower grade was that of Superintendents holding charge of Sections. The third grade was that of Assistant Superintendents, who were expected to function as Senior Assistants in larger sections and as Assistants-in-charge in smaller ones. The lowest grade in the service continued to be that of Assistant. Provision was made for direct recruitment in the grades of both Assistant and Assistant Superintendent. In the case of Assistant, 25 per cent of their posts were reserved for clerks promoted to their rank, the remaining 75 per cent being filled by direct recruitment on the results of the Ministerial Service Examination held by the Federal Public Service Commission. In the case of Assistant Superintendents, however, direct recruitment was limited to 50 per cent only. The direct recruits in this grade were to be drawn from the results of the combined competitive examinations for the IAS and Central Services, Class I. As the posts of Assistant Superintendents were Class II posts, it was agreed that candidates who secured positions immediately below those recruited for Class I posts should be appointed as Assistant Superintendents. The remaining 50 per cent of the posts were to be filled by promotion from among Assistants. The posts of Superintendents and Under Secretaries were, on the other hand, declared as selection posts, to be filled by promotion on merit from the next lower grade.

Detailed information was accordingly sought to be obtained from various Ministries about posts in the Secretariat that might be included in the cadre of the Central Secretariat Service. Lists were also prepared of candidates who were eligible for confirmation in the different grades of the service. These were considered ministry-wise by Departmental Promotion Committees designed to formulate their recommendations for approval by the Federal Public Service Commission which interviewed candidates for the posts of Under

Secretary, Superintendent and Assistant Superintendent. Their interviews were completed and appointments made by the middle of 1949[9].

2.11 The constitution of Grades I to III of the Central Secretariat Service was completed by the end of 1953, as the last instalment of the gradings of the departmental officers by the Union Public Service Commission (UPSC), was received in March 1953[10]. The grading showed that the service as a whole did not require reinforcement from outside. A sufficient number had in fact been recommended for each of the three Grades by the UPSC from among the existing officers eligible for these Grades. As a matter of policy, however, it was decided that the women candidates from outside who had been considered suitable by the Commission for the Central Secretariat Service should be offered appointment to this Service. One such appointee joined Grade I as Under Secretary and four joined Grade III as Asstt. Superintendents. The constitution of Grades I to III of the Service having been completed the provisions in the Central Secretariat Service Scheme for the maintenance of the Service now came into operation. In accordance with these provisions a panel was prepared for promotion from Grade II to Grade I and appointments to the higher Grade were made from this panel. A panel was also prepared for the promotion of Grade III officers to Grade II in consultation with the UPSC. The scheme also provided for promotion from Grade IV to Grade III, partly on the results of a departmental competitive test and partly on the basis of seniority subject to fitness.

A Selection Grade representing Deputy Secretaries was formally added to the CSS from October 1, 1955, and it was visualised that those who were recruited directly as Assistant Superintendents, would be eligible to rise to Deputy Secretary's rank and beyond. Further changes took place in the structure of the Service on implementation of the recommendations of the Second Central Pay Commission. In accordance with the recommendation of the Second Pay Commission, Grade II (Superintendents) and Grade III (Assistant Superintendents) of the Service carrying the scale of Rs. 530-30-800 and Rs. 275-25-500 respectively were merged into a single Grade of Section Officers with a revised scale of Rs.350-25-500-30-590-EB-30-800-EB-30-830-35-900 with effect from 1st July, 1959[11]. The merged Grade Section Officer was classified as Class II Service but persons who were already members of Grade II of the Central Secretariat Service retained their Class I status.

### The Central Secretariat Service, 1962

2.12 The Central Secretariat Service was last reorganized in 1962, into the following four grades:

1. Selection Grade (Deputy Secretary and equivalent)
2. Grade I (Under Secretary and equivalent)
3. Section Officers Grade
4. Assistants' Grade

While 50 per cent of the posts of Assistant were filled by direct recruitment through UPSC (now through Staff Selection Commission) and 20 per cent of Section Officers posts by direct recruitment through Civil Services examination conducted by UPSC. Promotion to the grade of S.O. is made on the basis of Select List prepared from two sources viz. (i) on the basis of limited departmental competitive examinations for Assistants and Grade C of Central Secretariat Stenographers' Service and (ii) on the basis seniority-cum-fitness, in equal ratio. The posts of Under Secretary and Deputy Secretary continued to be filled by promotion. An extract of the main provisions of the Rules is at Appendix 2.1.

2.13 In the Central Government, higher post were as a rule specifically not included by name in the authorized strength of any Service. All such posts have been filled under the Central Staffing Scheme by the Establishment Officer of the Government of India. The Scheme was governed by the broad principles suggested by the Study Team on Personnel Administration, according to which a small part of the Deputy Secretary level posts is provided by a permanent group consisting of Selection Grade officers of the CSS. An authorised strength of 45 was fixed for this purpose.

2.14 After the last reorganization in 1962 there has been a visible rise of the Central Secretariat Service in terms of both quantity and functional elevation. The former Imperial Secretariat Service in the Government of India had been designed merely to man lower positions in the Central Secretariat, seldom rising beyond the level of Asstt. Secretaries. As heads of Sections and Branches their duty was to assist those operating at the 'consideration' and policy-formulation levels by bringing to their notice relevant facts and precedents. The breakdown of the tenure system at the level of Under Secretary following the acute shortage of officers in the higher services led to the gradual elimination of the so called distinction that earlier existed between Assistant Secretaries and Under Secretaries.

The Study Team on Recruitment, Selection and Training of ARC, in its report (June 1967) recommended that the practice of bringing officers of the IAS and Central Service Class I as Under Secretaries in the Central Secretariat should be discontinued, and these officers should be brought in to the Central Secretariat only at the level of Deputy Secretary and above after a strict selection and specific training[12].

2.15 When the Central Secretariat Service was formally re-constituted, the original purpose remained unchanged but the old barriers were removed so that some positions at the Under Secretary's level and fixed number of Deputy Secretary's posts came to be included in the cadre of the Service so constituted. The result was that, while members of the Service swamped the bulk of the Under Secretary's positions, by 1974 they came to hold 35.5 per cent of the positions of Deputy Secretaries. But in subsequent years the increase in the cadre strength has been very slow, as can be seen in the table below:

**TABLE 2.1**
**CSS Authorised Strength**

| *Grade* | *Initial Constitution* | *1-1-54* | *1-5-61* | *1-7-94* |
|---|---|---|---|---|
| Selection Grade | 45 (1-10-55) | ... | ... | 132 |
| Grade I | 180 (22-7-50) | 225 | 375 | 668 |
| Grade II | 300 (22-7-50) | 389 | | |
| | | + | 1400* | 2243 |
| Grade III | 400 (1-11-51) | 540 | | |
| Grade IV | 1819 (1-11-51) | 2500 | 4250 | 4789 |

*merged into Section Officers' Grade w.e.f. 1-7-59

*Source.* Annual Reports of MHA 1953-54 and 1960-61

Cadre-wise break up the strength may be seen at Appendix 2.2

**Desk Officer System**

2.16 The Deshmukh Study Team of ARC on 'Machinery of Government of India and its procedure of work' had proposed doing away with the Section-centered pattern and recommended adoption of 'desk officer system' under which each executive is allowed a defined area of functioning and handles all correspondence and problems relating to that area. When a communication is received, the executive concerned drafts a reply and issues it in simple situation. He submits otherwise the draft to the head of the division for signature without any recommendation or note.[13]

The Third Central Pay Commission had also gone into the question and observed: "In regard to the Secretariat there has been a consensus of opinion that there should be reduction in the level of consideration and decision-making and also in the number of persons of Departments responsible for taking a decision. The Pilot Officer Scheme and Officer-oriented Scheme have been in force in some Ministries. The ARC recommended a modified version called the 'desk officer system'. We endorse the recommendations..."[14]

There seems to no divergence of opinion that there is a direct relationship between work-system and office procedure and the pattern of staffing. Also, there is a consensus that there is need for re-inforcing qualities in this grade and hence it was held in many quarters that desk officers should not be conventional Section Officers but should be officers with difference of course from the quality angle.

2.17 Although most of the direct recruit Section Officers rose to the posts of Joint Secretary and Additional Secretary in the Ministry, this threw a challenge to the members of the service to make themselves suitable for higher level posts through appropriate in-service training and planned career development. Of late, the number of CSS officers at the higher levels particularly those of Additional Secretary and Secretary has been reduced to none.

**TABLE 2.2**

**No.of CSSOfficers occupying senior positions in the Central Secretariat**

| *Post* | *As on: 1.1.61* | *1.1.65* | *1.7.95* |
|---|---|---|---|
| Secretary/ Special Secretary | 1 | 2 | 0 |
| Additional Secretary | 1 | 1 | 0 |
| Joint Secretary | 6 | 18 | 17 |
| Director/Dy. Secretary | 93 | 155 | 184 |

## CSS CADRE MANAGEMENT

### Assistant's Grade

2.18 As already stated, 50 per cent of the substantive vacancies in the Assistant's Grade are filled by direct recruitment through open competitive examination, till 1987 conducted by the UPSC and from 1988 onwards by the Staff Selection Commission. The numbers of vacancies notified to the Commission to be filled through examinations held for the last five years are as under:

**TABLE 2.3**

**No. of Vacancies of Assistant Notified**

| Year of Exam. | 1988 | 1989 | 1990 | 1991 | 1992 | 1993 |
|---|---|---|---|---|---|---|
| No. of vacancies | 322 | 816 | 493 | 247 | 251 | N.A. |

All vacancies of the above 'direct recruitment' quota remaining unfilled in addition to equal number of vacancies are filled by promotion from the grade of UDCs of CSCS on the recommendations of the DPCs convened by the decentralised cadre units of CSCS.

### Section Officers' Grade

2.19 Direct recruitment to the Section Officers' Grade is made on the basis of Civil Services Examination to the extent of 20 per cent of the substantive vacancies in the grade. The remaining 80 per cent of the vacancies are filled by promotion from amongst persons from the Assistant Grade included in the Select List every year. The year-wise appointments made by direct recruitment and promotion for the last 5 years are as under:

**TABLE 2.4**
**No. of Section Officers Appointed**

| *Year of Exam./ Select List* | *1989* | *1990* | *1991* | *1992* | *1993* |
|---|---|---|---|---|---|
| Direct Recruits Joined* | 13 | 07 | 18 | 27 | |
| Promotion Select List* | 236 | 326 | 304 | 187 | 241 |

**Grade I**

2.20 Appointment to Grade I of the CSS and the Selection Grade are on the Central Staffing pattern. The panel of Grade I of CSS for the years 1987 to 1994 (8 years) could not be prepared on account of a dispute regarding seniority between directly recruited Section Officers and promotee Section Officers, which had been the subject matter of litigation for the last several years. The related Civil Appeal No.3797/91 (UOI & Ors Vs Amritlal & Ors) has been moving between the Supreme Court and Central Administrative Tribunal for all these years. However, in accordance with the direction of the Supreme Court given in their interim order dated the 20, September 1991, promotions to Grade I of the CSS have been made subject to the approval of the Union Public Service Commission and the decision on the above petition.

**Selection Grade**

2.21 The number of promotions of CSS officers approved in Selection Grade during the last five years is as under:

**TABLE 2.5**

| *Year of Select List* | *1989* | *1990* | *1991* | *1992* | *1993* |
|---|---|---|---|---|---|
| No. names included* | 40 | 40 | 40 | 40 | 23 |

**Source:* Annual Reports of Ministry of Personnel, PG and Pension

## Cadre Review

2.22 The Government agrees that periodical review of the cadre strength of a regularly constituted Service/Cadre is an important element of cadre management aiming at rationalisation of the existing cadre structure based on manpower projections[15]. However, as regards Central Secretariat Service is concerned no formal cadre review has been conducted ever since the Service was reconstituted in 1962, giving rise to the dispute regarding allocation of quota to direct recruitment and promotion of substantive vacancies.

## Provision for Training

2.23 Neither the Central Secretariat Service Rules, 1962, nor any of the Regulations under them provided for any compulsory training for the members of the Service. To look back into the history of the training practices for the officers of the Imperial Secretariat Service, it may be recollected that in pursuance of the recommendations of the Maxwell Committee (1937) the then Home Department drew up a scheme for training of freshly recruited Assistants and Clerks by the experienced Superintendents and Senior Assistants in their respective organizations[16]. This worked well during those days when the pace of development was slow and the world was moving at a rather leisurely pace. Even today, it must be admitted that there is no substitute for on-the-job training or learning as no amount of institutional training would give a civil servant the real feel of the job. However, in view of the accelerated pace of development particularly after independence, the on-the-job training to all the newcomers was neither possible nor effective.

It was therefore considered necessary to set up a specialised training institution with a view to making the staff fully useful to the government. A concrete step in that direction was, however, taken in pursuance of the recommendation of the First Central Pay Commission (1947), which endorsed generally the views expressed by the Assheton Committee on British Civil Service (1944) and underlined the need for civil servants to be more consciously directed towards higher ideals and standards of service, which could be achieved only by planned and purposeful training. The Secretariat Training School (now ISTM) was thus set up in May 1948 on a temporary basis with one part-time Director and two Instructors. Gradually, it placed itself on a permanent footing, in 1957, as an Attached Office of the Government of India under the Ministry of Home Affairs (now DoPT).

2.24 Later, rules 15, 16 and 17 of the CSS Rules, 1962 made the following provisions :[17]

> 'Every direct recruit Section Officer/Assistant is initially appointed on probation for a period of 2 years from the date of appointment. The period of probation can be extended by not exceeding one year. Similarly, the promotee officers of the CSS are placed on a trial for a period of 2 years on their appointment to a particular grade. During the period of probation or trial, the officer concerned can be asked to pass such test or examination as the Department of Personnel & Training (DoPT) may prescribe. In case the probationer or the promotee fails to complete the period of probation satisfactorily, he is discharged from the service or reverted to the lower grade as the case may be. In the case of probationers, they are confirmed after the completion of probation period satisfactorily.'

In pursuance of the above provision, the practice of sending directly recruited Assistants and Section Officers to ISTM for the foundational and in-service training was followed by the Ministries/ Departments before making confirmation. However, there was no statutory force under which the Ministries/ Departments would be obliged to send each of the directly recruited Assistants for training in time. As a result there has been a lopsided approach to the training scheme provided for these officers inasmuch as some Ministries insisted for passing of ISTM examination before considering them for confirmation while some did not even feel the need of training at ISTM.

2.25 In 1988, the CS Division of the DoPT which is responsible for the control and management of the Service, issued[18] a comprehensive Cadre Training Plan for CSS officers (Appendix 4.3). Again, since the Training Plan neither had proper authority for enforcement in the Ministries/Department, nor was in consonance with the provisions of the Service Rules, the Plan could not be implemented either by the Cadre Units or by the CS Division itself. For example, the Cadre Training Plan has provided that

> " ...all directly recruited and promotee officers appointed to various Grades, shall be required to undergo the Foundational, Refresher and Professional Development Training Courses prescribed therein, within one year of their regular appointment failing which their next increment shall be withheld."
>
> " The seniority of directly recruited Section Officers shall be determined on similar lines as in the case of IAS, in accordance with the aggregate marks obtained by the probationer; (a) at the Competitive Examination and (b) at the foundational Examination conducted by ISTM."

However, in the absence of a corresponding provisions in the Service Rules, the above provisions would have no meaning.

Therefore, if the DoPT, in principle, intend to plan for effective training scheme for these officers, it would be necessary to make suitable provisions in the Service Rules and derive adequate authority to make such rules or regulations as would be binding on the Cadre Units.

Further, the Cadre Training Plan may include only a broads Scheme of foundational and in-service training to be followed by examinations, wherever necessary, with prescribed time-frame in each case for various levels of the Service, and may not venture into the training methodology and session-plan which are for the training institute to decide. A model cadre training plan for CSS has been suggested at Appendix 4.5.

It may be necessary to take all Cadre Units into confidence and ensure their commitment for implementation of the Plan before it is finalised and prescribed.

## Conclusion

2.26 The Central Secretariat Service is one of the oldest civil services in the Central Administration of the country. Over a period of more than three quarters of a century the Service has had undergone several reorganization and restructuring to partly suit the need and structure of the administrative system at the Ministry level and partly the convenience and interest of the other All-India and Central Services at the higher levels. The Service remained disorganized and disintegrated into different classes and categories of recruits which made room for other Services in the precincts of the Central Secretariat. For this degeneration of the CSS, the members of the Service who had played its role at the 'consideration' level, were equally responsible. Nevertheless, the dependency on these (CSS) officers of the officers at the policy making level cannot be overemphasised because of the continuity and consistency provided by them to the system in general. And thus, the need for professionalism in the functioning at the 'consideration' level cannot be overlooked. Analysis of the foregoing facts, however, reveals that there has not been any integrated approach to the training and development of these officers at the initial entry level. Training at the earliest stage of the entry into the service will prove to be more effective and would help in development of the officer in the long run.

## References


1. Mishra, B.B., *Government and Bureaucracy in India—1947-76*, p.197.
2. *Report of the Study Team on Machinery of the Government of India and its Procedure of Work* (Part II, Vol.I), ARC (1968).
3. Mishra, B.B., *Government and Bureaucracy in India—1947-76*.
4. *Ibid.*
5. *Report of the Study Team on Machinery of the Government of India and its Procedure of Work* (Part II, Vol.I), ARC (1968), pp. 25-29.
6. Mishra, B.B., *Government and Bureaucracy in India 1947-76*, Oxford University Press, New Delhi, 1986, p.119.
7. *Ibid*, p.120.
8. *Review of Activities of MHA for the year 1948*, paras 8-10.
9. *Review of Activities of MHA for the year 1949*, para 7.
10. Ministry of Home Affairs, *Annual Report (1953-54)* (1957-58) (1959-60).
11. Ministry of Home Affairs, *Annual Report (1960-61)*.
12. *Study Team on Recruitment, Selection, UPSC/State PSCs and Training*, Report on, ARC (1967), para 3.8.2.
13. *Study Team on Machinery of the Government of India and its Procedure of Work*, Report on, ARC(1968), para 4.29.

14. *Report of the Third Central Pay Commission*, 1973.
15. Ministry of Personnel Public Grievances and Pensions, *Annual Reports, 1988-89 to 1994-95.*
16. Secretariat Training School, Annual Report (1962), Feb' 63.
17. Central Secretariat Service Rules, 1962.
18. Deptt. of Personnel & Training (CS Division), Cadre Training Plan for CSS (1988).

# 3

# The Training Institute—Its Organization and Functioning

3.1 Dr. Joseph R Starr, UN Consultant in Public Administration observed:[1]

> *"Among the different kinds of training institutes, it is probably the schools and institutes of public administration which have attracted the most attention and which seem to promise the most in the way of solutions of training problems. After more than half a century of experience in the operation of institutes, an experience which has been shared by at least a dozen countries for more than a decade, no general agreement can be recorded as to the organization and functioning of these institutions. The pattern which seems to be emerging in many countries is the multipurpose institute, whose activities may include teaching of several different educational levels, research, consultation, documentation, publication and many tasks of in-service training. These institutes may even exercise authority in the selection and promotion of civil servants, especially of the higher grades. Some schools and institutes are asked also to engage in extension activities and to operate training centres for civil servants at various locations in the country. These institutions have taken a wide variety of forms to meet differing conditions. The time has come, perhaps to consider the structure and scope of activities of these institutions with a view to strengthening them as agencies in the realizations of comprehensive plan of training."*

3.2 The analysis of the organization, structure and functioning of ISTM as one of the institute of public administration in India, is undertaken in this chapter. The chronological evolution and the major problems relating to the structure and functioning of the institute are brought under consideration.

Besides analyses of the various aspects of the Institute, this chapter aims to provide an operational guide to persons who are directly concerned in the organization and operation of similar training institutes, such as Directors, faculty, instructors, administrative officer and other member of staff; the controlling Ministries/Departments, advisory committees, consultative bodies and ministers concerned. At the first place focus is drawn on the mission or scope of functions of the institute; the structure and organization come next.

## OBJECTIVES AND FUNCTIONS OF ISTM

### The Objectives

3.3 The task of defining the objectives of an institute ordinarily arises at the time when the creation of such an institute is first under consideration based on felt need of imparting training to the specific civil servants. It is usually necessary to formulate the objectives as a Resolution, Article or any other similar basic documents which serve as the Charter of the Institute[2]. Reconsideration of the objectives may arise at a later date with expansion and modification in objectives and functions. The need of training for the CSS officers and the need for a formal training institution have already been explained in Chapter 2 .

3.4 The Secretariat Training School, as originally set up, had the following objectives to start with:

(i) training of new entrants to the Grade of Assistants recruited through Federal (Union) Public Service Commission

(ii) training of Assistants and Lower Division Clerks in English Typewriting and

(iii) providing refresher courses for Assistants and Assistant-in-charge (later called Section Officer).

3.5 Though the aforesaid objectives served the requirements of the Secretariat reasonably well for quite a time, the School found itself overrun by new and more exacting demands. It can legitimately be proud of the growth, development and resilience displayed by it over the years in the face of increasing challenges It was in recognition of the vastly enlarged scope of the activities that it came to acquire in November 1971 its present name—the *Institute of Secretariat Training and Management (ISTM)*[3]. The new name sought to bring to a sharp focus the altered role of this training body which now operates against the backdrop of a wider canvas. Far from being an institution catering to the training needs of a select band of ministerial staff from its inception, it had by now, within its reach, officers working as Deputy Secretary and Directors in the Secretariat. The range of courses cover practically the entire gamut of administration from secretariat rules and procedures to modern discipline of management and training of trainers.[4]

3.6 The objectives of ISTM as redefined in the context of its enlarged activities have been as follows:[5]

1. To plan, design and conduct post-entry foundational, refresher, and specialised training courses for different grades of officers up to the middle management level to enable them to perform their duties, work more effectively and to prepare them for greater responsibilities in future by increasing their professional competence;
2. To assess the training needs at various levels in the Secretariat as well as the related field organizations and organize training programmes to meet these felt needs;
3. To create and foster among the participants a positive and innovative outlook to work, and a sense of fraternity and team-spirit;
4. To provide peripatetic faculty support to State Government and Union Territories in areas like Office Management, Rules and Procedures, Behavioural Sciences, O&M and Work-Study, Financial Management and Training of Trainers, and to assist them in designing their training courses and help them in preparing their training materials; and

5. To produce monographs and other training literature/ materials (including audio-visual aids) relevant to the training courses designed and conducted by the Institute.

During 1974, the Institute was awarded an emblem with "Efficiency and the Public Good" as its motto[6].

## Functions and Activities

3.7 In order to achieve its objectives the Institute of Public Administration are required to perform certain prescribed functions and activities. The functions of ISTM have been analysed and discussed under the following broad headings:

I. Major functions
   - (a) Training.
   - (b) Research.
   - (c) Consultation, also known as advice or service.

II. Complementary functions
   - (a) Documentation, including the establishment of a specialised library in public administration.
   - (b) Publications.
   - (c) Serving as an information centre or otherwise disseminating literacy in public administration.
   - (d) Extension service or extra moral activities of an informational or educational character.
   - (e) Promoting the organization and activities of professional association of civil servants.

III Other activities
   - (a) Organization and conduct of conferences and seminars.
   - (b) Promotion of good relations between the government departments and similar training institutes in the country.

## The Major Functions

3.8 The three major functions—training, research and consultation—have been referred to as the trilogy of activities which least express the role of an institute of public administration.[7] Thus, there is some implication that the three major functions together represent an irreducible minimum, and that each institution should be endowed with at least these responsibilities.

**Teaching or Training**

3.9 Institutes of public administration, specially a training institute would primarily engage itself for all time in the function of imparting training, though it may or may not perform any of the other functions. This is the one function which is common to all these institutions. Great variety is exhibited, however, in the kind and level of instructions provided. An institute may be limited to pre-entry training or it may be engaged in instructional activities which range all the way from the lower operational level through the supervisory and middle and senior management levels of civil services.

The danger is that the training/teaching activities of an institute may touch upon so many subjects at different levels as to result in a dispension of the abilities and energies of the training faculty while great variety in training activities always presents organizational problems, the results may not be had if a specialized staff can be provided for instruction for different subjects at different levels. These institute, however, are seldom staffed so fully as to provide teacher who might concentrate on instructions at a given level. The result is that trainers are asked to teach at widely differing levels and in classes composed of students of different experience and preparation.[8]

3.10 The Secretariat Training School, the precursor of the ISTM, which started in 1948 for training the new entrants to the grade of Assistant in the Secretariat, was also no exception in exhibiting its capabilities in diversification of training areas soon after it was placed on a permanent footing in 1957. Till early sixties the school completed the coverage of *ab initio* and in-service refresher training to all upto the level of Section Officer in general areas of Secretariat rules and procedures. For the first time in 1961, the School started specialised training course in Cash and Accounts.[9] Thereafter, in 1965, first time the course of Work-Study training was launched.[10] Even after more than 30 years these two courses are considered premier and one of their kind in the country. Thereafter, the Institute progressively diversified year by year in its range of subject areas as well as level of officers. A progressive list of course added to the Institute's training calendar in different years is shown in the Table 3.1 below.

**TABLE 3.1**

**Year-wise inclusion of number and titles of courses in ISTM**

| *Year* | *Titles added/deleted/changed* | *Total No. of titles* | *Total No. of courses* | *Year and changes* |
|---|---|---|---|---|
| 1961 | Cash and Accounts Course | * | * | |
| 1962 | Special short courses for S.Os in: | * | * | |
| | -Central Registry/Typing Pool | | | Discontinued |
| | -Admn./Estt. Section | | | |
| | -Cash and Accounts Sections | | | |
| 1965 | Work-Study Training | * | * | Renamed in 1972 |
| 1966 | Commercial Accountancy | * | * | Discontd. |
| 1968 | Performance Budgeting | * | * | Discontd. |
| | Vigilance | | | |
| 1969 | IES/ISS (Probationers) | * | * | |
| 1971 | Orientation course for USs | * | * | |
| 1972 | International Course in Management Techniques (12 weeks) | * | * | Modified and renamed |
| | Advanced Management Services Course | | | (Renamed) |
| | Basic Management Services Course | | | (Renamed) |
| 1974 | Performance Budgeting | * | * | Discontd. in 86-87 |
| 1975 | Training for Staff Car Drivers | 27 | 63 | Discontd. |
| | Productivity in Project Management | | | Discontd. |
| | Orientation course for CVOs | | | |
| | Workshop on Programmed Learning | | | |
| | Records Management for IAS officers | | | |
| | Training on Desk Officer System | | | Discontd.in 92-93 |
| | Course on Personnel Management | | | |
| | Course on Records Management | | | |
| | Training of Trainers' in Desk Officer System | | | Discontd. |
| | Management of Field Organizations | | | |
| 1976 | Management Development Programme for CSS Grade I (Under Secretary)-shifted from IIPA | 34 | 88 | |
| | Training of Trainers in Pub. Admn. | | | |
| | Seminar on Identification of Training Needs | | | |
| | Seminar of Designing Effective Training | | | |
| | Seminar on Implementation and Evaluation of Training | | | |
| | Training of Trainers for LDCs | | | |
| | Behavioural Sciences Courses on: | | | |
| | Public Relations, PA/PSs, Reception Officers | | | |
| 1977-78 | Management Information System | 28 | 82 | |
| 1978-79 | Management Accounting | 31 | 81 | |
| | Reservation in Services | | | |

| | | | | |
|---|---|---|---|---|
| 1979-80 | International Course on Financial Management for National Development (8 weeks) | 35 | 100 | |
| 1980-81 | Post-training evaluation seminars of past participants of:<br>-S.O/ACSO (Probationers) Course<br>-Management Development Programmes<br>-Administrative Vigilance<br>-Desk Functionaries Course<br>-Advanced Management Services Course<br>-Behaviour Oriented Courses for PA/PSs<br>-Training of Trainers for Jr. Level | 41 | 102 | |
| 1981-82 | International Courses: | 42 | 111 | |
| | 1. Development Admn.—Approaches Planning and Management | | | Discontd. in 91-92 |
| | 2. Training of Trainers in Development Administration | | | Discontd. in 92-93 |
| 1983-84 | Recruitment Rules<br>Establishment Rules | 39 | 105 | |
| | Effective Writing —Official Noting and Communication | | | Discontd. in 92-93 |
| 1984-85 | Technical Workshops on<br>-Pension and other Retirement Benefits<br>-Conduct Rules | | | Converted into regular courses from 91-92 |
| 1985-86 | | 44 | 123 | |
| 1986-87 | | 42 | 106 | |
| 1987-88 | Direct Trainers' Skills (DoPT) | 40 | 116 | |
| 1988-89 | Course on Forms Design and Office Layout | | 88 | Discontd. in 91-92 |
| | Special Course for O&M Officers | | | Discontd. in 91-92 |
| | Zero Based Budgeting | | | Discontd. in 92-93 |
| 1989-90 | | | 102 | |
| 1990-91 | Quality Circle | 47 | 88 | Discontd. in 92-93 |
| 1991-92 | Computer Application Packages (DOS)<br>Computer Appreciation Course | | 62 | |
| 1992-93 | Design of Training (DoPT)<br>Handling CAT Cases<br>Database Management System<br>Word Processing in Hindi<br>Computer Application Packages (Unix) | | 99 | |
| 1993-94 | | 45 | 84 | |
| 1994-95 | | 38 | 65 | |

* Not available.

*Source:* Annual Reports 1962 to 1990-91 and ISTM Training Calendar of 1991-92 to 1994-95.

3.11 As could be observed, upto 1981-82 there was a gradual increase in the number of course titles, number of courses and in some cases the duration of the course. Thereafter, the number of course titles were more or less maintained, but there was some increase in the number of courses and participants in a year till 1990. The year 1991-92 onwards there has been sudden and steep declination in the activities of ISTM, except in foundational and refresher courses, inasmuch as all international courses which had been conducted since 1972 were discontinued, due to financial resource crunch, and the number of courses and participants reduced by more than 25 per cent of those in 1990-91, which has been attributed to depleted faculty strength. The work-load and faculty strength has been discussed later in this Chapter.

### *Computer Training*

3.12 With the introduction of computers in the Secretariat, imparting training in the use of computers to the officers of the Secretariat was of special significance in the mission of the Institute. Though the need was felt early in the year 1986-87, ISTM took some time to introduce computer learning in a meaningful manner for want of basic infrastructure, equipments and competent faculty. It was only through the dynamic leadership of the then Director, that some enthusiastic and potential faculty members were made to take up the task in a modest way in 1987-88 and introduced training on "Introduction to PC" in some of the in-house courses of the Institute. Consequent to gradual induction of more faculty members in the area and with a full-fledged Computer Laboratory (with 8 Nos. stand alone PC/AT 286 and one unix based 'Orbit 386' multi-user system with 8 terminals funded by UNDP ) ISTM introduced full-time courses on Computer Appreciation, Computer Application Packages and Database Management System.[11] The MIS course was further enhanced to full-fledged computer based course with an application development project work. The participants feedback for the past five years revealed that the teaching methodology of the computer faculty were highly effective and comparable with many computer professional institutes like NIC, CMC etc.. A new post of Assistant Director (Computer Programming) was created in 1989, and with gradual increase in the courses, in 1990-91 ISTM mooted proposal for upgrading the post of AD (PC) and further augmentation of the computer faculty. However, due to sudden turn-over of the faculty in the Computer Wing, the computer courses were gradually reduced, and the only faculty member with professional qualification in computer in the post of Assistant Director (Computer Programming) was repatriated without any replacement and ultimately the post was abolished in the name of economy.

### *Peripatetic Training*

3.13 As a result of the recommendations made at the Conference of Chief Secretaries held in New Delhi during May, 1976 the Institute set up a Peripatetic team of faculty to assist State Governments/ Union Territories in running model courses, helping with course design, training the trainers and providing faculty for running other specialised programmes.[12] The ISTM faculty have conducted a number of courses every year in various States in the areas of Behavioural Sciences, O&M and Work Study, Office Management and Procedure, Financial Management, Training of Trainers, Reservation in Services for SC/ST etc. One post of Joint Director and two posts of Deputy Director were sanctioned specifically to cope up with the extra work-load due to these additional courses.[13] However, of late, the number of courses conducted in States have reduced considerably for a number of reasons such as gradual development of faculty in the State Training Institutes, considerable increase in the travel expenses to be borne by the State Government ( as many State Administration do not value such expenditure as investment in HRD), and partly due to ISTM's cold responses to State Governments requests for such courses. The details of number of peripatetic training courses conducted year-wise are as under:

| *Year* | *No. of Courses* |
|---|---|
| 1977-78 | 10 |
| 1978-79 | 19 |
| ... | |
| ... | |
| 1986-87 | 19 |
| 1987-88 | 27 |
| 1988-89 | 22 |
| 1989-90 | 15 |
| 1990-91 | 17 |
| 1991-92 | 25 |
| 1992-93 | 13 |
| 1993-94 | 05 |
| 1994-95 | Not reported |

It was observed that no evaluation of the scheme had ever been conducted in the last 20 years of its existence. Many of the State Governments have, by now, got their own training institute and training faculty. In view of this, the scheme of peripatetic training which was introduced long ago needs to be reviewed in consultation with the State Governments.

### *International Programmes*

3.14 As a part of Technical Cooperation among the Developing Countries (TCDC), Department of Personnel & Administrative Reforms (now Deptt. of Personnel and Training), had, for many years, been organising, in collaboration with faculty of ISTM, training programmes specially designed for young Overseas Administrators in the developing countries at the middle management level who were engaged in the challenging tasks of socio-economic development in their respective countries. In this series, ISTM have conducted two to three courses every year since 1972 in the areas of (i) Management Techniques, (ii) Financial Management and (iii) Training Techniques, till 1992. Discontinuation of these courses has definitely brought down the name and status of ISTM amongst the training institutes (similar courses have been introduced at the same time in other training institutes), and thus the morale of the training faculty.

### Research

3.15 The background to research function is to be found in the long established marriage between research and university teaching. Any subject worthy of being taught in a university must be firmly grounded in research.[14] The UN and groups of experts under its auspices have long recognised the importance of research as a foundation for the improvement of training in the public service. The working group of experts emphasized the importance of research as an adjunct of the teaching of public administration, and it recommended that the institutes should be made responsible for the "long-range research programme to suggest improvements in the administrative system of the country" and to publish "authoritative monographs on administrative problems".

3.16 Research is known to be specified or recognized as part of the charter of most of the training institutes in India. The bulk of the research, so far, has been devoted to the production of manual and other instructional materials. The preparation of instructional materials entail a great deal of basic research In many Ministries/ Departments in Central and State Government organization charts of the various Departments. have not been prepared, and descriptive writing of an authoritative and objective nature on the administrative system was also unknown. The preparation of such materials, of great importance in training programme, required the collection and verification of a great deal of data.

3.17 ISTM did its first effort in May 1957, by bringing out a cyclostyled pamphlet on "The Organization of the Government of India".[15] The first edition of the book entitled "Organizational set-up and functions of the Ministries/Departments of GOI" was published in January 1962. Subsequent publications viz. "Notes on Office Procedure", "Notes on Financial Rules" were not only recognized as reference manuals and training guides but also prescribed as syllabi for departmental competitive examinations for various secretariat services conducted by UPSC.

However, except for the Notes on Office Procedure, the other books were not revised for many years, although an interview survey revealed that the other book viz. "Organisational set-up.." and "Notes On Financial Rules" are equally in great demand by the users in Ministries as well as in other statutory and autonomous public bodies. Therefore, not only these books need be revised and published but more of such manuals on Establishment Rules, Admv. Vigilance and other areas may be published for general use.

## Consultancy

3.18 The research function merges into consultation or advisory services. By exercising an academic freedom to engage in research in any subject deemed to be of importance, and institute may bring its recommendations for improvement to the attention of government departments or the general public. The term "consultation" is applied to this process only in the case that the institute has been requested to undertake the inquiry by the government[16].

3.19 ISTM had never taken any initiative of its own in extending consultancy services to the government organizations perhaps because it was never in its charter of functions. However, its expertise in the area of Office Management,Work-Study techniques and Training Methodology have always been in great demands in various State and Central Government Department and public sector undertaking and requests have been received not only for designing and conducting training courses in these areas but also for conducting studies on various management problems.

During 1990-91, on a request from Kendriya Bhandar, New Delhi, ISTM conducted two studies, one in the area of Manpower Planning and Personnel Administration and the other on Restructuring of the Cadres and their Pay Scales. Also, a three member team of faculty members from ISTM conducted a study on identification of training needs of the employees of the Government of Mizoram, which helped the State Government and Government of India (Training Division) in designing suitable training courses for the employees of the State.[17]

ISTM may consider including "consultancy services" in its Charter and provide consultancy services in its specialised areas in a more recognized form, as is being done by IIPA, NPC, etc.

## Library and Documentation Services

3.20 Any school or institute of public administration, whose activities, besides training and teaching, research and consultancy in the areas of specialisation cannot afford to restrict its library facilities to mere maintaining collection of books and literatures, but to provide complete information and reference facilities to its users. The ISTM Library, which is in existence eversince the setting up of the Institute formally in 1957, occupies a place of special importance in the Institute. A library of this nature could mainly have the following broad objectives:

(a) Provide reference and reading materials to the faculty and trainees in the functional areas of training;

(b) Keep the faculty and trainees informed about the various events of development taking place in areas of public administration, politics, science and culture through periodicals and journals; and

(c) To promote reading habits among the faculty, trainees and staff of the Institute.

### *Growth and Content*

3.21 The School started its Library in 1957 with a collection of about 5,500 books mostly instructional, which grew by the next five years to 20,000 of which about 15,000 were instructional[18]. Thereafter, there has been gradual increase in the books of general interest including management topics, encyclopedia and instructional books.

**TABLE 3.3**
**Addition of Books in ISTM Library**

| *Year* | *No. of Volumes* | *Year* | *No. of Volumes* |
|---|---|---|---|
| 1957 | 5,500 | 1986-87 | 43,380 |
| 1962 | 20,000 | 1987-88 | 50,000 |
| 1967 | 21,853 | 1990-91 | 52,500 |
| 1972 | 29,912 | 1992-93 | No charge |
| 1977-78 | 38,352 | 1994-95 | No charge |

*Source.* STS/ISTM Annual Reports of the respective year.

Besides this, the collection included various reports like All-India Reporter, Supreme Court Cases, Service Law Reporter, Administrative Tribunal Reporter, etc.

The Library is subscribing various national and nternational journals on training and management, periodical and magazines of scientific and general interest and all important newspapers for the faculty members and trainees.

### *Management and Staff*

3.22 The Library of ISTM functions with a staff of one Librarian (Junior Grade) and one Library Attendant under the supervision of one faculty member (as additional charge). The management of the affairs of the Library including policy matters is regulated by a Library Committee comprising the Director as the Chairman and four Joint Directors, Dy. Director (Admn.) and Dy. Dir.(Lib) as members. It has been observed, so long the Director has the will to uphold the interest of the Library and its users and functions in a democratic manner, the system worked well. But of late, it was alleged by members that the decisions already taken by the Director were often imposed on the members and got ratified.

### *Documentation*

3.23 This is one area of ISTM Library which has been neglected, partly due to inadequate staff and partly due to lack of awareness on the part of the faculty members. Till 1984, there was a system of circulating and maintaining clippings containing important information from newspapers and journals for information and reference of the faculty members. Such clippings were quite useful resources for conducting research and developing training materials. Such clipping were maintained subject-wise for future reference. However, on the recommendation of the SIU study the post of Research Assistant for this work was abolished in 1985 for upgrading the post of Director ( to JS level) and the work relating to paper clipping was discontinued.

### *Clientele*

3.24 The ISTM Library is primarily meant for the use of the faculty members during their term of deputation and participants of various courses during the period of their training. The facility of borrowing books is not available to the ex-faculty members and past participants of the Institute though there has been demands from such readers.

### *Budget*

3.25 There is no separate budget for the Library and the purchase of books and furniture is made under the head of Office Expenses, as the practice followed in the Ministries/Departments. It is felt that the Library of a training institution cannot be treated on the same footing as those in Ministries/Department. It should be on the lines of the libraries of universities and colleges. Providing library facilities to its trainees and its faculty members is one of its primary functions and unless there is separate budget allocation for the development and growth of library there could always be the possibility of incurring expenditure on non-essential items at the cost of development of the Library.

### *Publications*

3.26 Many training institutes are directed by the terms of their charters to prepare and issue publications relating to public administration. Even though there is no specific statement to this effect, it is generally taken for granted their publication is a legitimate function. The preparation of publications is closely related to the research functions and also the collection of documentation and library materials. These functions go together in a natural series, as quite obviously there could be few publications of much value without the performances of research, which in turn requires the collection of documentary and other material of research. The publications of schools and institutes seem to fall into a few well detained classes, which are identified and explained below.

### (a) *Information Brochures*

3.27 Perhaps the first publication which should be considered by a established school or institute is a brochure or leaflet describing its objectives and activities. This very necessary piece of informational literature should then be revised and reissued in preparation for the new terms or on other appropriate occasions. A collection of publication of this type appearing in a number of countries reveals that almost everywhere an effect is made to bring out a pamphlet which is attractive in format and llustrated with photographs. The contents are fairly standardized and may be summarised under subheads like; historical note (genesis), objective of the institute, description of accommodation and equipment including library and facilities, teaching faculty, plans of shed and description of courses. A well-written brochures of this type will give prospective students a good understanding of the facilities and purposes of the training institute.

The "Information Brochure" published by ISTM in 1976 may be revived and revised to modify the format on the above lines.

## (b) *Annual Report*

3.28 Another important document which provide progressive information year by year on activities and performance is the "Annual Report" of the Institute. It is rather unfortunate for any Institute or for that matter any public organization to consider publication of Annual Report as an unproductive and unnecessary expenditure and thus discontinued as has apparently happened in ISTM since 1992. As a matter of fact, the concerned Department should insist on such reporting of its activities before sanctioning funds for each of its attached and subordinate offices under its control. The format adopted by STS (later ISTM) from 1962 to 1976 would provide good guidance.

## (c) *Instructional Material*

3.29 Almost every training institute has been preparing and publishing large quantities of instructional materials. The first such material to appear is usually the cyclostyled summaries of lecture, prepared and released by the individual faculty members. Perhaps next in frequency come summarised compilation of notes from different text and rule books on the subject to provide supplementary reading material. Many training institutes have published collections of articles from professional journals or excerpts from published works in the form of "readers" for use by students. Instances are known of the publication of such material without any regard to copyright or obtaining permission of the author or publisher. The authorities in charge of training institutions may be cautioned against pirating publications in public administration, as in practically all cases, if permission is requested, it is freely given.

3.30 ISTM has achieved remarkable distinction in preparation of training material such as exercises, handouts, quizzes, case-studies in good number and quality in the areas of Office Management, Management Techniques, Financial Rules, Establishment Rules etc. for various courses conducted by it. Some of the case-studies in noting and drafting were prepared so painstakingly that they have been used by generations of training faculty for the last 15-20 years. However, instances have come to notice that some of the existing handout/write-ups prepared by ex-faculty have been used by substituting the authors names by his own, because such people believed that the faculty who takes a session on a given topic must use his own handout otherwise he may lose credibility. Such mistaken belief need to be corrected, as there is no greater credibility of a faculty than his intellectual honesty. Survey of opinion was conducted among the faculty members on the question whether a trainer should always use his own training handouts/materials (Appendix 3.1). Some of the senior members expressed their views as under:

> "The training handout/ material is impersonal. If it is well prepared and cogent it would serve the purpose...Once a handout has been prepared by a team of faculty member on the subject, they can be used by any faculty member on the subject, unless there is major change in the subject matter..."
>
> When a trainer goes to a class, his objective is to help his trainees learn, and the objective of a handout is to provide information in written form rather than to provide evidence of the faculty members' ability to prepare a handout, which in any case would be summarisation of portions from rule book, as in no handout a faculty member would be providing his own theory or researches on the subject.
>
> In view of this, ISTM may consider standardising the training handout and material prepared by a team of experts from the faculty and develop a system of up-dating it from time to time.

### (d) *Monographs*

3.31 The publications of products of research is a sign of maturity in a school or an institute of public administration. ISTM has brought out, from time to time, a number of monographs on various areas for the benefits of its participants. These monographs were also in great demand from various training institutions and government departments. It was observed that after 1986, there has not been many original monographs published by the Institute except in the area of computers. A list of original important monographs is in Appendix 3.2.

## (e) *Professional journals*

3.32 There is no better way to provide an outlet for the product of research and other matter of professional interest than to publish a "public administration review or other periodical".

Materials of great value in the comparative study of public administration appears in professional journals of various state and central training institute in the country. A less demanding publication venture is to prepare and issue regularly a Newsletter. It is high time that the ISTM Newsletter which has been on the anvil for quite sometime should be brought out forthwith.

### Informational activities

3.33 Rarely are institutes of public administration changed in a formal way with responsibilities of an informational nature, except that some of these institutions have been directed to issue publications concerning public administration. Many of these institutions, however, assume as a matter of course that they have responsibilities in the dissemination of information on public administration. This may be considered a part of the broad functions of furthering administrative reforms[19]. In addition to issuing publication some institutes like IIPA, IAMR etc. have offered public lectures as a means of stimulating interest in administrative improvements. ISTM may also arrange such public lectures/ seminar on topics of common interest, which not only help in sharing information at a common forum but also bring the public employees closer to the Institute. Lectures from eminent scholars can later be published in the ISTM journal.

### Extension Service

3.34 Many schools and institutes are required by circumstances to engage in extra curricular activities which are informational or educational in nature[20]. Some schools and institutes in many parts of the world offer a substantial part of their instruction in off-duty hours for the convenience of civil servants who could not otherwise attend. Training institutions which operate in this manner undoubtedly perform a valuable service to public employees and open opportunities for self-development.

Every year, large number of CSS Assistants etc. prepare themselves for departmental competitive examination for promotion to the grade of SO. It would be great service to the community if part-time classes of such employees are arranged by the institute. For such classes even ex-faculty experts in their subjects may be associated.

## Fostering a Professional Association of Alumni

3.35 Some institutes of public administration have been instrumental in founding and sponsoring associations of persons interested in good administration. The sponsored society is sometimes made up of the graduates or former students of the training institutions. This has been found to be good method of stimulating the continued interest of person who received some training and obtaining their participation in the affairs of the school. An active society of this kind may hold frequent public lectures, discussion groups, seminars or panels which contribute to public understanding of administrative reforms and professional development of the member[21]. Though there is no recognized official sponsored body in the name of association of ex-faculty or past participants of ISTM, there has been a natural affinity among them for the past so many years. It has been proverbially often said that once enter the portals of ISTM, become a member of the ISTM family. A formal recognition of the ex-faculty and past participants in the family of ISTM may be a welcome gesture of goodwill on the part of the Institute. Such members may be extended library facilities and invited to all academic, literary and ceremonial activities of the Institute. A small membership fee may be raised for the development of such facilities.

### *Annual Day*

3.36 One of the easiest way of bringing the past participants and former faculty members together at least once in a year is by celebrating the Annual Day of the Institute every year. For any institution of learning, the Annual Day or Foundation Day has a special significance and importance, as much for the faculty as for its students. Generally, distinctions achieved by the students during the course of the year are honoured with prizes by the Chief Guest, usually an important person to recon with. Secretariat Training School eversince its inception has been celebrating its Annual Day for this purpose. The trainees who stood First, Second and Third in the final examinations of various qualifying examinations held during the preceding year are given prizes in the form of books of specified values on this day. The Chief Guest is generally the Minister-in-charge of Training or in his absence the Secretary (Personnel). However, there has not been any fixed day of the year for Annual Day, but is placed on the availability of the Minister to preside over the function, whose presence and addressing the gathering of past and present trainees and faculty members had always been a source of inspiration. The activities of the Institute during the past one year are reviewed and the Annual Report of the Institute is presented by the Director.

Since publication of Annual Report has been dis-continued, the celebration of Annual Day of ISTM has also been stopped in 1992. Whatever be the reason this was most unfortunate from the participants' and faculty's point of view.

## STRUCTURE AND ORGANIZATION

### Status of the Institute

3.37 No problem relating to the organization and functioning of institutes of public administration has let to wider differences of opinion and greater variety of solutions than that of locating the training institutions, that is, placing it in organizational relationship with elements of the government and educational system[22]. Underlying some of the phases of the problem is the concept of *autonomy*. The persons who are directly concerned with the success of these institutions are anxious to see them endowed with enough freedom of action to make possible for them to realise their goal. The Geneva Working Group of 1957 said, "This independence is an elusive concept", but concluded that " some independence is essential".

When an institute is first created, it is necessary, to put it somewhere in the governmental structure. Where it is placed will have profound effect upon the way in which it will function and its success in realizing the mission assigned to it.

In view of the objectives and functions of the Institute which was primarily imparting training of officers of Secretariat Services being controlled and managed by the Ministry of Home Affairs, ISTM was created in 1948 as a Subordinate Office of the Ministry of Home Affairs. Later, when the staff and Instructors of the School were taken from the officers of the Service and also in view of the Schools acquiring expertise in the area of training it was upgraded to an Attached Office in 1957.

## The Charter of the Institute

3.38 As a general rule each institute of public administration can point to a basic document, which creates the institution and gives formal statement to the fundamentals concerning its mission and organization. While there is a great deal of variation in terminology such as, Rules, Resolution, Memo of Association etc., this basic document may be referred to as the Charter[23]. Most official (government funded) institutes are created by executive orders issued by the President or other Ministerial level. Institutes of an autonomous and voluntary nature have charters and by-laws of their own adoption. In many cases, these basic documents become public records by reason of being filed as part of the Articles of Association to comply with law relating to voluntary association or a society under Society's Act. Like IIPA.

3.39 ISTM, even after 38 years of its existence as a formal training institute of public administration and an Attached Office of the Ministry of Home Affairs (now of DoPT) has no such formal document which a new Director or any authority in the Department can lay hands on if one desires to give a right direction to the Institute.

On search of old records, the earliest Annual Report of the Institute which could be retrieved were of 1962 onwards, which reasonably provide a wholesome information on genesis, objectives and functions of the then Secretariat Training School. Later, in 1976, an information brochure was brought out containing the objectives, functions and details of various training course conducted by ISTM. The subsequent issues of 1980 onwards were further abridged and eventually, its revision and publication was discontinued. Thus, on this date, there is no document available other than the back cover of the Annual Training Calendar which gives a sketchy outline about ISTM for the prospective participants and their sponsoring organization.

However, these information brochures, pamphlets or even the Annual Report of the Institute is not a substitute for the Charter of Institute. A summary of the content of a charter is given below. It is recommended that ISTM in consultation with the DoPT (Training Division) may create such a document for the benefit and guidance of all concerned.

***Summary of the Contents of a Charter***

3.40 The normal contents of the Charter, as laid down in the UN handout (Para 394) may be summarised under the headings which follows:

(a) *Style and Location*

The charter normally creates the training institution giving its exact name and geographical location.

(b) *Attachment*

The location of the training institute within the administration or academic structure is clarified by stating that it is an attached or subordinate office of a Ministry/ Department, a statutory or an autonomous society as in a part of an university or faculty.

(c) *Control and Supervision*

The Charter should also lay down the matters in which the Institute will consult its nodal Department, client Ministries and other agencies of the Government or statute like UPSC, SSC etc. in the matter of its activities of training, research and consultancy as also administration and personnel matters like appointment of faculty members, training associates, etc.

(d) *Internal Organization*

The Charter normally deals with the fundamentals relating to the structure of the training institutions, including the manner of appointment and the function of the principal officers, such as Director, Additional Director, Heads of Departments, Director of research, library, administration, etc. The Charter normally names the internal sub-division of the training institution, such administrative office, library, research unit, department of in-service course.

(e) *Objectives*

The objectives or mission and main activities of the institute would be defined in the Charter.

(f) *Programmes and Courses of Training*

Since teaching/training is usually considered the main element of the mission, it would be normal to specify in the Charter the programmes of instruction/training courses which the institute is expected to offer.

(g) *Selection of Participants*

It is most important that general rules be clearly stated in this regard. The responsibility of the Ministry/ Department the exact authority of the Director or Staff of the institutions, the DoPT or other agency should be clearly stated in the Charter.

(h) *Financial Provisions*

The Charter should contain a general specification concerning the financing of the training institutes by providing the initial or a minimal annual budget or by pleading to the Government to provide adequate operating funds. This is important in order to give assurance for the long range planning which is necessary in the operation of such an institution. The financial provision of the Charter should not be considered as taking the place of the necessary annual budgeting arrangements.

**The Direction**

3.41 The direction of an institute should be confided to an officer of sufficiently high rank to reflect the prestige of the institution, and to enable him to communicate on an equal plane with the head of the element of the administration which are served by the institute.

The determination of just what this rank should be is a matter to be decided with reference to the levels of participants and course[24]. There seems to be a general understanding that the head of an institute need not be a Minister. The leadership is looked upon everywhere as a non-political appointment, corresponding to the key position in the permanent civil service.

The manner of appointing the Director is usually stated in the Charter, and this determines, at the same time, the channel of reporting to be employed by the Director. In an institute created as integral part of a Department, the appointment of the Director, receives the personal attention of the Minister in-charge of that Department. It may be that the appointing authority is required by the terms of the Charter to consult in advance with the governing body of the institute or some other authority, but the appointment is made in the name of the head of the state.

3.42 The Director, ISTM, has all along been an officer of the Central Secretariat Service from its very inception, except for a couple of spells in the recent years when the post was manned by IAS officers. However, each one of them has provided unflinching leadership to the Institute and contributed towards its development and growth.

On its creation in May 1948, the Director, Secretariat Training School had combined the duties of a Deputy Secretary in the Ministry of Home Affairs[25]. Only by 1955, the School had a full time Director, an officer of the level of Deputy Secretary of CSS[26]. In 1970, the post of Director was upgraded to the level of a Director in the Secretariat alongwith creation of an Additional Director to assist him[27]. In July 1985, for the first time, ISTM had an IAS officer as the Director. In February 1986, another IAS officer of the level of Joint Secretary to the Government of India was appointed for a full term of four years upto May 1990.

If growth and development of an institute are the indicators of the quality of leadership provided by its Director, then all these years the Institute has seen growth all round—upto 1985 in terms of training programmes and activities and during 1986-90 in terms of infrastructure and building facilities. It is, however, seen that in terms of both development and activities, the Institute started declining from 1993 onwards. An interview survey of the faculty revealed that there has been, of late, general dampenness in the morale and motivation among most of the faculty due to growing indiscipline and lack of interest on the part of the management. It was pointed out that during a period of two years from July 1993 to June 1995 as many as four faculty members sought voluntary repatriation before completing their terms of deputation, and unfilled vacancies could not be filled for want of sufficient applicants. One of the reasons for such decline was apparently the appointment of a non-trainer on the verge of his retirement as the head of a training institute.

### *Review of the Status of the Director*

3.43 As stated above, the post of Director, ISTM was upgraded to the rank of Joint Secretary in the Ministry in 1986 on the recommendation of SIU. The upgradation of the post was justified on account of the following:

(a) Greater responsibility on account of the very appreciable increase in the number and variety of training programmes;

(b) The increase in the number of International Training Programmes for Overseas Administrators, at middle and senior management levels;

(c) Training programmes for senior officers at the level of Under Secretary, Deputy Secretary and Directors, in areas such as Reservation in Services; Training Methodology, MIS, Management Development, Behavioural Skills, Management Accounting and Financial Management; and

(d) The peripatetic programme in the area of Development Management, for Joint Secretaries, Directors, Deputy Secretaries etc. of State Governments and Union Territories.

On review of the existing activities of ISTM it could be concluded beyond doubt that none of the above conditions are any longer existing inasmuch as (i) the number of courses have reduced considerably, (ii) no international courses have been conducted since

1993, (iii) number of officers of the levels of Deputy Secretary and Director have also reduced to negligible, and (iv) number of peripatetic courses have also reduced and no course on development administration has been conducted in States after 1985. In view of this, it should be reviewed whether a full time officer of the rank of Joint Secretary for the position of the Director would continue to be justified or the responsibilities could be combined with the office of Joint Secretary (Training) in the Department. In that case the post of Additional Director will have to be revived. He will discharge the functions of the Head of the Department. The other hard option would be to resurrect the activities and courses of ISTM to pre-1992 days to justify the present faculty strength and the status of the Head. The Director must also take some training sessions, at least with senior groups, to justify his position as head of a training institute.

## The Administration

3.44 The Administration is generally placed in charge of an officer of the title of Registrar or Administrative Officer. A question of some importance arises with reference to the ranges of responsibilities to be confided to the Administration. A good guide upon this matter would be to say that the Administration may well be entrusted with all the administrative affairs of the institute, but to exclude professional matters from its jurisdiction. The Administration or the non-teaching staff of ISTM, headed by the Director, broadly consist of three categories of staff viz. Housekeeping and Establishment, Stenographic Assistance and Group D staff. At the time of creation of STS with teaching faculty strength of four including the Director, the following complement of staff was sanctioned for the Office[28]:

| | |
|---|---|
| Supervisor | - 1 |
| UDC-cum-Librarian | - 1 |
| LDCs | - 3 |
| Stenographer | - 1 |
| Class IV including Chowkidar and Sweeper | - 9 |

Over the period of last 47 years, with diversification and

expansion of the activities and faculty strength, the size of non-teaching staff has also grown proportionately. The existing strength of Administrative staff of ISTM is at Appendix 3.3.

After the recent expansion of building plant of the Institute the areas like hostel and classroom maintenance remained neglected for want of adequate supervision. There is a general opinion of the staff and faculty that the present supervisory levels in Administration including the DD(Admn) and Director are so busy in procurement of furnitures, equipments and other fixtures that they get little time to decide about their gainful utilisation for the benefit of trainees and faculty. The only Section Officer, after attending to management of store purchases and deployment of Group D staff, hardly gets any time for looking into the various personal matters and welfare of the staff and faculty. For proper supervision and accountability of the affairs of training facilities (including classroom management) hostel facilities and personnel management, there should be one supervisory level officer each in the grade of Section Officer for these units.

3.45 For the purpose of effective supervision and accountability the Administration of the Institute can be divided into three distinct units:

1. Personnel Administration and Establishment of staff and faculty of ISTM;
2. Training Facilities—stores relating to training material and classroom management; and
3. Hostel and Hospitality - arranging meetings, conferences, workshops, etc.

Each of these units should be placed under the charge of separate supervisory officer of the level of Section Officer. The nomenclature of the post of Section Officer in ISTM which is an attached office of Government of India does not seem to be appropriate, as there is no concept of Section in the Institute. On the analogy of the practice followed in other attached offices of Government of India, such as National Crime Records Bureau (Ministry of Home Affairs) or the Directorate of Estates (Ministry of Urban Development) the designation of Administrative Officer or Assistant Director respectively may be adopted.

## Internal Structure

3.46 The internal structure of the training institution normally corresponds to the range of instructions offered by it. If the instructions could be limited strictly to the professional field, the institute would be clearly seen recognised as department of instruction, and it would need an internal subdivision except for the performance of non-teaching functions. In fact, functions such as research, preparation of manuscripts for publications and consultation could be regarded as so closely related to the teaching function that the internal sub-division would not be necessary for handling these functions[29]. The internal organization of an institute should be kept as simple as possible. There is nothing to be gained, and much to be lost, in the multiplications of internal departments, divisions or sections, each with its head or other chief offices. If the ideal of a simple departmental organization as described above cannot be realized, a minimum organization is not more than three/ four branches set up[30] corresponding to the specialized areas of training, such as Foundational and In-Service Training Research and Development, Management Services, Financial and Personnel Management etc. Research branch could be responsible not only for the planning and conduct of research, but also for the direction of the library, the preparation of publications, the supervision of the service functions and the performance of the informal functions. The function of the In-Service Training branch would be clearly indicated by its title.

3.47 Internal structure of ISTM (earlier STS) has always been with minimum number of departments and functional distribution, or in other words could be called as "most flexible". One of the reasons therefore could possibly be the nature of persons appointed as the faculty members of the Institute. Though the faculty members are appointed against posts sanctioned for different subject specialisation like Joint Director (Financial Management), Deputy Director (Office Management), Asstt. Director (Accounts) etc. but since most of them come from the Secretariat their personal experience and expertise could be used in other areas as well. This system of one single team of faculty with the Director as the leader has always worked well in the past. In the beginning, the school started with broadly two disciplines viz., founcational and refresher training and typewriting and shorthand training. The Cash and Accounts training started in 1961 was handled by the faculty for Foundational and Refresher Training. In 1965, inclusion of training in Work-study in the Charter of the School gave rise to the creation of another specialised area and eventually a separate wing. The faculty in this area must have had either the special qualification in Management Techniques or had undergone Work-study training in the School.

## Examination Wing

3.48 Quite distinct from the normal training functions of the School holding of examination for recruitment to lower grade staff in the Central Secretariat and its Attached office was transferred from UPSC to the School in 1969 (exams conducted from 1.4.70) to create a new wing named Examination Wing in the internal structure of the STS[31]. By then, the School had proliferated into four distinct wings:

1. Examination Wing
2. Work-study Wing
3. Shorthand and Typewriting Wing
4. Foundational and Secretariat Training Wing

Later, the Examination Wing began functioning independently with a separate budget of its own with effect from 1 4.1975, and which eventually emerged as Subordinate Service Commission on July 1,1976 and thereafter as Staff Selection Commission in September, 1977[32].

3.49 Upto the year 1980, it can be observed that there has been a gradual and continuous diversification in the training areas and activities of ISTM creating five different wings on the basis of subject grouping, each headed either by the Additional Director or one of the four Joint Directors. However, the concept and practice of one team and one leader for the faculty had continued inasmuch as there was inter-mixing of the faculty in courses of different wings and the performance report of all faculty up to the level of Deputy Director was written by the Director and those of Assistant Director by the DD(Coord)/JD(Coord) as the case may be. The system worked well where the Director had maintained direct and one to one relationship with each of the members of the faculty with increased feeling of satisfaction and rapport.

3.50 The seeds of bureaucracy was sowed for the first time in the structure of ISTM in 1986, when the new Director, a bureaucrat by profession, declared each of the Joint Directors as respective Wing Head and asked for reporting through the hierarchical layers. However, discussions with faculty members of his time revealed that having the background and experience of training and being committed to the cause of training, he himself (the then Director) ultimatly choose to function only by way of one-to-one relationship at every level breaking all hierarchical barriers of bureaucracy. This worked well to enthuse the commitment of the faculty members. But by then, some of the Joint Directors had tasted the latent "power of exploiting" in the hierarchical system and wanted the authority of writing ACRs of Deputy Directors and Assistant Directors under them. With this design, they could prevail upon the new Director (1990-91). Before he could get into the processes and pitfalls of training, the organization of the Institute was once again re-structured on the analogy of the structure and functions in the Secretariat. ISTM was divided into the following four new wings[33]:

1. General Management and Office Administration
2. Personnel Administration and Training Methods
3. Financial Administration and Management
4. Behavioural Science and Training Research

The new Organization Chart of the Institute is at Appendix 3.4.

The Joint Directors, as Wing Head, were declared as Reporting Officers for the purpose of ACRs of DDs and ADs of his wing. There were representations from DDs against this new reporting system, which were referred to the Training Division. But no decision was taken by the Department till the representationists repatriated after completion of their deputation.

Finally, during the period 1992-95, the Institute had another Director, who set aside all norms of organizational structure for expediency of personal convenience and established functional relationship on personal allegiance.

### *Opinion Survey*

3.51 A survey of opinion of faculty was conducted, which revealed the following view of some (about 40 per cent of those who responded to the questionnaire at Appendix 3.1) faculty members: "..for training functions there should be no hierarchy particularly as in many cases subject areas of training fall in different wings". Another member feels "... all faculty members are specialised in their respective fields, and they should look at each other as equals, thus enabling in the sharing of ideas". One old timer has suggested that the earlier system of supervision and reporting by the Director in respect of all faculty members had maintained better harmony in the faculty. However, decision making in the matter of management of courses, research and publications, may continue through the respective Wing Heads. The remaining faculty members are, however, satisfied with the present system of hierarchy.

### Advisory Bodies/ Committees

3.52 Since training institutes are treated in many matters like academic institutes the Charter normally creates one or more boards, councils or committees. The type of councils commonly are: (i) a governing council, having powers of supervision; (ii) an advisory council or committee, having merely consultative and coordinating powers; (iii) an academic council or faculty meeting, usually having some authority or internal matters, such as course and discipline of students; and (iv) a liaison or coordinating committee, which may be necessary for maintaining continuous relations with other agencies, such as the Ministry/Departments in matter of in-service training, or with a university or other institutions.

With a view to facilitate intra-institutional discussions and decision making on various matters of the ISTM following committees have been in existence, at least for the last 20 years of its functioning:

1. *Policy Advisory Committee*: All decision on matters of policy on training programmes, training methodology and course content, etc. were within the purview of the Policy

Advisory Committee comprising the Director as the Chairman and all faculty members of and above the level of Deputy Director as members. The system of collective decision making process bring all the faculty members closer to the Institute's functioning. However, since November 1992 till July, 1995 i.e. during the tenure of this Director not a single meeting of the PAC was held though there was no formal orders issued scrapping the Committee.

2. *Library Committee*: The decisions regarding maintenance and development of library facilities are supposed to be taken by this Committee. The Director is the Chairman, and all JDs, DD(Admn) and DD(Lib) are members.

3. *Hostel and Catering Committee*: The matters regarding hostel and catering facilities are within the purview of the Hostel and Catering Committee.

4. *Monthly Faculty Meeting*: Like every training institute, the monthly faculty meetings of ISTM has always been considered as the most important forum for free discussion on various administrative and functional matters of the Institute and important decisions have been taken in the interest of one and all. However, it was perhaps the most unfortunate thing ever happened to the Institute when such a meeting could be degraded by discussing the household problems of individuals. When some faculty members raised serious administrative matters for decision, such meetings had to be declared as undesirable interference and questioning the propriety of the Administration by faculty members and disbanded for future. There has not been any faculty meeting since October, 1994 till 31 July, 1995.

5. *Official Languages Committee:* This is an obligatory Committee for implementation of official language policy of the Government in training. This is the one Committee in ISTM which has met regularly and religiously.

## The Training Faculty

*The Source*

3.53 The professionally trained persons needed in the operation of a training institute include teachers, research workers and subject specialist within the field of public administration. The problem of staffing a school or an institute consists, in the main, in finding the professional personnel possessing these capabilities. Such professionals and experienced personnel can be made available from two sources; first the teachers in university or professional institute, and secondly, experienced administrators having expert knowledge of administration specialities. Professors are recruited to teach in the training institute the subjects which they are already teaching in the university/ college, such as language, history, geography and mathematics. Teachers may also be found from the same sources for some specialized subjects related a little more closely to the work of the civil service, such as administration, law and statistics. The experienced administrators are brought in to teach special knowledge related directly to their work, such as financial legislature, tax administration and office management[34]. It is safe to say that an institute of public administration cannot be conducted at all without relying in large measure upon experienced civil servants in the faculty. There is no other way to relate the instructions directly to the administration practices of the country concerned and to prepare students specially for the tasks which will fall upon them later in employment[35]. Some observers have been strongly impressed with the necessity of having persons of practical experience in administration as training officers. Most Governments use their own employees as instructors, rather than looking to the academic world for teachers. One group of experts felt that instructors should be drawn from the line, and should return to the line after a few years, except for the small number who might wish to make training their career. In criticism of this view, one authority had said: "The belief appears to be held in the [British] Civil Service that no one should remain on training duties for more than about three years—just long enough, I should think, to enable them to learn how to do the job."

3.54 ISTM has always drawn its faculty from the Secretariat or other Government organizations on deputation for a specified period of three to five years. Most of the trainers who were interviewed by the researcher are of the view that the five years' period is just adequate while some were in favour of permanent faculty in subjects like behavioural techniques, public administration, etc. The researcher, who has had three stints (of about four years each) in ISTM, strongly felt that a civil servant whether in operation or in training puts his best for not more than four years at one stretch, thereafter he must have a change. A permanent faculty in a training institute would in any case be harmful.

### *The Rank and Status*

3.55 To look back at the gradual development in the faculty since its inception, it has been observed from the records that in the beginning when the STs started its training course with three Instructors—one each in Office Procedure and Financial Rules, the third for typewriting training[36], the appointments were on tenure basis of eminent scholars from among retired or working government servants. Later, Instructors were appointed on cadre posting of Under Secretaries and Section Officers of CSS. In 1966, the Instructors of the level of Under Secretary was designated as Assistant Director[37]. With effect from April, 1973, the posts Assistant Directors and Instructors were re-designated as Deputy Director and Assistant Director respectively[38]. In 1975, all posts of Deputy Directors and Assistant Directors in ISTM were made ex-cadre posts with a view to attracting suitable officers on deputation with requisite aptitude, proven caliber, tested talent and acknowledged accomplishment[39]. By then the faculty strength of ISTM had already risen to include besides the Director, one Additional Director, one Joint Director, 12 Deputy Directors, six Assistant Directors (from Section Officers) and 14 Assistant Directors (from Selection Grade of CSS). Since then, many changes took place in the range of functions of ISTM and the size increased many fold with some reductions here and there to the present strength of 33 as shown in Appendix 3.5.

### *The Work-load*

3.56 In any discussion on the question of faculty strength of a training institute, on one side it is generally argued that the academic work of training and teaching cannot be measured in any quantitative term as it involves lot of mental activities in research, thinking and preparation ahead of every lecture, while the other side, setting aside such expressions concludes that lecturing is a highly repetitive task without any definite outcome and therefore the strength of the Institution can be easily assessed on the basis of number of hours of lectures conducted during a specified time taking into consideration some extra rest allowance. However, the Staff Inspection Unit of the Ministry of Finance, in 1982, had studied the whole process of training activities in ISTM with a view to laying down norms for teaching and non-teaching staff of the Institute. As regards fixing of teaching norms for the faculty, their job was divided into the following parts[40]:

(i) Teaching time (actual classroom contacts),
(ii) Preparation for teaching time, and
(iii) Other allied, incidental, complementary and supplementary activities connected with the course, including course designing, course coordination, course correspondence, feedback analysis, appraisal, updating of training material, preparation of exercises, case studies, monographs, training aids like slides, charts etc., conducting of examination/tests, setting of question papers, evaluation of answer scripts, invigilation etc.

A detailed proforma indicating the various activities performed by each faculty member is placed at Appendix 3.6 for reference. On the basis of the data supplied by the working faculty members during the period of study, the Study Team prescribed the classroom time, which could be expected on an average from a faculty member, as 475 hours per year, which would include, inter-alia provisions for leave and training reserves[41]. For the purpose of calculating teaching hours, the total teaching hours as per the time-table for various courses (or training calendar) including peripatetic and specially designed courses would be taken into account. Dividing the total teaching hours by 475 would give the required faculty strength. It has been agreed by one and all that the norms are highly liberal by any standard. On conversion of 475 hours to course week on the basis of average 25 hours of teaching per week, every faculty member is expected to take up minimum of 19 course weeks per year. The actual assessment of work-load for the last five years from 1989-90 to 1993-94 may be seen at Appendix 3.7 which reveals considerable spare time with most of the faculty members. But this fact is not in the knowledge of the management. It has been observed that there is no system of monitoring the activities of the faculty members on daily-diary basis which may enable the management to ensure proper distribution of work to the faculty members. If one has the will, with the use of computer, analysis of the nature and distribution of work is not difficult. However, allocating training sessions of one specialization area to a member of faculty of different area/wing would also not be within the professional ethics and good management practices. A Deputy Director (Behavioural Techniques) cannot be asked to take classes in Constitution because there is not enough classes in Behavioural Techniques to keep him busy. This only indicates that the work-load assessed at the time when the post was sanctioned is not existing today. Same is the case with the posts of Joint Director and Deputy Directors (Peripatetic Training) and number of posts Deputy Director (Foundational Courses) and Deputy Director (Management Services). To sum up, the whole faculty strength of ISTM may be reviewed in the light of the present activities of the Institute, because insufficient and inequitable work also makes the organization inefficient.

***Faculty Development***

3.57 A number of civil servants have had to assume the title and duties of trainers often with little experience fit for the post. Training officers do not begin their careers equipped with an advanced academic degree which might be taken as badge of entrance into that profession. Many officers upon whom these responsibilities fell had little confidence in themselves as being equipped to perform the tasks, although probably without exception they have been anxious to improve themselves and to learn to do their jobs better. On the whole, training officers have been at a loss as to where to turn for self-development or advice.

### *Monetary Incentive*

3.58 With a view to attract better talented civil servants to training, the government, in 1986, introduced monetary incentives[42]. In the modalities the then existing trainers were required to be replaced with more talented recruits who deserved them. But, it was not easy to identify really talented without having tested them on the job. In the process, many of the genuine trainers got weeded out to make room for those who ultimately proved to be mercenaries.

The survey of the reasons for the faculty members joining ISTM (Appendix 3.1) has revealed that while for majority of them it was liking for teaching/training and yearning for an academic environment and for an experience of sharing with others, for a number of them it was the "extra money" as training allowance or a "foreign jaunt" which attracted them to ISTM, out of which some eventually proved to be committed trainers also. In this regard, someone has rightly said that morale and attitude of the faculty to a large extent could be atuned by the leadership of the Head of the Institute. If the Head is not fully committed to the objectives and purpose of the Institute he cannot demonstrate the expected behaviour in his juniors.

### *Training of Trainers*

3.59 Another important aspect of the development of the faculty is imparting them the "trainer's skills". They need to know the modern techniques of training, be skilled in the conduct of classes of adults and able to stimulate their interest and encourage them to think for themselves. The trainer should have a good educational background, some years of experience in government work, and instruction in the new and sophisticated method of training. Training has become a highly specialised and professional undertaking. Training is a skill.

Ever since the introduction of the "Direct Trainers' Skill" (DTS) package developed by the Thames Valley University (formerly Slough College) Slough, in 1987, ISTM has subjected every new trainer, soon after his joining, to this one week course. This has been quite useful for the development of the novice into the skills of training. But most of the trainers feel that since the fresh trainers in the absence of earlier exposure to training would not know the practical problems and pitfalls in the training process and could not assimilate the whole package at that stage, the same needed to be repeated (as a refresher course) after say one year or so. The ISTM trainers who have done the DTS are now also required to undergo a new package on "Design of Training (DoT)". However, the transfer of learning these packages can be ensured through a close monitoring by the Head of the Institute and other senior members of the faculty.

***Training Abroad***

3.60 In 1964, the STS sent one of its faculty member to USAID Programme on Training on Administrators and Instructors of State Training Institute[43]. During this time, a committee in the UK recommended that the British experience on techniques and instructional methods be extended to other countries and a three month course for training instructors to which developing countries including India would be invited to send participants. This led to the preparation and offering of a course in training techniques by the Royal Institute of Public Administration, London. This course was widely used by the ISTM faculty since 1970 onwards under the Colombo Plan. This was one of the useful courses for the trainers of training institute in countries like India. Later in 1983, a Trainers Development Project was launched by the Government of India (Training Division) in collaboration with ODA of British Council Division. As many as 30 slots in courses on Training of Trainers, Management of Training, Management Information System and other allied matters were made available to the Trainers of various Central and State training institutes in India. However, these courses were attended by participants from other developing countries of Asia and Africa. During the last phases of TDP from 1992 to 1995, two programmes on Special Training of Trainers (SToT)[44] and one Special Management of Training (SMoT)[45] were conducted with the assistance of the Thames Valley University, Slough, for the trainers and training managers from India only. ISTM got as many seven trainers trained under these course in the last four years. In addition to these ISTM produced seven Recognised Users for conducting the DTS and DoT courses mentioned above as part of the TDP. These Recognised Users will further train trainers of various institutes in India.

## The Physical Plant of the Institute

3.61 Any training institute needs a building or other premises suited to the variety and range of activities which it is expected to carry on. Ideally, the accommodation should be planned and prepared before the creation of the institute. A good many schools and institutes had to begin operation under makeshift arrangements in premises that were not at all suited to their needs and purposes. Quite often, an institute has been assigned the premises used formerly by some other educational institution. It is only by chance that such premises are sometimes well suited to the needs of an institute of public administration and several cases the new institute was faced at the outset with the problem of making extensive changes and renovations.

However, in the matter of allotment of accommodation for ISTM, the history of the past had been unfortunate and painful. In 1948, when STS was set up on a temporary basis, it started its training classes at Block "A", Curzon Road Barracks, near Constitutional Club[46]. Later,it was shifted to Mettcalf House, near Old Secretariat. Sometime in 1950 or so the School came down to B-Barracks, Queensway (now Janpath). As the barracks were later in 1963 declared dangerous by CPWD the School was allotted four Wings in the prefabricated office building (West Block) in R.K.Puram, and the School was shifted in July 1964. As R.K.Puram was too far away from the Secretariat Complex ( North Block and South Block) for the part time classes in English Typewriting and Hindi Typewriting and Stenography, an alternative accommodation in 2-A Prithviraj Road was allotted to the School. The accommodation with ISTM was neither sufficient nor congenial for the instructional activities of the Institute. During this time, with a view to bring down the National Academy of Administration from Mussoorie to the capital, a huge campus was raised on the south of Outer Ring Road near Munirka.

However, NAA did not come back to Delhi and while most of the Campus was allotted to the newly created Jawaharlal Nehru University a small portion comprising two classrooms and half of Hostel Block 1 was allotted to ISTM for its Management Services Wing and hostel. The new academic environment was at least face saving before the overseas participants for the International Course in Management Techniques launched in 1972. But the Institute's scattered classes at three different places gave rise to a number of administrative and management problem. Being a research and training institute, it needed to be located in a campus of its own in an environment which was conducive to its academic requirements. After a long struggle for about 20 years, consequent upon shifting of JNU completely to its own new campus, in 1991 the entire ISTM was brought into one campus still known as Old JNU campus.

3.62 In general, it may be said that a training institute of public administration needs accommodation similar to those of a small or medium sized college with differences in some respect. Like any organization, an institute also in the first place require adequate office space, a room to be used as the office of the director, and with need of other rooms to accommodate administration and the clerical and secretarial staff. What such an institute would be different from a college is in respect of the end of office space for its professionally trained staff on a scale allowing more commodious quarters that are provided in colleges, a common room for use by all members of teaching staff and cupboard where the teacher can keep his papers. An institute of public administration is expected to introduce certain renovations, which have implication with reference to the accommodation provided. Each member of the teaching staff is expected to perform research and, in many cases, to share in the service activities. At the same time, there is general intention to break down the staff and formal relations between trainer and trainees and to encourage informal conferences between them. To discharge their duties each member of the teaching staff needs a private office, or at least a semi-private one. This means that such an institute needs a more generous allotment of office space in proportion to the number of members of the staff than would be provided in many other kinds of educational institutions. In the case of shortage of space, it has become necessary to share the rooms by two faculty members. In such a situation, sharing should be as far as possible should be by faculty members of the same discipline and wing of the institute, and rooms of the same discipline close to each other on the same floor. Floor demarcation on the basis of level or rank is not good in an institute. During the course of the study it was observed that at the levels of Deputy Directors and Assistant Directors, faculty members are required to share rooms on the basis of socio-political behaviour viewed by the Administration. The surveillance network planted by the administration has been telling upon the morale and spirit of the faculty.

3.63 As for rooms of the general nature of classrooms, an institute will ordinarily require at least one fairly large assembly room or auditorium, a few medium sized classrooms of ordinary design, and a number of smaller rooms suitable for use as syndicate or seminar rooms for groups instructional learning. Of late, such institutions ideally have a committee or conference room with facilities of wider projection and public address system With respect to the furnishings of rooms, an auditorium may have fixed seats, but the chairs of classrooms and committee room should be movable preferably with coaster wheels in order to adjust in different arrangements to accord with the method of instructions being used. Seminars and syndicate rooms should be equipped with chairs and a large table, as this arrangement is the best known for the encouragement of full discussion.

## Residential Facilities

3.64 Learning is a continuous process undertaken over a period of time as opposed to a nine-to-five business. A congenial atmosphere and informal environment for free and open interaction between trainees and trainers outside the classroom helps in the enrichment of the learning process. Thus, campus of a training institute can play an important role in promoting not only esprit de corps amongst the trainees from different parts of the country but also free communication with the trainer regarding their goals, expectations and problems.

***ISTM Hostel***

3.65 In the name of hostel, initially when the Secretariat Training School was shifted to R.K. Puram in 1964, three Type II residential quarters were allotted in the adjacent residential complex for accommodating the outside participants. The trainees used to take their meals in the nearby market. Later, in 1972, half of a hostel block in the Old JNU campus was allotted for the participants of the 'management' and 'senior' courses being conducted in the JNU campus. Here, boarding as well as lodging facilities were available to the participants. Beyond this, however, any campus culture was not visible amongst the inmates of the hostel. The improvised dining room, makeshift common room and lack of recreational facilities had kept the community disintegrated. Generally, the interaction in a training institute takes a two way course; one in the classroom sessions and the other during informal mixing outside the class which include the evening tea sessions, dinner meetings, Sunday breakfast table, etc. Such fora contribute a lot in a learning process and developing self- confidence among the individuals. In most of the State and Central training institute located outside the Capital this has been working well, but in the case of ISTM where the majority of the participants for in-service training are local residents and faculty members are on deputation from various Ministries/Departments and are permanently local residents, the campus culture has not been possible so far. As a matter of fact, some observers insist that newly recruited probationers (the direct recruit Assistants and Section Officers) must compulsorily be made to reside in the hostel so that they can get maximum opportunity for free discussions and concentrate in their studies. It also helps in maintaining punctuality and discipline in the classroom. The course director is expected to have informal discussions with the participants off the training hours.

***Working Lunch***

3.66 For the above reasons, a working lunch as part of the course instead of leaving the participants hunting for a meal, would definitely contribute to the learning tempo and environment particularly for specialised courses for senior groups. The practice of serving course lunch and tea to the participants of specialised courses existing from 1976 to 1990 needs to be revived.

## Financial Resource

3.67 Like any other developmental activity, one of the major components in the business of training is adequate source of funds. Every training institute need its financial resource, and if necessary it may be allowed to generate it. But ironically, ISTM being a attached office of the Department of Personnel and Training, Government of India, has to depend like any other public office on the money of the tax payers through the Consolidated Fund of India duly sanctioned by the Parliament in the Annual Budget of the Department of Personnel and Training ISTM's budget includes expenditure on the various activities and supporting machinery of the Institute. It comprises disbursements on the Institute's infrastructure, training materials, salaries, training research and publications, social activities and other unscheduled expenditure. The real cost and expenditure (Annual Recurring) on the training function at ISTM include:

1. Salaries of faculty and staff
2. Salaries of Section Officers (Probationer) for six months of their training period
3. Training materials for participants including training aids (consumables) for faculty
4. Office management expenses
5. Hostel : store and maintenance
6. Library : books and periodicals
7. Printing and Publications
8. Meetings, Conferences, Annual Day, etc.
9. Faculty development

Generally, the expenditure on the above items are required to be met from the non-plan fund of the general budget for the Institute. In addition, suitable fund is provided from the plan fund for development of infrastructure, library and equipments.

Left to the Institute, its faculty has adequate potential for earning money through consultancy services like designing and organizing customised training course for non-governmental bodies, conducting management studies, etc. This source was tapped for the first time 1990 with a view to generate extra resource at the disposal of the Institute for development (beyond governmental red-tapism), and a separate account was created in the name of "Personal Deposit Account" of the Director, ISTM. The money earned through the consultancy services including that received as course fee from the DoPT sponsored courses are deposited in this account, and after meeting the related cost, the savings could be used for infrastructural development.

3.68 On the question, whether the budgetary provisions be made under the Plan head or the Non-plan head, the Working Group on National Training Policy, looking to the fact that training is an investment in Human Resource Development, recommended that much of the training activities should be funded from plan budget. However, if the Government's guidelines on funding, in the National Training Policy, that each Department should set apart 1.5 per cent of its salary budget for the sole purpose of training is implemented, the training institutes can generate most of its required resource direct from the client organization.

**Evaluation of Training Institutions**

3.69 The Working Group on the National Training Policy has touched upon the need of evaluation of training institutions focused on building the internal structure and processes of the training institutions in harmony with the requirements of the training programmes in view. However, if the training institutions are to be considered as one of the important partners in the training system, the need for standardization of training institutions in terms of infrastructure, design of courses, quality of trainers and training evaluation practices, cannot be overemphasised. The evaluation of the institutions would be on those standard parameters, and would act as a driving force towards the standardization.

**Conclusion**

3.70 Every institute or school of training has two principal elements- faculty and participants (or students). In order to function smoothly and to realize the aims for which the institutions was created, these two elements have to be organized and subjected to a degree of discipline. Further, in order to function effectively, every school and institute will need a premise, in which will be placed certain equipment and supplies needed in operations. In brief, an institute is itself a unit of public administration, and it presents the usual problem of leadership, staffing, funding and supply without which an agency cannot succeed. Since these institutes are intended as forces for improvement of administration in all public offices in general, it is highly important that they themselves represent the best in modern ideas of organization and administrative procedures. If the internal organization is streamlined and efficient, if the offices and classrooms are examples of good modern layout and planning, and if the office and teaching equipment is of the most up-to-date design, the school or institute may serve as something of a model or demonstration of good administrative practice. The school or institute should practice what it preaches, that is good administration; and there is no better way for it to teach its lesson than to stand as a good example of an institute well-organized and well-run. The necessity of recruiting persons who have genuine qualifications and aptitude as Training Officers is observed everywhere. Training programmes can be no better than the persons who plan and execute them. The time has passed when the training of civil servants could be safely left in the hands of amateurs. Many observers therefore feel that it is time to promote a feeling of professional solidarity among training officers and to offer to such officers easy access to courses designed for their development.

## References


1. Starr, Joseph R., *Schools and Institutes of Public Administration—a Coparative Study*, Knoxville, University of Tennesse, 1960.
2. United Nations, *Handbook of Training in the Public Service,* New York, 1966, para 327.
3. ISTM—*Annual Report 1971.*
4. ISTM—*Annual Report 1975,* p. 1.
5. *Ibid,* p. 2.
6. *Ibid,* p. 3.

7. Davy Thomas J., Reining Henry—*Education for Administrative Careers in Government Service*, Sweeney Stephen B (ed.), University of Pennsylvania Press, 1958, p.191.
8. United Nations, *Handbook of Training in the Public Service,* New York, 1966 para 336.
9. STS—*Annual Administration Report 1962.*
10. STS—*Annual Administration Report 1965.*
11. Ministry of Personnel Public Grievances and Pensions—*Annual Report 1990-91,* Para 7.47(ii).
12. ISTM—*Annual Report 1977-78,* Para 4.1.
13. ISTM—*Annual Report 1978-79.*
14. United Nations, *Handbook of Training in the Public Service,* New York, 1966, para 339.
15. ISTM—*Organizational set up and Functions of the Ministries/ Departments of the Government of India (First Edition)*, 1962, Preface.
16. United Nations, *Handbook of Training in the Public Service,* New York, 1966, para 344.
17. ISTM—*Annual Report 1990-91.*
18. STS—*Annual Administration Report 1962.*
19. United Nations, *Handbook of Training in the Public Service,* New York, 1966, para 354.
20. *Ibid,* para 357.
21. *Ibid,* para 360.
22. *Ibid,* para 368.
23. *Ibid*, para 390.
24. *Ibid,* para 399.
25. Ministry of Home Affairs—*F.No.20/26/48-Appts.*
26. MHA—*F.10/17/55-S&NG.*
27. STS—*Annual Administration Report 1970.*
28. MHA—*F.No.20/26/48-Appts.*
29. United Nations -*Handbook of Training in the Public Service,* New York, 1966, para 408.
30. *Ibid,* para 409.
31. STS—*Annual Administration Report, 1969.*
32. Deptt. of Personnel and AR Notification No.
33. ISTM—*Annual Report 1990-91.*
34. United Nations, *Handbook of Training in the Public Service,* New York, 1966, para 411.
35. Menier,*Education in Public Administration*, pp. 53-60.

36. MHA—*F. No. 20/26/48-Appts.*
37. STS—*Annual Administration Report 1966.*
38. ISTM—*Annual Report 1975* para A3.
39. SIU (Min. of Finance, Deptt. of Expenditure)—*Report on Study of ISTM,* October 1982, p. 7.
40. *Ibid* p. 8.
41. DoPT—O.M. No.
42. STS—*Annual Administration Report 1964.*
43. Ministry of Personnel Public Grievances and Pensions—*Annual Report 1992-93,* Para 7.27.
44. Ministry of Personnel Public Grievances and Pensions—*Annual Report 1994-95,* Para 7.31.
45. MHA—*F.No.14/3/48-NGS.*
46. STS—*Annual Administration Report,1964.*

4

# Providing Training Opportunities

## The Scope and Purpose

4.1 In the broader sense of the term, "Training Opportunities" in the context of this study, will include the function of survey and assessment of training needs, the training facilities made available and the will of the organization for providing training. More the need, more will be the opportunities for training. More the availability of training facilities, more will be the opportunities to the employees to avail themselves of such facilities. And greater the will on the part of the organizations to provide training to its employees, greater will be the opportunities for their training. In this three dimensional function of training interventions in an organized civil service like CSS, there are mainly three partners to perform their roles, namely,

(1) The organization (the concerned Ministry/Department),
(2) The individual officers (the prospective trainees), and
(3) The training institution ( the training courses).

In this Chapter, an attempt has been made to conduct a survey of existing training opportunities available to the officers of the service, and study the role and expectations of the above three in the context of the "training opportunities" for the officers in various grades of the Central Secretariat Service.

## The Existing Training Practices (for CSS)

4.2 As already stated earlier, the Secretariat Training School (later ISTM) was primarily set up in 1948 for imparting training to the Assistants and Section Officers of the Central Secretariat

Service. Broadly, training courses conducted by ISTM for the members of CSS can be placed in the following three categories:

(a) foundational and induction training which is imparted to the fresh entrants of the different services,

(b) in-service and refresher training to officers who have put in few years of service and need further knowledge and skills, and

(c) specialised training to officers who are required to handle new programme and new methods and procedures.

**Fundational and Induction Training**

4.3 The objective of foundational training is to prepare the new entrants to an environment in which they will be placed, to acquaint them with the system of work and rules and procedures applicable in respect of functions which they would hold after completion of the training. Such training, apart from imparting knowledge and skill to the new entrants, give them certain measures of confidence to perform their tasks and create the necessary background for learning on the job.

The *ab-initio* training for the direct recruit called as Foundational Course aims to provide a mix of Orientation and Induction training to the newly appointed to the public service. The kind of training known as Orientation is a general introduction to public employment. It should provide them with an understanding of the aims and purposes and the social usefulness of the various departments as a whole. It has been found that a broad knowledge of public administration, history and cultural heritage of the country, the socio-economic environ and the general laws relating to a public servant will be useful in orientation of a newly appointed Assistant and Section Officer.

4.4 Direct recruitment to CSS has been made only to the grades of Section Officers and Assistants. As already stated earlier, prior to merger of Grade II and Grade III to the Section Officers in July 1959, direct recruitment was made in Grade III of Assistant Superintendent and Assistants.

The *ab initio* training (as it was called then) to the Assistant Superintendent (and later Section Officer) and Assistant directly recruited through Federal (Union) Public Service Commission was conducted by the Secretariat Training School. In the beginning, the course of study prescribed for these freshly recruited Assistant Superintendent (later SO) and Assistants covered the following subjects[1]:

(i) Office Procedure;
(ii) Rules of Procedure and Conduct of Business in Parliament;
(iii) Organisation of Govternment of India Secretariat;
(iv) Constitution of India—Parts V and XIV;
(v) Financial Rules;
(vi) General rules and Orders governing the recruitment conditions of service, conduct, discipline etc. of government servants; and
(vii) Typewriting.

### Training for Section Officers (Direct Recruits)

4.5 The whole course of theoretical training mentioned in the preceding paragraph is covered in three months. Towards the end of two months, however, the Section Officers are required to appear at a preliminary examination. After the completion of three months training they are posted for practical training in Secretariat work in the different Ministries/ Departments for three months. During this period, weekly progress reports were submitted by the probationers through their Ministries and a watch was kept by the School on the progress of the training received by them. On completion of the practical training, the Section Officers returned to the School for a further period of two months for general instructions which may be found necessary in the light of their practical training. Towards the end of this period, the Section Officers appeared at the final examination. Thereafter, they were posted to different Ministries for another four months. During this period, the probationers are attached to senior Section Officers as far as possible, and encouraged to perform all the duties of a Section Officer under his guidance. After completing the one year's training as above, they are posted against regular duty posts of Section Officers and they continue to be on probation for a further period of one year before they are considered for confirmation[2].

## Training for Assistants (Direct Recruits)

4.6 The training course for Assistants (Direct Recruits) at the School was initially spread over a period of six months. At the end of about six weeks, they were required to appear for a preliminary examination. The final examination was held towards the end of the three months period, and before they were posted to different Ministries for three months for practical training. The course of instruction in the School, combined with three months' practical training, is designed to give the trainees a full and comprehensive idea of the work which they will normally have to attend to in a Secretariat office. At the end of six months' training the Assistants were posted to a regular Section in the Ministry where they were entrusted with regular work which Assistants were normally required to perform. At the end of one year, if their work and conduct during probation have been satisfactory, and they have passed the final examination conducted by the Secretariat Training School, they were confirmed in the Assistants Grade of the CSS.

The Assistants who, on their recruitment, were initially posted to the Ministries due to limited training facilities in the School were, however, given only three months' theoretical training in the School where they had to take the preliminary and final examinations as indicated above. As they had already spent some time in the Ministries, no further practical training is considered necessary for them[3].

## Refreshers Courses for Section Officers and Assistants

4.7 In spite of the emphasis on *ab initio* training, there has been no lessening of the importance of "in-service" training of personnel at the middle and lower levels. It is almost axiomatic that time taken out to survey one's work from a distance always ends in making one a better man and worker as it gives him the much needed break to get acquainted with all that has been happening around him and which he, in his engrossment in the daily work, may well have missed. The STS has, therefore, always attached considerable importance right from the beginning to these Refresher Courses for Section Officers and Assistants[4].

The Refresher Course for Section Officers which started in 1960, continued thereafter as a regular feature of the training programmes of the School[5]. The Refresher Course for Assistants, which was in the original charter of STS from its inception in 1948, had been discontinued in 1955 in order to cope with the training of the large number of persons recruited to the grade of Assistants on the basis of the competitive examination held by the UPSC in 1955, 1957 and 1959 were revived in October, 1962 as by then the training of the Assistant (DR) had almost been completed[6]. The Assistants who have had no training at all in the school as well as those who had not attended a regular course in the recent past viz., within the last five years or so, were eligible to be deputed to these Refresher Courses. The duration of these courses were specially reduced from two months to six weeks each to enable the Ministries/Departments to spare these Assistants without any serious difficulty[7]. But in 1963, the duration was again restored to two months[8].

The original syllabii of the *ab initio* and Refresher Courses for Section Officers and Assistants of CSS are at Appendix 4.1.

4.8 The Estimates Committee in its 93rd Report (1965-66) reviewed the course of study of the Secretariat Training School and observed[9] as under:

The Committee considers that as Section Officers and Assistants constitute the base of the Central Secretariat, it is imperative that their training receive careful attention. The Committee would suggest that the syllabus for their training may be suitably enlarged so as to give them a better understanding of the social and economic problems of the country. Government may examine in this context what portion of the Foundational Course for Class I Services conducted by the National Academy of Administration could, with suitable modifications, be filled into the programme of training for Section Officers and Assistants. Apart from training in rules and office procedure, the Committee would like Government to impress upon the young recruits, the imperative need for proper husbanding of Government's limited resources by effecting utmost economy consistent with a high level of efficiency, as also the idea of service to the public and of helping in the onerous task of development of the country.

The Committee would also like the Government to review the refresher courses for Section Officers and Assistants so as to provide them with an opportunity to equip themselves better to discharge their duties.

In pursuance of the above recommendations the course content of the *ab initio* as well as Refresher Courses for Section Officers and Assistants were enlarged, in 1968 to cover subjects like history, culture, public administration, law, etc. The revised list[10] of subjects covered in *ab-initio* and Refreshers Courses for Assistants and Section Officers is at Appendix 4.2. Consequently, the duration of the courses were also revised.

Subsequently, in November 1973, in order to cover the maximum intake of direct recruits in various grades every year, the duration of training for these courses were further reduced[11]. There was further revision of the duration and contents of these courses in 1976 and 1979.

**Specialised Courses in Functional Areas**

4.9 Besides *ab initio* foundational and in-service Refresher Courses, Specialised Courses in the functional areas like Cash and Accounts, administrative vigilance, establishment rules etc. have been conducted for these officers since 1961. A list of such courses is available in Table 3. However, these courses have been designed to cover the general assumed need of employees of various Central Government offices. The selection of trainees have not been made on the basis of the required need. Thus, the courses do not meet the specific need of the participants who are actually working in the relevant functional area, and those who are not actually working in that area but get themselves nominated for the course do not have a need.

**Field/Study Visits**

4.10 One of the most fruitful methods of reducing the monotony of class-lectures and of appetising the mind has been found to be an educational visit to places of interest[12]. The participants get an opportunity to have first-hand experience of different culture and work system in the States. With similar objectives the participants of all Foundational and in-service as well as long duration Specialised Courses in ISTM were taken on a study-tour to various public sector projects, State Secretariat, etc. These study tours were discontinued gradually since 1987-88 onwards except for the Foundational Courses for Assistants and Section Officers. There has been continuous demand from other participants of such study-visits as a part of the training course. The matter needs a review.

## Management Development Training

4.11 "Of recent years", says one authority, "the term management training has been used loosely to cover all training above the supervisory level"[13]. The term is so used here also, but it is given some precision by identifying the different levels and the major purposes of training in management in the civil services. In the Central Secretariat Service, such training for the officers above supervisory levels have been sub-divided into two steps and named as "Professional Development Programme for Under Secretaries" and "Management Development Programme for Deputy Secretaries" and the latter is conducted in the IIPA.

In some respect, managerial training may be viewed as not basically different from supervisory training, as the first line supervisors are unquestionably identified with management, rather than with the rank and file which constitute the greater body of workers. They need training in handling their subordinates, planning work, making work assignments and other matters which are the common responsibilities of managers of all grades. Managerial training is understood to include a good many matters which are and beyond those suitable or necessary for supervisory training. Managers of grades above first-line supervisors have responsibilities for planning and coordinating on a vastly broader scale. These differences, and their implications in training, maybe seen in the usual distinction made as to the levels of management[14].

### *The Levels of Management*

4.12 In the public service, three levels of management are

usually identified. The lowest level can be fairly sharply distinguished as consisting of the first-line supervisors as defined above[15]. The highest level, often referred to as "top management" is usually defined as including the principal officers who are continuously involved in the formulation of policy, and includes heads of main sub-divisions of the Departments, known as Wing, principal advisors and other staff officers. Since the training for such "top level" of civil servant is not within the scope of this study it may not be necessary to elaborate further in the matter. The middle level may then be defined as from a point just above the first-line supervisors to a point just below Head of the Wing[16].

In the Central Secretariat, the levels of Under Secretary or Branch Officer and Deputy Secretary/ Director (inter-changeable) or Divisional Head are identified as the middle level of management, which assume the day-to-day performance of the work of a large organization like a Ministry or Department, and as a pool or reserve from which were drawn recruits for appointment to the higher positions.

*In-Service Training for Middle Manager*

4.13 In a typical civil service, like the CSS, the position of middle management present such great variety in functions and responsibilities as to challenge the ingenuity of the officers responsible for planning suitable training. A first view of the training needs for the middle management level officers of the Secretariat may leave the trainer into a chaotic condition, because of the great variety of responsibilities and occupational specialities[17]. In general, in-service training for middle managers must offer many opportunities for specialisation. A sound approach in planning training for middle managers is to identify sub-groups which have similar needs and recognise certain cases or situation which have important implications with reference to the types of training to be provided.

4.14 The MDP for empanelled Under Secretaries of CSS has been conducted by ISTM since 1976[18]. To begin with, the Training Division envisaged different programmes for different categories based upon the mode of appointment to the grade of

Section Officers as also the age group to which the officers belonged as indicated below:

(a) Management Development Programme-I for promotee Section Officers below the age of 50 years at the time of empanellment (6-7 weeks)

(b) Management Development Programme-II for officers directly recruited as Section Officers and below the age of 50 years at the time of empanellment (3 weeks)

(c) Management Development Programme-II for officers above the age of 50 years at the time of empanellment (2 weeks)

The programme mentioned at (a) above was held in the Indian Institute of Public Administration in Jan-Feb 1976. Later, the Training Division felt that the distinction sought to be made between the programmes was not necessary and it was, therefore, decided to give up different groups. It was also decided that the Management Development Programmes would be held only at the ISTM. The objectives of the programme are primarily:

— to widen the perspective and conceptual abilities of the participants;
— to acquaint them with the latest social, economic and political environment in the country;
— to familiarise them with the quantitative technique and tools of modern management; and
— to expose them to modern concepts of behavioural sciences.

These programmes have helped create a sense of camaraderie and esprit de corps amongst the Under Secretaries working in various Ministries/Departments and provided a forum for learning from experience of colleagues in sister Departments. After return to their Ministries, they are able to meet more often in groups, discuss matters of common interest and solve their problems in the "Management Way" through a systems concept of thinking and a Task Force approach.

**Cadre Training Plan**

4.15 In August 1988, a comprehensive Cadre Training Plan

for CSS officers was prepared and issued by the Department of Personnel and Training (CS Division), according to which the Foundational Course for Section Officers (Probationers) comprises four specially designed modules to expose the participants to public administration, Office Management and Procedure and socio-economic development of the country:

— **Module I :** Four weeks; followed by one week attachment to a Voluntary Agency/village in a remote and backward area. (5 weeks)

— **Module II :** Four weeks; followed by a two weeks' study tour to a State capital to visit, among other places, the Secretariat, a nearby public sector undertaking and a Rural Development Project. (6 weeks)

— **Module III :** Four weeks; followed by 07 weeks "On-the-Job Training" (11 weeks)

— **Module IV :** Two weeks (2 weeks)

In an inter-department meeting held in August 1990, it was decided that a field component of 12 weeks will be provided in the training programme for Section Officers. This would provide for briefing at the State capital, if necessary, through Administrative Training Institutes (two days) and they would then be attached to different districts for training. A posting in a village for about a fortnight would also be included. However, it seems the above decision was not implemented by ISTM till the 1995 batch of directly recruited Section Officers.

The broad course content and duration of the Foundational Course for Assistant (direct recruits) and Refresher Courses for promotee section Officers and Assistants, Professional Development Programme for empanelled Under Secretaries and Management Development Programme for empanelled Deputy Secretaries (being conducted at IIPA) were also prescribed in the Cadre Training Plan at Appendix 4.3.

### The Session Plans

4.16 The Session Plan for the above mentioned Foundational and in-service courses for all levels of officers of CSS as followed by ISTM and IIPA may be seen at Appendices 4.4 to 4.9.

At this stage, a comparative study of the syllabii and content of the courses for the Section Officers and Assistants followed prior to 1988 (i.e. pre-cadre training plan), those given in the plan and those being followed at present by ISTM would reveal that the course content, particularly for the Foundational Course for Assistant (direct recruits), has deviated not only from the original scheme as modified from time to time but also from the Cadre Training Plan, so much so that the course no longer remains foundational in nature. The subjects like Public Administration, Indian history and culture, national integration have been deleted and inputs on specialised topics like, project planning, role and functions of DDOs, income tax calculation and handling court cases have been added.

**Training Methodology/Tools Used in ISTM**

4.17 For an effective transfer of professional knowledge and skills, the Institute employs a wide range of training techniques, varying from the age-old lecture method to modern practices like syndicate discussions, role-playing, in-basket exercises, the case-study method etc. By adopting suitable training techniques, the Institute endeavours to create a learning environment where the active participation and involvement of the participants is ensured. Keeping in view the level of the participants, the objectives and the theoretical inputs, the following techniques are liberally used, as a supplement to the lecture method[19]:

(i) *Practical Exercise*

In order to provide the desired expertise to the participants of the kind of work they have to perform in their work situation, they are given practical exercises, following the theoretical exposition in various rules/regulations being followed in Government office and disciplinary procedures, parliamentary procedures, conduct rules, preparation of bills, etc.

(ii) *Syndicate Paper*

This method is being employed by the Institute primarily with a view to expose the participants to the method of working in groups. The entire batch is divided into viable syndicates as soon as the course is launched, and they choose a subject of contemporary interest. One of the syndicate members is chosen as a leader for conducting and moderating the discussions of the syndicate prior to the finalisation of the paper. The syndicates work more or less on their own, while preparing a paper on the allotted subject. The faculty provides only academic support in directing them to literature available on the subject chosen by them. After the report is ready, the syndicate presents the paper, on an appointed day, to the class as a whole. The paper is discussed by the class, providing opportunity for active participation by every member of the class. The faculty present monitor and facilitate the discussions.

Besides, this method is also used as a sequence to the lecture method. After having presented a theoretical proposition, the participants are divided into syndicates and are expected to find solutions to the specific problems raised by the faculty and their peers.

(iii) *Case Studies*

The Institute has prepared a few case studies based on actual incidents from the Central Secretariat, with suitable modifications for discussion in the class.

(iv) *Workshops and Project Work*

These are being profitably used in Foundational Course for Section Officer (probationer) and Section Officers (refreshers) course and Professional Development Programme for Under Secretaries.

(v) *Role-Play Exercises*

This technique is being effectively utilized in the Behavioural Training as also in the programmes on Administrative Vigilance.

In the area of behavioural skills, the participants are required to play roles, normally of an official and a member of the public and deliberate on a given situation. Later on, the behavioural aspects of the discussions are brought out, not only through an analysis from the role players themselves but also from the participants who are observers. This exercise has been of considerable use in bringing out finer elements of human behaviour and attitudes in inter-personal interaction.

In the case of administrative vigilance, this exercise is done in the form of a mock enquiry. The participants play different roles such as the charged officer, enquiry officer, presenting officer and assisting officers. This method gives a practical orientation to the participants who are able to get a fair idea of the procedure followed in the actual conduct of an enquiry.

(vii) *Book Reviews*

With the multiple objectives of inculcating the habit of reading, assimilating what has been read and presenting it before a forum, the participants in Foundational Courses are asked to review certain books of an academic and contemporary interest. This has also helped in enhancing the public speaking and debating abilities of the participants, and ensuring greater involvement in the programme. For Foundational Courses the objectives and goals of training are by and large more specific and pre-determined as compared to management development programmes.

## Executive Training in States

4.18 With a view to providing an orientation and exposure to the district administration, its problems at village, block and district level in implementation of various Central/State schemes, to the officers of the Central Secretariat Service, the scheme of deputation of these officers, at levels of Section Officer and Under Secretary, to work in one of the States, was introduced in 1953[20]. Initially the duration of the course was of two years, but the duration was reviewed from time to time, and currently the duration of the course is nine months, commencing once in a year in July. The curriculum of the course has been structured so as to provide an indepth knowledge and expertise in the areas of revenue administration, police and judicial administration, development administration and functioning of BDO. The course includes specialised attachment depending upon the Ministry/Department where the officer has been working, to give him an indepth exposure to the problems faced by the States in various scheme and projects. Trainee officers are required to work on a project/specific assignment allotted by the State Government. The detailed curricula of the Executive Training Programme is at Appendix 4.10.

4.19 The course being purely voluntary, not many officers have ever been opting for this course. On an average not more than two or three officers volunteer every year for the course. Another reason for the poor response is the condition that an officer cannot opt for his home state for the training. Apparently, the DoPT (particularly at the higher level of bureaucracy) have not attached enough importance to such training opportunities for the CSS officers, as, of late, the Annual Reports of the Department are not getting mentions about the scheme.

The scheme needs to be reviewed by the CS Division in the context of training and developmental need at the levels of Section Officer and Under Secretary, and may be considered if the same could be made a part of the Cadre Training Plan.

## Training Abroad

4.20 The training of civil servants including those of CSS by taking them out of their homes and sending them to Institutions in the advanced countries is a post-Independence phenomenon of the last forty years during which technical assistance and economic aids have been offered on the grand scale. For many countries training abroad has been a principal method of acquiring modern technology and expertise for national development. The choice of civil servants to have the experience of going abroad for some months or years of study has dramatic elements. For this and other reasons, it attracts a great deal of interest. For many persons concerned with training in the public service, training abroad seems to be the most important phase, and the approach most likely to bring quick results in national development[21].

### *The Advantages of Training Abroad*

4.21 The training of civil servants abroad, principally the civil servants of the developing countries who go to the more technologically advanced countries for training, is an outstanding part of technical assistance. It involves the travel of thousands of civil servants each year. The subjects of training defy description because of their great variety[22]. Generally, one of the advantages claimed in favour of this kind of training abroad is the gains in technologies on the part of the developing countries. However, today after 48 years of Independence, how far this defence is valid in respect of public administration in India, is a matter of further analysis and evaluation. This apart, training abroad is looked upon as a broadening experience. It gives the visitors the opportunity to see how other people live and observe the material and cultural aspects of life. A civil servant returns from his foreign travel, it is said, with a broader horizon and a better grasp upon his mission. Even if he learns little of immediate application in his work, he is thought to be a better civil servant as a result of his experience.

*Selection of Civil Servants for Training Abroad*

4.22 The unerring choice of the right civil servant to profit from a training experience abroad is an ideal which is probably impossible to attain in practice. The number of misfits and wasted training opportunities can be reduced, in part, by an understanding of the abuses which have accompanied appointments in many places. A determined effort must be made to eliminate favouritism, partisan politics, nepotism and the similar abuses which have vitiated civil service appointments at many times and in many places. The natural tendency to choose a person because he is available must be resisted. Repeated applications for training grants must be scrutinized carefully, in order to avoid overtraining selected individuals at the expense of others.

In making selections, a balance should be maintained between the interests of the individual and the good of the service. In the past it has often been asserted that a civil servant is not sent abroad to earn an academic degree, or to enhance his standing in the community. Undoubtedly, the good of the service is paramount over the desires of the individual. In case of divergence of interest, there comes a point where the civil servant must confirm to the needs of the service or take the obvious course to dissociate himself from it. Up to this point, everything possible must be done to conform to personal wishes[23].

Of late, the Government of India in its National Training Policy guidelines has prescribed that overseas training shall be need-based and shall predominantly aim at drawing lessons from successful cross-country experiences. Only institutions which are reservoirs of knowledge and data-base on relevant experience shall be used.

## SYSTEMATIC TRAINING—AN ACTION RESEARCH

### *Systems vs Systematic Approach*

4.23 Buckley describes[24] system as a "a whole which functions as a whole by virtue of the interdependence of its parts." Interdependence or interaction of its component parts is thus a prime characteristic of systems and organizations. The organization as a whole may be described in systems terms or its component parts e.g. training, recruitment, etc., characterised in the same way[25]. Looking at training as a sub-system of the organization, it receives personnel, materials and information from other functional sub-systems as "inputs". The transforming mechanism in this training sub-system produces outputs that include the knowledge, skills and attitudes acquired by trainees. The user i.e. other sub-systems, should then provide the training system with appropriate feedback. This kind of model, Buckley has described as an "open" training system which requires a proactive approach from the trainer. A "closed" system would confine itself more to the activities with the training department/ institution. Presently, most training has been of the "closed" system variety which has made it unresponsive to organizational needs. To operate effectively in an "open" system trainers have to be aware of and alert to the realities of, and the changes in the user organizations beyond their own which may impact on the form, content and conduct of their training efforts. In addition, the trainer must consider both direct and planned outputs and the possible side-effects of training that may influence behaviour in the place of work.

4.24 Another way in which the term systems approach can be interpreted is as a logical relationship between the sequential stages in the process of investigating training needs, designing, delivery and validating training. Atkins believes[26] that emphasis on logical and sequential planning and action makes it more appropriate to describe this process as systematic.

An attempt has been made to apply a systems approach at the organization (user Ministry) level to examine the broader issues of the aim, function and appropriateness of training for the CSS officers, and develop a training model by applying systematic approach directly to day-to-day functioning of the training departments of the organization and institute (ISTM).

The decision to apply a systematic approach to training is made when the trainer is convinced that training is the most appropriate way to overcome a current or anticipated shortfall in performance. Performance problems, whether actual or anticipated involve people, and very often, it is people, as a group rather than as individuals who have performance problems. The need for training can occur in every area of organizational activity which involves people. Therefore, a trainer is likely to become involved with designing training programmes in a wide variety of situations and needs. A reference may be made to Chapter 1 (Conceptual Framework —Training Needs).

4.25 Induction training needs are probably short-term and the purpose of an Induction training programme is limited to helping a newly appointed person adjust to a new working environment. Those who are appointed for the first time in the government, like directly recruited Assistants and Section Officers fresh from college, need in addition, orientation (called Foundational Course) to the system and environment in general. Induction training programmes, from the organization's point of view, are concerned with helping people attain satisfactory performance as quickly as possible.

4.26 The process that help to identify training as the solution to actual or predicted performance problems may generate sufficient relevant information for the trainer to move on to subsequent steps in the systematic approach. Job Analysis is one process of examining a job in detail in order to identify its component tasks, including identification of the main objectives of the jobs, conditions under which it is performed, responsibilities, difficulties and distastes, supervision, etc. The information gathered during the analysis is used to draw up a job description. In addition to job analysis, part of the further investigation might include a close examination of data provided by reviews or previous training programmes which were designed to tackle the performance problem currently being studied.

A natural extension of the preparation of the job description is the job specification. When drawing up a job specification the trainer uses information which has been confirmed or collected previously and analyses the knowledge, skills and attitudes (KSA) associated with each task that makes up the job.

### The Job Description of a Secretariat Officer[27]

4.28 The starting point of almost all the work in all Wings of the Central Secretariat is a receipt, which could be a letter from a government office (a non-secretariat organization, a sister wing in a Ministry, a sister Ministry of a State government) or from a private source; or it could be a note from the Minister or the Secretary. A major part of the Manual of Office Procedure describes the methods and procedure of dealing with a receipt. The Section Officer is supposed to see all fresh receipts; separate those that can be seen by the officers straightaway, mark the rest to the Assistant. The Under Secretary and Deputy Secretary who see the former lot are required to dispose off on their own the receipts on which assistance of the Section is not required. The come down again to the dealing hand. Before the dealing Assistant examines the receipt, he would connect the papers located in the current and old records. After getting such papers, he is expected to summarise the case, bring out the issue for decision, quote precedents and even suggest a course of action. This is checked for facts and thoroughness by the Section Officer and submit the case to the officers. Each officer through whom the case travels is entitled to add something to the basic note prepared by the Assistant. Depending upon the nature of the case a decision is taken at the appropriate officer level and the file then comes back to the Assistant, who prepares a draft based on decision taken and submits through Section Officer to the higher officer for approval. If a case calls for consultation with another Ministry, the file of noting is ordinarily marked by the sender to the appropriate officer in the concerned Ministry where it becomes a receipt and is examined in the same way as mentioned above.

## Survey on Organizations' Role in Training

4.28 As is common knowledge, training in civil services in India has been highly deficient at least for the last two decades or so. With the exception of the Defence Services and perhaps also in civilian establishment under that Ministry training has been given very little attention in government organizations, particularly in the Central Secretariat. The Ministries have not only been lacking initiative in the past but in many cases have shown positive apathy towards sparing personnel for training courses or earmarking funds. Even while sponsoring personnel for training courses offered, several organizations have been reluctant in sending good workers under the mistaken notion that work would suffer during their absence and hence had sponsored those who they considered sparable, thus paying a lip-service to their contribution in the training effort as ritual.

*Management of Training*

4.29 In any training process the organization plays an important role in identifying the organizational requirements and the individual's training needs before providing training opportunities to the latter. As a matter of fact, all training process not only begin but also end in the organization, as the organizations (here the Central Ministries/Departments) are the main beneficiaries of the outcome of the total process. But the question arises, how far are these Ministries/Departments concious of this fact?

4.30 A survey was thus conducted to assess the willingness on the part of the Ministries/Departments in creating and providing necessary training opportunities for the officers of the Secretariat, the practices of selecting/nominating trainees, post-training follow-up and other training activities as practised by them. Due to constraints of time and large number of participating organizations, a questionnaire on Management of Training was devised and sent to all the 33 Ministries/Departments, Cadre Units of CSS with a forwarding letter from the Director, ISTM to all Joint Secretaries in-charge of administration.

In spite of reminders and personal follow-up, after four months of its sending, response to the questionnaire was received from only 12 out of 33 Cadre Units. This fact itself gives an indication of the degree of importance attached to training and development of its officers in Ministries/Departments. It shows that not more than 35 per cent of them are conscious of the requirement of training and thus willingness to see adequate opportunities. One of the reasons for such a state of affairs could be, as most management theorist and practitioners have said, the lack of awareness and commitment of the Heads of organizations for development of its subordinates, towards efficiency of the organization and ultimately providing better service to the people. This attitudinal behaviour transmitted down through various levels in the organization which ultimately gives rise to a particular environment, be it of discipline, corruption, service or efficiency.

*Number of officers sent for Compulsory Training Courses*

4.31 The survey results (last three years data) showed that in the case of promoted Assistants on an average only 10 per cent of persons appointed in a year receive their in-service (Induction) training in ISTM, in the case of direct recruit Assistants, up to 38 per cent of the new entrants received their Foundational Training in ISTM, and 50 per cent of them as late as two years after their appointment.

The training opportunities made available to Section Officers ten promotee as well as direct recruits have been comparatively better during the last three years ever since they are being nominated by the CS Division. Upto 70 per cent of the promotee Section Officers have attended Section Officers (Refreshers) Course at ISTM within one year of their promotions. The directly recruited Section Officers being small in number and since they are directed to report to the ISTM first (before they join the service) for Section Officers (Probationers) Course, the situation seems to be within control and satisfactory, though a good number of direct recruits Section Officers are yet to complete their Foundational Training but joined their Ministries for some personal reason or other.

As reasons for not attending to these Assistants their compulsory training, about 70-90 per cent of the Ministries have stated that (i) being large in number sometimes, ISTM could not accept all of them in a course, (ii) the Ministry sometime could not relieve all of them together due to exigencies of work, or (iii) their supervisors have not relieved them.

*Practice of selecting and nominating officers for training*

4.32 The responses to the questionnaire reveal that mostly officers are nominated for various training courses (i) on the basis of the performance and need of the existing job and (ii) to learn new systems and procedure in the organization. Sometimes, persons are identified for training keeping in view the future promotion and posting or on identification of specific weakness which could be rectified through a particular course. The Ministries did admit that sometimes officers are nominated at the initiative of the individual officers or when he could be easily spared. Thus, in most of the cases the officers himself had the decisive role in identifying his training requirements and in other cases mostly the Training Unit or Administration decided. The role of immediate superior or the highest level in the organization has been rare and negligible.

*Knowledge of Objectives*

4.33 A factor which enhances the learning process and its transfer is the congruency of training objective between the trainee, his boss (representing the organization) and the training institution. A variable which brings about this congruency is a pre-training discussion between the trainee and his boss about their objectives from training and the training objectives as stated by the training institution. As a matter of policy, in none of the Ministries, either the supervisor or any other training officer generally discuss the training objectives and training needs of the individuals or those of organization before the officer is deputed for training. Unless there is clarity of objectives the training will not gain insight into the total training process and will not be able to derive maximum benefit from the training course. At the training institutions, however, objective congruency, as an aid to increasing the effect of training, could be achieved through the process of pre-training evaluation which has been discussed later in this report.

*Training Manager in the Ministry*

4.34 According to the survey, none of the Ministry/ Department is having any officer designated as Training Manager or Training Coordinator for the Department. Only two out of 12 Ministries are having a separate Training Unit under the charge of a Section Officer who are also doing routine matters regarding issuing training circulars and nominating officers for various courses. It has been observed that in some of the large Cadre Ministries, the training desk is being handled by an Assistant or UDC.

*Interaction with ISTM*

4.35 One of the major drawbacks in training institutions as perceived by the organizations was the inability of the training institution to keep abreast with practical problems and the growing needs of the sponsoring organizations. They felt that the training not fully geared to their real life problems had very limited value to them. The training institutions in turn feel that a factor contributing to the dissatisfaction with the prevailing standards of training was due to the organization themselves adopting a lax attitude towards training and not being very serious in their efforts to maximise the benefits of training. They felt that there was lack of communication and coordination between the training manager, the trainer, the supervisor and the top team.

4.36 The survey has revealed that more than 80 per cent of the Ministries/Departments are willing to arrange interaction between the officer, the training managers and training faculty of ISTM for the purpose of (i) drawing up the plans for identification of training needs, and (ii) details of the course. Some of them may use such exercise for identifying specific performance problems of the individuals as also setting competence standards on job/tasks or even for selection of participants.

About 20 per cent of the organizations have stated that such interaction may not be possible due to time constraints or due to lack of initiative from officers/staff of the Department.

However, to bridge the perception gap a certain amount of liaison between training institution and sponsoring Ministry/

Department is required. It is accordingly suggested that a meaningful procedure of periodical interaction be initiated by ISTM to understand the changing system, procedure and requirements of both the parties. The interaction process could be carried out through personal discussion, use of questionnaires, visits to Ministries and feedback obtained from preceeding courses. In addition, periodical workshops/seminars may be conducted to sort out common problems of the Ministries and ISTM, where the CS Division and Training Division may also be associated.

*Post-Training Follow-up*

4.37 Relevance of any training is tested on transfer of learning to job, and such impact of training can be assessed through systematic training follow-up of the trainees. The follow-up study can give an insight into the relevance and applicability of the training offered and the organization has the most important contribution to make.

The survey revealed that only a few Ministries had a system of follow-up after the training by either holding discussions with the trained officer or are asked to submit a report on his training alongwith an Action Plan for changes/improvements to be introduced. However, there is no system of assessing the impact of training on the performance of the officers subsequent to training or of actual transfer of learning, nor the ISTM is presently conducting any follow up exercise. The Ministries/Departments may carry out post-training follow-up of the trainees on a regular basis and inform/discuss their finding with ISTM to enable them deciding whether training courses need modification or the concerned individual may be given further training on the specific deficiencies.

## Survey of Training Needs

4.38 One of the most important activities which the proposed training manager can undertake is the survey of training needs for collecting information to be used in deciding upon the kind of training to be provided to the officers. "Unless careful analysis are made to find out training that is really needed, there is grave risk of leaving essential training undone while relatively inconsequential activity is engaged in."

The training need survey should normally be made at the time when the Department decides to embark upon a programme of in-service training. Thus, the survey is intended to lay information about the Civil Service to be used in planning. The appointment of a new training officer or a decision to have a better training programme than in the past may also be occasions for making a training survey.

Many executives, when asked to furnish information about needs for training, are quite ignorant of the whole subject, and tend to answer the questionnaire with the first ideas that come to mind. It is probably rare that the Head of a Department, when first asked to furnish such information conducts anything like an objective survey is his own organization to identify the kinds of training most needed. Distrust of the result is common, although the persons in managerial positions in the Civil Service should be the best source of information about training needs. In the absence of the consultation of management in matter, relating to training decision on what training to offer are likely to be merely the intuition of training officer.

4.39 As part of this study, a questionnaire (Appendix 4.7) was prepared as a means of conducting the survey of opinion of the officers of CSS at the supervisory / managerial levels on training needs. The questionnaire mainly seeks information on three aspects, first the amount of training these officers already had and their educational level and nature of work, second their perception /opinion about the need of training in improving efficiency and organization's concern about training and third, the officers' own opinion about the type and content of training they need for themselves as well as what their juniors require. The first is an effort to ascertain facts, while the second and third would be taken as the expression of subjective judgement and opinion.

The questionnaire was distributed generally among the Assistants, Section Officers and Under Secretaries who have some (2-3) years of experience of work in the Secretariat. The responses could be collected from about 200 Section Officers and 50 Under Secretaries from different Ministries/Departments.

*Existing Level of Education and Training*

4.40 A sample of about 200 Section Officers revealed that 65 per cent of them were only graduates and 35 per cent possessing post-graduate qualifications including degree in law and PG diploma in management.

55 per cent of the Section Officers have not attended any training course during the last five years, while 25 per cent have attended only one course and remaining 20 per cent have attended more than one courses during the past five years.

*Training Need Opinion of Individual Officers*

4.41 The responses received from 200 Section Officers and 50 Under Secretaries have been summarised below in percentage:

**TABLE 4.2**

| *The questions asked* | *Responses in per cent* | | |
|---|---|---|---|
| | *Yes* | *Sometime* | *No* |
| 1. Do you think, training is a must for improving performance on the job? | 92 | 04 | 02 |
| 2. Do you think that officers at higher/highest level in your Department believe in the need of training for improving performance? | 30 | 52 | 18 |
| 3. Do you think Induction/Orientation training is essential on promotion to the next grade? | 80 | 14 | 06 |
| 4. Do you think officers are nominated for training courses on the basis of— | | | |
| decisions exclusively by the Admn. | | 20 | |
| initiative taken by the supervisor | | 10 | |
| initiative taken exclusively by the officer? | | 70 | |
| 5. Do you think that a Foundational Training is must for newly recruited officers in CSS (Assistant and Section Officer level)? | 100 | ** | ** |

If yes, the duration of such course should be:

| 2 weeks | 4 weeks | 3 months | 6 months | more |
|---|---|---|---|---|
| 02 | 40 | 48 | 06 | 04 |

Analysis of the above data only reveals that majority of the individual officers believe in the need of institutional training at every stage, but the Ministries/Departments do not provide enough opportunities for the development of its employees. At least the officers feel that higher officers in the Department do not attach adequate importance to the need of training for development of their performance. In most of the cases the individual officers take initiative in getting themselves nominated for training courses. The very practice of circulating training courses inviting volunteers speaks about the Ministry's perception of training and development of its officers.

**Contents of Training**

4.42 The training of civil servants particularly in the Secretariat Service need to develop skills in two areas, one on specific rules and procedure of work, and the other the managerial and behavioural skills. At the operational level, the Assistants and Section Officers require rules and procedural skills, whereas at supervisory levels of Under Secretary and Deputy Secretary the officers need to apply more of managerial skills. With a view to conduct a survey of opinion of the individual officers of the Service about what they feel should be the thrust of the training for various levels of officers, the third part of the questionnaire contained the following question asking each individual's view in respect of all the officers with whom he is working, and the responses have been summarised in percentage :

**Q.** In your opinion, officers in the various levels require training on specific rules/procedure skills and managerial/behavioural skills in different degrees. Please indicate.

**R.** **TABLE 4.3**

| | Degree of training needed in rules and procedure skills | | | Degree of training needed in managerial/ behaviour skills | | |
|---|---|---|---|---|---|---|
| Level | High | Mode-rate | Negli-gible | High | Mode-rate | Negli-gible |
| Deputy Secretary | 20 | 65 | 10 | 85 | 10 | 05 |
| Under Secretary | 40 | 40 | 20 | 85 | 15 | ** |
| Section Officer | 80 | 20 | ** | 70 | 30 | ** |
| Assistant | 90 | 10 | ** | 15 | 60 | 25 |

The above data indicate that at the lowest level of Assistant, training input should be more in rules and procedure while at the higher levels of Under Secretary and Deputy Secretary training should be on managerial and behavioural skills. In the case of Section Officers, the opinion favours for both rules and procedure as well as on managerial/behavioural skills.

4.43 To supplement the above another question was asked to all Grades officers up to the level of Under Secretary to identify, not more than 5 topics, out of a list of 36 topics covered in ISTM training courses, the specific areas in which they think they need training and the areas which they suggest for their immediate subordinates. The responses collected were further tabulated below (Table 4.4), Grade-wise (vertical rows) and Topic-wise (horizontal rows) as the need felt by self and by his supervisor on each topic. Only 18 out of 36 topics have received consideration, while the response against rest of the topics were insignificant to indicate any inference, and thus have been ignored.

**TABLE 4.4**

**Training need data of the Officers of the Central Secretariat**

| | *For Asstts.* | | *For S.Os* | | *For US* |
|---|---|---|---|---|---|
| *Functional Topics* | *Self%* | *Boss%* | *Self%* | *Boss%* | *Self%* |
| 1. Noting and Drafting | 75 | 74 | 0 | 48 | 0 |
| 2. Secretariat Procedure | 45 | 62 | 20 | 42 | 0 |
| 3. Records Management | 25 | 58 | 26 | 66 | 0 |
| 4. Establishment Rules | 65 | 58 | 42 | 48 | 0 |
| 5. Computer Application | 40 | 56 | 56 | 48 | 36 |
| 6. Handling Court Cases | 25 | 38 | 18 | 0 | 24 |
| 7. Financial Rules | 40 | 24 | 16 | 30 | 24 |
| 8. Disciplinary Procedure | 25 | 12 | 0 | 0 | 0 |
| 9. Communication Skills | 30 | 5 | 0 | 20 | 24 |
| 10. Leadership Styles | 0 | 0 | 22 | 0 | 24 |
| 11. Time Management | 0 | 0 | 16 | 24 | 24 |
| 12. Grievance Handling | 0 | 0 | 20 | 0 | 30 |
| 13. Decision Making | 0 | 0 | 34 | 0 | 24 |
| 14. Personnel Management | 0 | 0 | 34 | 0 | 54 |
| 15. Management Concepts | 0 | 0 | 48 | 0 | 54 |
| 16. Financial Management | 0 | 0 | 0 | 0 | 30 |
| 17. Economic Policy | 0 | 0 | 0 | 0 | 24 |
| 18. Career Management and Training | 0 | 0 | 0 | 0 | 24 |

The above data indicate that 75 per cent of Assistants themselves as well as their supervisors (Section Officers) equally feel that they (Assistants) need training in Noting and Drafting, while the Section Officers have not felt that they also need training in Noting and Drafting but their supervisors (Under Secretaries) feel that their Section Officers need improvement in the skills of noting and Drafting. This may be further analysed by observations, case-studies and discussions with higher officers. On the other hand, it may be observed that there is general need at every level for training in Computer Application. Similarly, on various management topics, the Under Secretaries and Section Officers showed their interest in learning but have not recommended for their respective subordinates. This type of analysis can give a general idea about the need and interest of the officers in various functional areas and help the trainers in designing the courses.

4.44 One of the earliest report on training in public service well worth repeating for the guidance of training officers of the present, is as follows:

> Individual service or efficiency ratings have proved very useful in the isolation of training needs. Further significant clues to the need for training are provided by records of errors, accidents, discipline cases and complaints.... In many cases, of course, employees themselves have a clear idea of the training they need ... Selection and placement authorities are another important source of information.

However, training need survey is an not one step, one time activity of any training process. It can be spread over the various stages of training and development as an integrated element of the whole on-going activity, as the information gathered at the stage of evaluation of one course can be used for need assessment for subsequent course as also the performance assessment may include information on training need of an employee.

Departments may consider appending a separate sheet on training need suggestions from the supervisor, which should be detached soon after they are written (so that they don't have any reflection on the performance appraisal part of the individual) and collated and analysed by the Training Officer for planning future training programme.

*Training Plan*

4.45 As has already been mentioned, ISTM is primarily responsible for imparting all pre-entry and in-service training to the CSS officers upto the level of Under Secretary. Therefore, at the stage of survey and assessment of training need there should be close collaboration between the Training Officers of the Ministries and the faculty members of ISTM. The CS Division of the DoPT have prepared a training plan called Cadre Training Plan for the CSS officers prescribing the broad course contents and duration of various foundational and in-service courses for all level of Officers. Apparently the Cadre Training Plan has been prepared without any proper survey of needs either by the training institute or by the organisation. It may be necessary to review and recast the Plan after doing the survey of needs at the organizational level in close collaboration with the client organization and training institute.

4.46 A plan is in large part a formulation of policy and of intentions to do something in the future. It has no great value as a guide to a programme of action if these matters are stated vaguely without limitations as to time. To make the plan a bridge to a programme of action, it is necessary to formulate goals for expected achievement. Moreover, each goal must be accompanied by a series of dates to be understood as the target dates for the accomplishment of specified part of the course. The goals and their accompanying target dates should be realistic, that is, actually attainable with the disposable resources.

The next stage in preparation of Training Plan after survey of need is formulating the training programme by the training institute (ISTM) in collaboration with client organisations, Ministries/ Departments. The plan is a general consideration of all aspects of training while the programme is an indication of the work to be undertaken by the training institute. The programme is the culmination of all the processes which have been brought under consideration. The content of the programme depends upon the solution of all the different problems which have been mentioned.

*The Training Programme*

4.47 The design and delivery of the training programmes can be undertaken by the institute only when a well-written set of training objectives have been produced. These objectives state what has to be achieved by the end of training, they provide a sequence or order in which the training should take place and they give an indicator of what kinds of strategy and tactic should be used. They provide the basis for measuring the effectiveness of training in terms of the knowledge, skills and attitudes expected of the trainees, the minimum acceptable performance standards and the conditions under which the performance is measured. They provide link between training needs and the training which is delivered so that the training can be validated.

However, the training institute does not have complete freedom in designing of the courses and selecting the methodologies. There are a number of factors which would influence the design of a course like organizational constraints, target population and learning principles.

*Constraints*

4.48 One of the biggest constraints that has to be contended with is time. Trainers are usually expected to react quickly to meet the needs of the client organization, and after the initial survey and investigation, time has to be considered in a number of ways. There is the consideration of time span between the need survey, design training, prepare training material and scheduling the courses. There is the balance of the length of time that the officers can be spared for training and the length of time that is needed to achieve the objectives. In the case of CSS officers there is a huge backlog of personnel who need to be trained before the Cadre training plan takes on its expected pattern of frequency which means that deadlines will need to be set for clearing the backlog. The time constraints in the situation would also be linked with training facilities, accommodation and their availability.

*Target Population*

4.49 A close scrutiny needs to be made of the profile of the target population before the task of designing of courses is taken up. Particularly in the beginning for handling the backlog of untrained officers who have by now acquired experience of varied nature and duration. Officers recruited against reservation quota may need special additional care to bridge the gap, if any. The best that the institute is likely to achieve is a broad picture of the target population which is sufficient for planning in the initial stages but there are specific features which it is useful for trainers to know about when the training course is actually begin. These can be identified through the trainee's profile received from the Ministries before the course.

*Training Strategies and Tactics*

4.50 Training strategies can be categorised as centralised and decentralised, as trainer-centred and learner-centred, as on-the-job and off-the-job, etc. The strategy that is chosen will depend very much on what is being trained, knowledge of the target population and the constraints which the training designer has to work to. The training plan for the Secretariat personnel may adopt both strategies in the relevant context, for example trainees may undertake some form of self-learning through guided reading (learner-centred) and observation within the organization (decentralised) as a pre-requisite to attending a course at ISTM (centralised and trainer-centred). Similarly, there would be a judicious mix of on-the-job training between institutional off-the-job learning. Having decided upon the appropriate strategy, the trainer will select the most appropriate methods or tactics with which to apply the learning strategy.

*Consideration of Implementation of the Plan*

4.51 The most important and vital planning task is the consideration of the execution of the plan. This involves a number of matters, such as proper scheduling of the courses in order to cover all new entrants in a year in the case of Foundational Courses and availability of trainees in the case of in-service refresher training. The prior commitment of the organization in this regard is essential.

## Conclusion

4.52 The terminal use of training is to help achieve the goals of the organization through optimum use of manpower. As observed, identification of training need is not done at present in any systematic manner either by organizational diagnosis or job analysis. Training courses are offered on the perception of the training institutes about what the organizations need rather than on the basis of perceptions of organization or the employees themselves as that they need for achievement of their objectives. There is no follow-up to either to ensure transfer of learning to their respective job or to assess the benefits of such trainings to the organization. The skills acquired during the training are not always utilised in the field, as in many cases immediately after the training the officer is posted to assignments which has no relevance to the training undergone. This results in infructuous training efforts and also in the loss of morale and motivation of the participant himself and when seen by other it has an adverse demostrative effect on the zest for undergoing training. It is generally felt that proper training policy and planning for its implementation is needed in all government departments at macro as well as micro levels.

4.53 If there is any principle of universal recognition in the field of training, it probably is the belief that civil servants should always be released from duty to participate in formal training. Release from duty indicates that the highest officers in the organization recognise the value and the necessity of training and that they believe in the specific course to the extent of counting attendance as a duty. The recognition of this principle should not be looked upon as a special favour to the individual who receives his salary while occupied in schooling. It is to be remembered always that the interests of the organization are paramount in training and the civil servant takes the training, not for his own satisfaction but for the improvement for his functioning in the organization. Many trainers report unsatisfactory results when participants are released for training on a part-time basis for example, a half day in an intensive training course and the return to their desk. If the training activity is desired to be a period of intensive study and application to administrative problem, it is a mistake to plan it to occupy a part of the ordinary working day. Some observers go further and insist that training must be offered at a place far from the usual place of work, so as to remove the participants from the demands of the telephones and of secretaries and colleagues who may come for consultation.

## References


1. STS—*Annual Administration Report 1962* para 3.
2. *Ibid,* para 4.
3. *Ibid,* para 5.
4. STS—*Annual Administration Report 1966* para 6.
5. STS—*Annual Administration Report 1962* para 7.
6. *Ibid*, para 8.
7. *Ibid.*
8. STS—*Annual Administration Report 1963* para 8.
9. STS—*Annual Administration Report 1966* para 30.
10. STS—*Annual Administration Report 1969* Appendix VI.
11. ISTM—*Annual Report 1975* page 7.
12. ISTM—*Annual Report 1987-88* para 8.
13. Tickner F.J.—*Modern Staff Training : A Survey of Training Needs and Methods of Today,* University of London Press, 1952, p 139.
14. United Nations—*Handbook of Training in the Public Service,* New York, 1966 para 167.
15. *Ibid,* para 168.
16. *Ibid,* para 169.
17. *Ibid,* para 177.
18. ISTM—*Annual Report 1975* page 17.
19. ISTM—*Annual Report 1988-89.*
20. MHA—*F.No.1/10/53-CS(A)*
21. United Nations—*Handbook of Training in the Public Service,* New York, 1966 para 196.
22. *Ibid,* para 198.
23. *Ibid,* para 209.

24. Buckley, Roger Caple, Jim—*The Theory and Practice of Training*, Kogan Page, London, 1992, p. 26.
25. *Ibid*, p.28.
26. Atkins B.—*Programmed Learning and Educational Technology*, 1983.
27. *Report of the Study Team on Machinery of the Govt. of India and its Machinery of Work*—ARC 1968, para 4.5.

# 5

# Impact of Training

5.1 A training system should be maintained only as long as it produces the desired results. Therefore, assessment of the effectiveness of any training programme or its impact on the performance of the job-holder are vitally important. Assessment can be viewed as a method of measuring change in knowledge, skills and attitudes, job performance of the individual after training.

## Evaluation Practices in ISTM

5.2 ISTM, like all other training institutions, follows the traditional system of reaction evaluation based on the participant's feedback at the end of the programme. This feedback is mainly concerned with their reaction to—

(a) the various inputs given by faculty members,
(b) training methodology/tools used,
(c) reading material,
(d) duration of sessions/programme, and
(e) physical facilities.

The format of evaluation and validation feedback is given in Appendix 5.1. The participant feedback is discussed and programmes reviewed by the Policy Advisory Committee of the Institute. Since the Committees are at dormant state for the last three years no follow-up has therefore been done beyond the individual coordinators' level.

Besides this, for conducting post-training evaluation of effectiveness of various training programmes organized by the Institute, series of seminars were conducted[1] with the past participants of respective programmes viz. Section Officers/ACSO

(Probationers), Management Development Programmes and Management Services Courses, with a view to obtaining from them a feedback and objective assessment of the effectiveness of such programmes on administrative efficiency and managerial effectiveness and taking steps to revise/redesign suitably the training programmes, so as to make them effective, relevant and useful wherever necessary, in the light of the recommendations received from them. Such seminars of past participants have also been discontinued after 1986.

5.3 As a matter of fact, it was observed that the trainers and the course coordinator do not make the desired distinction between validation and evaluation in the real sense of the terms:

> 'Validation' refers to the measurement of a cause-and-effect relationship and consists of two discrete parts of the process which are described as internal validation and external validation. Internal validation is concerned with assessing whether a training activity has achieved its objectives, in other words, "did the trainees learn what they were taught?" External validation aims to find out if the trainees have applied what they have learned in training to the job context and whether they have been able to perform to the level expected of them after training. Evaluation is the process of attempting to assess the total value of training—that is the cost-benefits, and general outcomes which benefit the organization as well as the value of the improved performance of those who have undertaken training[2].

5.04 Measurement of knowledge and skill is done at the sessions through quizzes, written or oral and practicals at the end of the course (or Module) in a written, descriptive examination. However, the outcome has seldom been used as internal validation, since learning objectives were not written before imparting training in most of the cases. The results of examinations are attributed to the abilities of the trainees[3].

A survey was conducted through one of the questions ( in the Questionnaire at Appendix 3.1) as to whether the feedback form used in ISTM is adequate for improving the trainer's performance (or a training session). In reply to this, while most of the members have said in the affirmative, a good number of them feel that the form is too general on the course as a whole and does not indicate the efficiencies in the specific sessions. Often the feedback under the heads "content" and "presentation" is given on the basis of impression created by the faculty member(s) and on the basis of specific learning gained (or difficulties faced) by the individual. The opinion about training methods, training materials are asked in general in respect of the course, instead the participants may be asked to react on how the method used and material supplied helped him in learning.

Not only in ISTM but in most training institute in this country as well as in some developed countries, the trainers including those who are propagating the knowledge and skills in learning techniques are more conscious about their own performance during a training session rather than holding attention on what and how his trainees are able to learn. Hence, they ask for the trainees comments on the content and presentation by the trainer rather than asking them as to how much they were able to learn.

5.05 Survey was conducted through a questionnaire of the evaluation practices followed in ISTM and of suggestion of the faculty members on a systematic evaluation of training courses.

*Pre-training Assessment*

With regard to the pre-training assessment the survey reveals, the course coordinators in most (not in all) cases try to match the trainees' and their organizations' need with the course objectives and test the trainees pre-training knowledge and skills and attitude at the commencement of the course, and make necessary changes in input, context and methodology of the course suitably.

*Immediate Reaction*

The faculty members/coordinators use Immediate Reaction Questionnaire at the end of each course in case short courses, and at the end of each Module in the case of longer duration modular courses. Sometimes, some faculty members obtain feedback at the end of the session also.

The feedback received is used in bringing improvement, wherever possible, in the course input, training methods, presentation, training materials and physical facilities by the coordinators.

*Post-training follow-up*

As regards follow-up of trainees a few months after the training course, though there is no such system at present in ISTM, the faculty members have, by and large reacted positively. About 90 per cent of those who have responded have agreed that there is need of systematic follow-up of the trainees after their return to their jobs. Such exercise would help ISTM in knowing whether the course contents have met the training needs of the concerned officer and whether the transfer of learning to the job has taken place and problem therein, if any. They hoped that it would be possible for ISTM with the support of the Ministries to carry out such follow-up. However, one has felt that the benefits may not be commensurate with the efforts involved. The other faculty members strongly feel that there must be interaction with the trainees and their officers after the completion of the course through questionnaires, meetings, workshops, conferences, etc. This could be done through the joint effort between the ISTM and the Ministries having Training Coordinators.

5.6 In some organizations, it has been claimed that evaluation of training is too costly, it does not really prove anything or it isn't really applicable because training cannot be valued in financial terms. Some trainers have reflected a defensive approach to validation because they have felt that it invites criticism and apportions blame when training has not been as successful as it might have been. Even the head of Institute has been seen refusing to be present in validation session, or has even asked the coordinator to delete the negative points from being read out, where participants had been too critical about the training. However, if training is to enjoy a high profile, then thorough validation of its activities is vital so that, among the line managers who lack faith in training, the training institute can demonstrate its worth.

An attempt has been made, as a part of the research study to develop an "Assessment Model" and run it for one set of course with a view to study the feasibility and problems in conducting such an evaluation model for most of the courses in due course.

## AN ASSESSMENT MODEL

5.7 In a total measurement system, the assessment activities take place in four distinct but complementary stages:

- during the initial planning;
- throughout the learning experience;
- at the conclusion of training; and
- at periodical intervals after the programme ends.

Incorporating the above stages of training the Assessment Model developed for the study is shown in Fig. 5.1.

Assessment Model

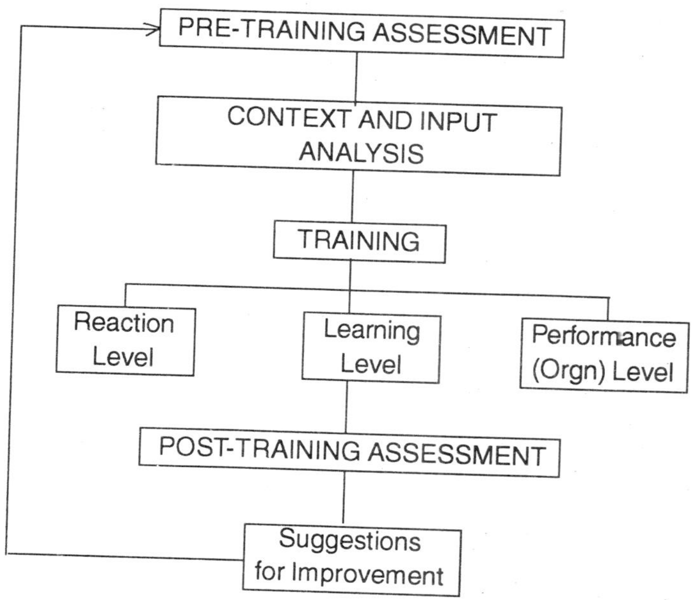


Fig. 5.1.

5.08 Most of the training coordinators in the ISTM have made use of only one tool of assessment i.e. the perception and reported reaction of participants after the programme. This method of self-reporting is liable to personal biases. While this method does at times reflect the general feeling of the participants about the programme, it does not lend itself to specificities and quantification. Some research and experimentation could be undertaken in order to evolve certain quantifiable measures of assessment particularly for skill oriented induction training programme for youngsters. It has to be remembered that the process of assessment is a part of the larger process of attempting to take corrective action and is not an end in itself. The success of any training activity has to be assessed in terms of the learning and its subsequent impact on organizational improvement. Therefore, the major thrust in this 'study-project' is to check the actual learning derived from training apart from the general feeling and reaction of the participants. Practical application of the research findings to improve subsequent programme essentially calls for the adoption of Action-research as the most appropriate method.

5.9 The Assessment Model presented in Fig. 5.1 encompasses three broad categories:

(1) Pre-training Feedback.
(2) Context and Input Analyses.
(3) Post-training Assessment.

In the pre-training stage, the concentration has been on matching the trainees' and organizational needs with the training objectives. Looking into the multifarious activities of the Ministries/ Departments of the Government of India, as would neither be possible nor would it be useful to have covered all aspects of activities through the Foundational training programme, efforts were made to match the training objectives and needs to the objectives of the sponsoring Ministries/Departments to the common functions only.

**Pre-Training Assessment**

5.10 Much of what the individual trainee gains through the course depends on his perception about the training, his existing level of knowledge, his attitude and his potential for improvement. The given batch of trainees being fresh from universities has hardly any idea about the role and relevance of training to its job performance. On the other hand, based on past experience, it has been observed that most supervisors and heads of organizations are vague about the objectives of training. The objectives of the supervisor (if he has taken the initiative) in nominating his Assistant for the course differ from those of the trainee, which in turn does not always concur with the programme objectives. This lack of goal congruence becomes a major problem because critical evaluation of the achievements of any training has to be done in the light of the objectives intended to be achieved. This understanding of the training objectives by the participants before commencement of training would be the initial step in achieving goal congruence.

The problem of goal congruence and matching of objectives does not merely remain an evaluation issue but becomes a part of the training and in fact is the first step towards motivation for learning[5].

At the pre-training stage the trainers ought to know more about the group of trainees on aspects like how well informed they are about various concepts and skills that the programme intends to offer.

## Input and Context Analyses

5.11 Since input assessment is to be done before the commencement of training, it can be considered as another aspect of pre-training assessment. Data obtained from the first aspect of the pre-training evaluation stage can give direction to the programme directors and the trainers in deciding their training inputs. It would decide the most appropriate training methodology for different subject inputs as also whether their input should be pitched low or high or whether they need special efforts to freeze the rigid trainees among other things so that the course contents are not rated either too high or too low by the group of participants at the end of the course and little is left in terms of modification for that group of participants.

## Assessment—An Action Research

5.12 Matching of training objectives can be done through mailing of questionnaire and /or through formal and informal discussions with the participants. Due to time constraints, a simple nine points questionnaire (Appendix 5.2) was got filled in alongwith the registration (basic-data) form by the participants on their reporting for training at the Institute. This questionnaire was used in the case of Assistant (direct recruits), Section Officers (refreshers) courses and Professional Development Programme for Under Secretaries. Since the participants of Section Officers (probationers) were mostly fresh from colleges and they had no knowledge about the work in the Secretariat, the pre-training questionnaire was not considered appropriate and in the case of Assistant (refresher) course at present the participants were other than promotee Assistants also the questionnaire was not used. The data obtained from the pre-training question-naire related to:

(1) The training needs of the individual and his organization as perceived by the participant and his supervisor;
(2) The information on whether they are rightly motivated to learn and their expectations from the programme;
(3) The level of knowledge, if any, of any of the subjects included in the programme.

*Analysis of Pre-training Data*

***Assistants (Direct Recruits)***

5.13 The data obtained through the pre-training questionnaires to participants of Assistants (DR) course has been converted into percentages in Table 5.1.

**TABLE 5.1**

**Response of Trainees to Pre-training Questionnaire**

1. Matching of the objectives of the course with the trainee's.

| | *Fully* | *Partially* | *No* |
|---|---|---|---|
| (a) Individual need for his work and professional development | 70 | 27 | 03 |
| (b) Organizational needs | 64 | 36 | * |

2. Who was involved in the decision to nominate him for this course?

| | |
|---|---|
| (i) Initiative taken exclusively by himself | 51 |
| (ii) Initiative taken by his supervisor | 20 |
| (iii) Decision left exclusively to admn | 29 |

3. Right at the time of joining this course whether, the trainee:

| | |
|---|---|
| (i) knew nothing about his job | 03 |
| (ii) was trying to learn the work | 33 |
| (iii) was already performing his job, by and large, to the satisfaction of his supervisor | 64 |

| | | *To great extent* | *To some extent* | *Not at all* |
|---|---|---|---|---|
| 4. | (a) The supervisor was giving necessary training on his job adequately | 20 | 65 | 15 |
| | (b) Learnt his job | | | |
| | (i) through observation/ imitation of peers | 50 | 47 | 03 |
| | (ii) through guidance from superior | 33 | 51 | 14 |

5. Trainees think that there is need of this foundational training programme to enable them to have the basic knowledge of their work and to learn the necessary skill.

| *Yes* | *To some extent* | *No* |
|---|---|---|
| 85 | 10 | 05 |

6. Trainees think they have been nominated for this course

| | |
|---|---|
| (i) at the right time | 52 |
| (ii) too early | 00 |
| (iii) too late | 48 |

7. Trainees think the subjects included in the syllabus would adequately cover the nature and subjects of their job back in the Ministry.

| *Yes* | *To some extent* | *No* |
|---|---|---|
| 70 | 27 | 03 |

8. Trainees think they have already some/adequate knowledge about some of the subjects included in the course, like economics, public administration, constitution of India, behavioural sciences and Indian history and culture, as also of Office Procedure, FR/SRs etc.

*Training needs and training objectives*

As regards matching of training objectives and training need it is observed that in view of 70 per cent of participants it was "complete", while in respect of remaining 27 per cent it was "partial". About 64 per cent of participants stated that the training objectives met the organizational needs "fully", and remaining 36 per cent only "partially".

*Motivation in participants*

Almost 51 per cent of participants had taken the initiative to get nominated for the course, in the case of another 20 per cent initiative was taken by their supervisors. In spite of the course being a compulsory one for all directly recruited Assistants, only 29 per cent have stated that the decision to nominate them was exclusively an administrative decision of their respective offices. However, most of them have also admitted that, had the training course been optional they would have opted for it for fulfilling their personal training needs.

*Need and timeliness of the training*

About 85 per cent of the participants have agreed fully and remaining 'to some extent' that there was a need of this programme to enable them to have a basic knowledge of their work and to learn the necessary skill.

52 per cent of the participants have found that the training is at the right time while 48 per cent of those and who have already put in some service feel that they are too late. None felt this training was too early.

This data confirms that majority of the participants are at the same level of training need. The experienced ones, in such a situation, could be involved in discussion in the class.

*The course input and Pre-training knowledge of trainees*

The responses reveal that while subjects included in the syllabus adequately covered the nature and functions of the job, a good number of participants have some knowledge of one or more subjects like the Constitution of India, public administration, Indian culture, behavioural sciences, economics, planning etc. included in the course, and another 25 per cent who have already put in some service have some knowledge of the functional subjects like office procedure, FR/SRs etc.

*Section Officers (Refreshers) and PDP for Under Secretaries*

5.14 Similar pre-training data for Section Officer (Refresher) course and Professional Development Programme for USs have been collected and tabulated in Appendices 5.2 and 5.3.

## Post-Training Assessment Steps

5.15 Post-training assessment as suggested in the model for this study comprises three levels:

(1) *Reaction Level*

The reaction of the participants to the training programme is obtained immediately after the completion of the training programme. This reaction is obtained through a proforma and through the observations and discussions, both formal and informal among the course director, faculty members and the participants about the programme.

(2) *Learning Level*

Since the programme under study is a foundational programme for the new entrants fresh from universities the level of functional knowledge and skill has been assumed as zero and actual learning subsequent to the training programme is measured on the basis of end-of-the-course test.

(3) *Performance (Organization) Level*

The third aspect of post-training evaluation is through follow up with the participant as well as with his supervisor on the job.

Learning has to be measured keeping in view the objectives of the course. Training objectives are sometimes very specific and facilitate the measurement of learning. But in most situations it is not so. It is in this context that studying the expectations of the group of participants from training and relating it with training objectives and inputs in the pretraining evaluation process gains significance.

## Reaction Feedback

5.16 It is the practice in almost all training situations to assess the effectiveness of a training programme at the end of the course. This is normally done through an Immediate Reaction Questionnaire which vary in size, content and format for different training programmes. By and large, these proformae elicit the trainee's viewpoint about the training programme he attended. The format used by the ISTM for foundational courses as in Appendix 5.1, covers the following :

(1) Attainment of the course objectives by the participant.
(2) Degree of achievement in certain specified skills.
(3) Amount of knowledge acquired on each of the input subjects.
(4) The views of the participant about the duration of the course, session timings and course coverage.
(5) The effectiveness of each pedagogical tool/method used in the training programme.
(6) Opinion on the reading material, library and other facilities provided by the Institute.
(7) Views on the study-tour, attainment of its objectives, its duration and arrangements.

No doubt, this type of feedback which is in fact, the reaction of the participant to the immediate academic and social surroundings of the training progrsme, has some apparent benefits. It provides a feedback to the programme director and to trainers about how well the course was received by the total group of participants. It also gives an indication of the frame of mind of the trainee after the course. This is important for implementation of the new ideas gained through training since a positive attitude at the end of the programme will enhance the commitment of the trainee to put to use the knowledge and skill acquired through training. The sample for the study comprises two groups, 137th batch consisting of 32 and 138th batch comprising 35 Assistants (direct recruits) undergoing training simultaneously from April 4, 1994 to June 17, 1994 at ISTM.

About 51 per cent of the 67 participants are fresh having joined the service during the last three months of commencement of the course, 33 per cent have put in one year's service and the remaining 16 per cent have put in about two years.

5.17 The data obtained through reaction feedback proforma, in respect of both the groups, has been summarised and converted into percentages in the Table 5.2.

**TABLE 5.2**

**Reaction Feedback and Rating of Subject input by Participants of Group I and Group II**

(a) How far has the course enabled him to acquire the necessary competence/ skill in:

| | *Subject* | *Fully* | | *Considerably* | | *Partly* | | *Vaguely* | |
|---|---|---|---|---|---|---|---|---|---|
| | | *Gp I %* | *Gp II %* | *Gp I %* | *Gp II %* | *Gp I %* | *Gp II %* | *GpI %* | *Gp II %* |
| 1. | Office Procedure | 19 | 40 | 62 | 43 | 19 | 13 | * | 03 |
| 2. | Noting and Drafting | 13 | 30 | 56 | 33 | 31 | 27 | * | 10 |
| 3. | Financial Rules | 10 | 16 | 56 | 43 | 31 | 27 | 3 | 14 |

(b) How far has the course added to your knowledge ofthe following:

| | | *To a great extent* | | *To a considerable extent* | | *To some extent* | | *Not at all* | |
|---|---|---|---|---|---|---|---|---|---|
| | | *Gp I %* | *Gp II %* | *Gp I %* | *Gp II %* | *Gp I %* | *Gp II %* | *Gp I %* | *Gp II %* |
| *Module I* | | | | | | | | | |
| 1. | Machinery of Govt. | 30 | 63 | 60 | 29 | 10 | 08 | * | * |
| 2. | Office Procedure | 16 | 37 | 60 | 45 | 24 | 18 | * | * |
| 3. | Noting and Drafting | 12 | 35 | 44 | 35 | 44 | 20 | * | 10 |
| 4. | Conduct Rules | 38 | 80 | 58 | 20 | 04 | * | * | * |
| 5. | Leave Rules | 40 | 60 | 50 | 34 | 10 | 06 | * | * |
| 6. | Estab. Rules | 20 | 26 | 60 | 44 | 20 | 30 | * | * |
| 7. | Fin. contl. and Budget | 15 | 20 | 61 | 50 | 24 | 30 | * | * |
| 8. | Provident Fund | 17 | 44 | 58 | 38 | 25 | 18 | * | * |
| 9. | Official Language | 30 | 51 | 35 | 34 | 35 | 15 | * | * |
| 10. | Security of Infn. | 34 | 63 | 50 | 31 | 16 | 06 | * | * |
| 11. | Records Management | 23 | 23 | 63 | 51 | 14 | 26 | * | * |
| 12. | Constitution | 21 | 18 | 45 | 42 | 34 | 30 | * | 10 |
| 13. | Eco.dev. and Planning | 14 | 17 | 58 | 49 | 24 | 34 | 04 | * |
| 14. | CSS Rules | 18 | 18 | 54 | 44 | 28 | 35 | * | 03 |
| 15 | JCM | 17 | 18 | 55 | 45 | 28 | 34 | * | 03 |

*Module II*

| | | | | | | | | |
|---|---|---|---|---|---|---|---|---|
| 16. Disciplinary Rules | 29 | 34 | 53 | 48 | 18 | 18 | * | * |
| 17. Parliamentary Proc | 55 | 65 | 41 | 31 | 04 | 04 | * | * |
| 18. Resvn.in Services | 18 | 18 | 54 | 44 | 28 | 35 | * | 03 |
| 19. Fundamental Rules | 39 | 48 | 48 | 43 | 23 | 09 | * | * |
| 20. T.A. and LTC Rules | 27 | 23 | 53 | 54 | 20 | 23 | * | * |
| 21. Pension Rules | 27 | 51 | 62 | 42 | 10 | 07 | * | * |
| 22. Project Planning | 25 | 50 | 70 | 40 | 05 | 10 | * | * |
| 23. Role and Functions of DDOs/HoOs | 15 | 20 | 62 | 50 | 23 | 30 | * | * |
| 24. Income-Tax | 27 | 23 | 53 | 54 | 20 | 23 | * | * |
| 25. Handling Court Cases | 40 | 75 | 56 | 20 | 04 | 05 | * | * |

2. Matching of individual's expectation from the course with course objectives—

| Positive | | Negative | |
|---|---|---|---|
| Gp I | Gp II | Gp I | Gp II |
| 82% | 79% | 18% | 21% |

| | | Gp I | Gp II |
|---|---|---|---|
| 3. Duration of the course— | adequate | 50% | 34% |
| | too long | * | 02% |
| | too short | 50% | 64% |
| 4. Time allowed for individual sessions | | | |
| | adequate | 79% | 68% |
| | not adequate | 21% | 32% |
| 5. Course topics sequenced logically | | | |
| | Yes | 58% | 84% |
| | No | 42% | 16% |

6. Training Methodology / tools—

| | Very Effective | | Effective | | Not Effective | |
|---|---|---|---|---|---|---|
| | Gp I % | Gp II % | Gp I % | Gp II % | Gp I % | Gp II % |
| Lecture | 36 | 60 | 61 | 40 | 03 | * |
| Syndicate | 17 | 29 | 62 | 71 | 21 | * |
| Exercises | 41 | 46 | 48 | 51 | 11 | 03 |
| Case Studies | Not applied | | | | | |
| Films | 30 | 21 | 30 | 51 | 40 | 28 |

7. Course material supplied, found relevant

| | Mostly | Considerably | Partly |
|---|---|---|---|
| Gp I (%) | 47 | 50 | 03 |
| Gp II(%) | 47 | 53 | * |

5.18 The analysis of the participants' feedback obtained by respective course directors (separate for each group) showed that there was lack of uniformity in the impressions/views among the two groups as well as among the trainees in each group. Reaction evaluation method has some inherent biases, such as:

(1) The course director is likely to get a relatively better rating as compared to other trainers, all because of being the course director.

(2) The ratings obtained for individual input sessions of the faculty are by and large directly related to the degree of socialisation and the efforts made to present an enjoyable lecture.

(3) The opportunity provided to the Assistant for attending a training programme thus relieving him of his office work can lead to a euphoric reaction about the course being very good, helpful and enjoyable.

(4) The mix of the training group (its homogeneity / heterogeneity) and the leader who normally during the course of training can itself colour the reaction of the participants toward the training programme.

(5) Besides these immediate perceptions of the participant, the reaction to the effectiveness of a training programme can be influenced by the factors like his expectations from the programme and how keen he is to optimise the benefits from training.

Since this kind of data did not give the evaluators a definite feedback, other measures had to be used so as to substantiate these findings. It was, in this context, thought appropriate to use the learning index and other measures with reaction evaluation to arrive at a definite feedback about the course for its subsequent improvement.

**Learning Measurement**

5.19 Coming to the actual measurement of learning, it is rather very difficult to devise any tools of measurement which would give a true picture of the extent to which a participant was able to learn in relation to the stated objectives of the programme. Mere expression from the participants that they have learnt from a particular programme may not be a sufficient indicator of learning derived from the course. Therefore, it was considered worthwhile to take into account the performance of the participants in the end-of-the-course examination in each subject covered in the training programme as an indicator of their learning.

Due to time constraints it was not possible to have measured the pre-training knowledge, particulary of those participants who have put in some service in the Ministry as Assistant and know somewhat more about their jobs than those who had joined recently. However, since majority of the participants belong to the latter category, for simplicity of analysis the pre-training knowledge of the group has been taken as zero and percentage marks secured in each subject as the 'index of learning'.

*Analysis of Data*

5.20 Since the total reliance on the reaction of the trainees as a method of evaluation was not valid in many situations, it is postulated that it was emotionally biased. To test this hypothesis a comparison of the reaction evaluation with the actual learning based on mean percentage marks secured by the group was made.

The evaluation proforma eliciting the participants' immediate feedback had as one of its columns a four point scale for each subject input. The four points of the scale to the acquiring of knowledge were "to great extent", "to considerable extent", "to some extent" and "not at all" which are attributed to "excellent", "very good", "good" and "poor" rating of the trainer. If knowledge of a particular subject input is acquired through the programme "to a great extent/ considerable extent" by 70 per cent or more of the participants in a group, then it is rated as "high". When the 50-70 per cent of participants have acquired the knowledge only "to some extent" it is rated as "medium", and if is less than 50 per cent the rating is "low". The rating then for each subject were compared with the learning index for the group against each subject as in the Table 5.3.

### TABLE 5.3
### Comparison between the Reaction Evaluation Feedback and Learning

| | | | *Rating from Evaluation Feedback* | *Learning quantified-% Relative rating as Learning index* | |
|---|---|---|---|---|---|
| 1. | Machinery of Govt. | | High | 76 | High |
| 2. | Office Procedure | | High | 42 | Low |
| 3. | Noting and Drafting | Gp I | Medium | | |
| | | Gp II | High | | |
| 4. | Official Language | Gp I | Medium | 63 | Medium |
| | Gp II High | | | | |
| 5. | Security of Infn. | | High | 59 | Medium |
| 6. | Records Management | | High | 57 | Medium |
| 7. | Disciplinary Rules | | High | 62 | Medium |
| 8. | Conduct Rules | V | High | 79 | High |
| 9. | Parliamentary Procedure | V | High | * | * |
| 10. | Establishment Rules | | High | 57 | Medium |
| 11. | Reservation in Services | | Medium | 51 | Medium |
| 12. | Fin. Control & Budget | | High | * | * |
| 13. | Fundamental Rules | | High | * | * |
| 14. | T.A. and LTC Rules | | High | 54 | Medium |
| 15. | Leave Rules | V | High | 56 | Medium |
| 16. | Pension Rules | V | High | 53 | Medium |
| 17. | Provident Fund Rules | | High | 59 | Medium |
| 18. | Public Administration | | Medium | 66 | Medium |
| 19. | Constitution of India | | Medium | 54 | Medium |
| 20. | Eco. dev. and Planning | | Medium | 59 | Medium |
| 21. | Indian Culture | | Medium | 66 | Medium |
| 22. | Behavioural Sciences | | High | 67 | Medium |

The above table shows that generally the rating given by the participants in the reaction feedback is one grade higher than relating rating of learning except in the case of Office Procedure and Noting and Drafting in which the learning was low whereas the reaction rating was high. Similarly, in the case of Financial Rules the ratings are very high but the learning effected was only medium. This variation between the rating in reaction feedback and actual learning only confirms the presence of element of bias in the reaction feedback. This should be noted by the course directors.

**The Training Tools/Methodology and Reaction Feedback**

5.21 In furtherance to the study of reaction level, the participants' feedback about the training tools/methodology was also compared with their learning. Most of the studies indicate that the lectures are the least effective method in terms of retention of learning, and therefore emphasis should be on other techniques/ tools such as group discussion, exercise, films and syndicate work. However, the participants reaction in the sample group was heavily in favour of method to be followed by exercises. If there is complete reliance on the reaction feedback, there will be a natural tendency to increase lecture input and decrease the use of other methods because participants have expressed their preference for lecture method and it has been shown to be comparatively less effective. It could be that the participants like lectures because it does not require much active involvement on their part.

The reaction questionnaire also gave a feedback to the faculty that many of the participants were not happy with the exercises and syndicate work because they were not properly conducted or structured (this was revealed in a discussion with the group) and they ought to be modified if the learning values haa to increase. The research indicates that unless the lectures are reinforced with exercises and job practicals (maybe in a simulated situation) there will be very little learning and its consequent application on the job.

## On the Job Assessment

5.22 After having acquired the essential knowledge and skills, trainees have to ensure that they apply this learning to the job and thus increase organizational effectiveness. An important element at this stage is a supportive organizational climate which is very essential for introducing changes/innovations in the organization. But the training institution's, like ISTM's, responsibility is not merely imparting knowledge. They play an equally important role in the post-training stage of transferring learning to the job. Since any training loses its meaning, unless it is transferred to the job and since the ultimate goal of any training programme is application of training to the job for improved functioning, the training institution has an important role in ensuring that knowledge acquired at the training institution finds sufficient application. Study of transfer of training to the job gives an in-depth analysis of the factors within the organization helping or hindering the transfer of training.

As a measure of post-training assessment of the effectiveness of the various training programmes, the ISTM conducts periodical seminars of past participants of the respective programmes with a view to obtaining feedback from the participants on the basis of their experience of transferring their learning to their jobs. The assessment is subjective from the individual participant's point of view, however, no, evaluation has so far been made from the organizations, and the bosses' point of view. Moreover the assessment of the nature and degree of change in job-performance is difficult because it involves many varying factors like different organizational tasks, nature of job of each individual organizational requirements.

5.23 In this study, the major tool for assessing the transfer of training and improvement in job performance was not only the perception of the Assistant himself but also the opinion of his supervisor. For the purpose of collecting data, a set of follow up questionnaires (Appendices 5.5.a to 5.5.f) was prepared, which attempted to measure the extent of transfer and investigate factors which affect the transfer of learning to the job. The follow-up questionnaire was supplemented by informal discussions with the supervisor. The questionnaire included the following aspects:

(1) Improvement in conceptual knowledge and skill, and his overall personal and professional development.

(2) Transfer of various aspects of training with specific reference to the aspects covered in the programme.

(3) Reasons due to which he could not or did not bring improvement, which fell into four categories of

— organizational constraints, e.g. the organizational factors not within the control of individual,

— individual constraints e.g., the factors generated within oneself

— training input insufficient or irrelevant,

— job characteristics not related to training inputs.

(4) Degree of cooperation received by the Assistant from his supervisor and colleagues.

*Analysis of Data*

5.24 The first stage of measuring the impact of training on the job was to ascertain the applicability of the subjects covered during the training to the kind of job the Assistant does. One of the criticisms often levelled against any evaluation of transfer of learning is that there is no definite method of ascribing learning only to training and that improvement could also be due to some organizational and individual factors and time. In this study, attempts to overcome this problem were made by specifying clearly in the questionnaires sent to the supervisor and the Assistant that the information was sought with particular reference to the training and as a result of training. The aspects of follow-up were specific to the training input which were covered and not any other general subjects.

## Improvement of the Job Performance Attributed to the Course

5.25 The reported improvement of the participant in eight main functional subjects covered in the course and attributed to the training is given in the Table 5.4.

## TABLE 5.4

### Areas in which Trainees and their supervisors reported improvement

| *Function* | *Improvement seen and attributed to training* | | *Reasons for no improvement* | | | | | | |
|---|---|---|---|---|---|---|---|---|---|
| | | | *Indiv. cons-traint* | | *Orgn. cons-traint* | | *Input insuffi-cient* | *Function not relate to job* | |
| | *% Trainee* | *% Boss* | *% T* | *% B* | *% T* | *% B* | *% T* | *% T* | *% B* |
| 1. Office procedure | 77 | 95 | 10 | 5 | * | * | 13 | * | * |
| 2. Noting and drafting | 82 | 100 | * | * | 09 | * | 09 | * | * |
| 3. Records Management | 63 | 40 | * | * | 10 | 20 | * | 27 | 40 |
| 4. Handling classified information/ papers | 54 | 43 | * | * | 05 | * | 05 | 36 | 57 |
| 5. Disciplinary/ Vigilance matters | 27 | 20 | * | * | * | * | * | 73 | 80 |
| 6. Dealing with parliamentary papers/questions | 50 | 40 | * | * | * | * | * | 50 | 60 |
| 7. Dealing with establishment matters regarding: | | | | | | | | | |
| (i) Recruitment/ promotion/ reservation in services | 45 | 40 | * | * | * | * | * | 55 | 60 |
| (ii) Pay fixation/ leave | 45 | 35 | * | * | * | * | * | 55 | 65 |
| (iii) Pension cases | 36 | 25 | * | * | * | * | * | 64 | 75 |
| (iv) TA/LTC | 27 | 10 | * | * | * | * | * | 73 | 90 |
| (v) GPF | 25 | 05 | * | * | * | * | * | 75 | 95 |
| (vi) CAT cases | 40 | 35 | * | * | * | * | * | 60 | 65 |

| | | | | | | | | | | |
|---|---|---|---|---|---|---|---|---|---|---|
| 8. Preparation of Budget | 14 | 05 | * | * | * | * | * | 86 | 95 |
| 9. Project Planning | 05 | 10 | * | * | * | * | * | 95 | 90 |
| 10. Dealing with Cash and Accounts matters | | | | | | | | | |
| (i) Calculate Income Tax | 15 | 10 | * | * | * | * | * | 85 | 90 |
| (ii) Conduct Audit | 05 | 05 | * | * | * | * | * | 95 | 95 |
| (iii) Assisting DDOs | 05 | 05 | * | * | * | * | * | 95 | 95 |

What is immediately noticeable is that there is a definite improvement in the performance of the Assistant after the training in particular areas of office procedure and Noting and Drafting and records management but in 50-90 per cent of cases the subject input was not related to the job. The instances of organizational constraints and individual constraints were very few, maybe that the trainees have not able to identify them properly. A glance at the data suggests that more often the supervisors report greater improvements than the participants themselves. A plausible explanation for this could be that either the Assistants themselves are not conscious of the improvement or that they rate themselves more moderately or the boss is giving an over rated response because of social desirability. However, the response to the post-training questionnaire was only 40 per cent of total population and moreover because of time constraints the questionnaire was sent too early, the findings need to be verified in subsequent studies.

The feedback from the participants on the input modules will be very useful in inferring whether the emphasis of the programme was in keeping with the training objectives or had to shift more in favour of some other aspects or whether the relevance of a subject to the total organizational functioning was not brought out well or not stressed enough. These details go into making subsequent programmes more meaningful.

**Realisation of Course Objectives**

5.26 While the objectives of the course have been translated into various inputs and subjects, the realisation of these objectives in their broad form is necessary. Table 5 below gives the realisation of objectives as reported by the trainees in the follow-up questionnaire.

**TABLE 5.5**

**Realisation of Course Objectives**

| | *Objectives* | *Increased* | *Same as before* | *Undecided* |
|---|---|---|---|---|
| 1. | Overall feeling of satisfaction in work after training. | 85 | 10 | 05 |
| 2. | Ability to examine cases and apply rules correctly. | 85 | 10 | 05 |
| 3. | Ability to record notes and drafts. | 80 | 20 | * |
| 4. | Efficiency in dealing with bosses and peers. | 60 | 30 | 10 |

The analysis of the above data indicates that, by and large, there is a feeling of satisfaction except in the case of human relations. Trainers must take note of it.

**Transfer of Training—The Related Aspects**

5.27 In any transfer of training process there are, by and large four factors which can help or hinder the application of learning to the job. The first aspect is personal development and attitudinal changes. This would include improvement in self-confidence, open-mindedness, increase in the level of aspirations, etc. The assumption here is that with the personal development, the executive will also make an attempt to change his style of functioning in the organizational context.

The second factor is the perception of the managers about the training process. If participants and their organizations have a positive approach to training then, not only will the participants imbibe more during the training process but also have the commitment to transfer the same to the job. The organization will, because of their positive attitude to training, provide good support to the trainee to apply training to the job. It is here that it becomes necessary to ensure a positive approach to the training process and belief that training will help in bringing about personal and organizational improvements.

The third aspect is the organizational climate which is conducive to the introduction of changes by Assistants. In other words, and environment where the participants do not have too many restrictions on them thereby encouraging the transfer of learning to the job.

5.28 The Tables 5.6 to 5.9 give the response of the participants to the various aspects covered under these three categories.

**TABLE 5.6**

**Training Programme and Personal Development**

| | *Aspects relating to Personal Development* | *Agree* | *Undecided* | *Disagree* |
|---|---|---|---|---|
| 1. | The programme has improved my status in the Section/Deptt. | 60 | 30 | 10 |
| 2. | The programme has raised my personal goals and levels of aspiration. | 60 | 20 | 20 |
| 3. | I do not find any change in my personal development. | 20 | 05 | 75 |
| 4. | The programme has infused a lot of self-confidence in me. | 75 | 05 | 20 |
| 5. | The programme made me more open minded. | 90 | 05 | 05 |
| 6. | My interaction with Assistants of other Ministries proved beneficial. | 95 | * | 05 |

The above data indicates that the trainers have succeeded in increasing the self-confidence of the trainees and there was an improvement in the aspects like increasing personal goals and aspirations, open-mindedness and in interaction with other trainees.

5.29 The Table 5.7 indicates that almost all the trainees had a positive attitude towards training as a whole. In other words they believed that training helped in improving the skills of the Assistants.

**TABLE 5.7**

**Perception of Training (by participants)**

| | Aspects relating to Perception | Agree | Undecided | Disagree |
|---|---|---|---|---|
| 1. | Assistants learn more by working on the desk and training makes little difference. | 10 | 15 | 75 |
| 2. | Assistants learn more from books and self-study than from attending courses. | * | 10 | 90 |
| 3. | The programme created interest for individual learning. | * | 80 | 20 |

5.30 The responses in the Table 5.7 and Table 5.8 indicate a favourable support of the supervisor for the training of Assistants. But, the informal discussions with the individual officers give an impression that in many cases, particularly where the Supervisor himself did not have the exposure to any training, there is no perception about the gains and utility of training programmes. Because of such indifferent attitude of the Supervisors the Assistants are not relieved for training courses.

**TABLE 5.8**

**Perception of Training ( by supervisors)**

| | Aspects of Perception | Agree | Undecided | Disagree |
|---|---|---|---|---|
| 1. | The training has improved the Assistants skill/efficiency in his job. | 90 | 05 | 05 |
| 2. | Programme placed much emphasis on such rules and procedure which are little use to him. | 25 | 40 | 35 |
| 3. | The programme cater to what the department expected. | 60 | 25 | 15 |

It was, however, encouraging to gather that the majority of them attach due importance to training and favour early Foundational Training Course to the newly recruited Assistants. Unless there is organizational support and recognition to the value of training, no amount of training can bring effectiveness in employee.

5.31 The Table 5.9 below indicates that the officers on principle favour innovations but in actual practice it is reported that the office atmosphere is not very favourable.

**TABLE 5.9**

**Factors of Organizational Climate**

| | *Aspects relating to organizational climate* | *Agree* | *Undecided* | *Disagree* |
|---|---|---|---|---|
| 1. | My officers stimulates and approves innovations. | 75 | 15 | 10 |
| 2. | The office atmosphere does not favour innovation. | 25 | 40 | 35 |
| 3. | I feel restricted by conventions/procedures prevalent in the Section. | 40 | 05 | 55 |

This phenomenon is peculiar to the Government organizations where people pretend to be pragmatic but tend to stick to prevailing practices and procedure and do not want to take risk of innovative trials. The whole purpose of spending so much time, money and effort in training the Assistants is defeated if the organization does not recognise that change, innovations and development are all parts and parcel of training.

## Conclusion

5.32 In any long duration Foundational Training Course or Management Development Programme, pre-training evaluation assumes an important role in the process of learning and its implementation on the job. The data indicates that while the trainees are highly motivated to fulfill their training needs, the supervisors do not attach much importance to the institutional training, though they do train their subordinates on-the-job. The pre-training evaluation went a long way in helping the trainers to pitch their course input closer to the specific needs of the participants and in selecting right learning methods for the given group.

5.33 For an objective assessment of effectiveness of training course, one of the major criteria is the measurement of learning that has been derived by the trainees rather than subjective reaction feedback taken at the end of the course. For any model of assessment, both qualitative and quantitative techniques can be used. The technique properly selected would support each other's findings. Though in this Chapter different methodologies which illustrate the various categories that could be used for a particular training course have been used, different methods of assessments can be used for the same course of training depending upon the criteria of assessment in order to gain information about the learning from the course from different dimensions. Thus, the course design and input can be modified suitably.

5.34 The follow-up data including the study of factors which help and hinder transfer of learning to the job also give some clues to the trainers in terms of training activities as well as its assessment procedure; such as improvement in the relevance of the course content to suit the need of the participants and their orgainzation, proper selection of the participants for specialised courses and the involvement of the top management and immediate superior of the Trainee during the various stages of training assessment and follow-up process.

## References

1. ISTM—Annual Report.
2. Buckley Roger, Caple Jim —*The Theory and Practice of Training,* Kogan Page (1992).
3. *Ibid.*
4. *Ibid.*
5. Virmani B.R., Seth P.—*Evaluation Management Training and Development*, Vision Books (1985).

# 6

# Summary of Conclusions

6.1 In the preceding Chapters, analyses have been made of the evolution and existing structure and organization of the CSS, its needs and problem in relation to the organizational environment, the role and functions of ISTM, the existing training opportunities available, and suggested a possible model of systematic training and its impact assessment of the organizational effectiveness of the Ministries. The description of facts are based on exploratory research of old records, experience survey and objective observation over a period of more than two years, and the conclusions are based on objective analysis of these facts and not on preconcieved values, bias or preferences for a particular set of models.

The important conclusions and suggestions for improvements and future research are summarised below:

### Cadre Training Plan as Part of Cadre Management

6.2 Timely and systematic training is one important aspect of the broader personnel system and therefore, it should be appropriately and systematically integrated with other personnel practices like manpower planning, placement, performance appraisal and career development. The Cadre Training Plan for the CSS officers incorporating compulsory Foundational and Induction Training for the direct recruits and in-service and Induction Training for newly promoted officers need to be drawn after proper identification of training needs in consultation with the Cadre Ministries/Departments and ISTM. Training on various subject specialisation may be designed after identification of specific needs by the respective Ministries/Departments, maybe on the basis of performance appraisal and recommendation of the supervisors.

The requirement of completion of training prescribed in the Cadre Training Plan should be incorporated in the Service Rules to ensure implementation. The DoPT (CS Division) should impress upon the Heads of various beneficiary Ministries/Departments for their direct involvement and cooperation in development of their officers. [2.22, 4.19 and 4.20] A model Cadre Training Plan for CSS has been suggested in Appendix 4.5.

**Training Managers**

6.3 The government (in the DoPT) should take steps to make Heads of organizations (Ministries/Departments) directly responsible for training and development of its employees, and the Cadre Controlling Department should monitor the training requirements in the Cadre through "Training Managers" appointed for each Ministry. For uniformity of standards an officer in the Department may be appointed as "Training Manager" in consultation with the DoPT (Training Division) and he must get the requisite training in "Management of Training (MoT)". [4.34, 4.35 and 4.36]

**Resurrection of the Institute**

6.4 The Institute (ISTM), it will be recalled, began its operation in early fifties, its objectives being limited substantially to the imparting of training to newly recruited Assistants and Section Officers. Later, on its own initiative, it had diversified its function far beyond imparting direct training to CSS officers. The expansion of functions is, on the whole a tribute to the success of the Institute. When able teaching faculty and experts assemble under the right leadership of the Head of the Institute, it is natural for the government to begin to look to the Institute for service of varied nature.

In Chapter 3, while the story of perceptible growth and development of ISTM speaks of the successive leadership of the Directors and dedication of the faculty in the last forty years, the same also tries to analyse the reasons for gradual degeneration of the Institute in the last 10 years or so. In order to resurrect the Institute to its pre-1990 level, the organization and functioning of the Institute need to be reviewed on the following aspects:

*Appointment of the Director*

6.5 The appointment of a Director is a matter of great importance in the development of an institute. It would be desirable to identify for this position an outstanding scholar in public administration, who has adequate exposure and positive attitude to training and development of civil servants and at the same time enjoys a reputation for practical skill in administration. [3.41 and 3.43]

*Review of the Internal Structure*

6.6 In order to regain the tempo of growth and development of the Institute, a complete review of the organizational structure and faculty strength of ISTM may be one of the imperative steps for its resurrection. [3.46, 3.51 and 3.52]

*Revival of Training Courses*

6.7 Though ISTM was primarily created for imparting Foundational and in-service training to the CSS officers, its diversification in the specialised areas of Management Techniques and Training Methodology had brought the Institute in the training map of the world. Discontinuance of these prestigious courses has not only been a setback to the image and status of ISTM but has also affected the morale of the faculty which had in the past proven its ability to organise series of International Courses with professional competence. It is only hoped that the new leadership of the Institute would not only revive the three International courses held till 1991-92 but also diversify the Institute's activities further qualitatively and quantitatively. [3.11, 3.13 and 3.14]

*Research and Consultancy*

6.8 Importance of research as an adjunct of the training in public administration and bringing out authentic documents containing suggestions for improvements in the administration cannot be overemphasised in the current senario of economic reforms in the country. Consultancy or advisory services emerges from the research functions. Every training institute should include Research and Consultancy in its Charter and provide consultancy services in its specialised areas. [3.15, 3.16 and 3.18]

**Providing Opportunities for Training**

6.09 Training is not only valuable but necessary. One may go so far as to say that every public employee fitted to be a civil servant, everyone who finds himself in the position of a civil servant must undergo a learning period, during which he works at something less than full efficiency and gives something less than the full value of his service to his employer. As an employee of the state, each individual must be the professor of certain knowledge and he must be proficient in certain skills, which are never needed in quite the same degree or quantity in other employments. The amount and kind of training needed by individuals to fit them as civil servants varies greatly, but all person are in need of some training. The minimum of training needed by all may be said to be the inculcation of attitutes which are consistent with the position of the individual as a public servant.[4.38, 4.43 and 4.44]

6.10 The availability of personnel for training depends upon numerous factors, such as the length of the course, the location at which the training is offered, and the hours and dates of attendance. It may be difficult to obtain the release of employees placed low in the hierarchy, because their services are necessary in maintaining the smooth functioning of the organization. It is perhaps incumbent upon the Heads of organizations to impress upon their officers to realise that a good officer, if he is better trained can, by improved performance make good the alleged loss of work by higher productivity. In the long run, the benefits that would accrue to the organization by higher productivity in subsequent years would be immense. The senior officers should be asked to inculcate such team spirit within their Branch, Division or Wing as to be able to spare one of their juniors for training once in a while without affecting the work system. Not relieving an officer by his supervisor may be construed as the latter's incapacity to manage his work and lack of team spirit and may be recorded against. [4.31, 4.32, 4.34 and 4.49]

## Review of Training Programmes

6.11 The distinctive things about Induction Training are, first, that it is given immediately or soon after the original appointment; and secondly, that it is designed specially to impart instructions in the tasks of the particular position which the recruit is to enter as his first assignment. An induction course, carefully designed to impart a body of knowledge necessary to the new recruit in the performance of his duties and at the same time to perfect skills which he will need, can materially shorten the period of time for learning the new job. One observer has expressed the belief that training can reduce the learning time by one third to one half of that required to learn the duties of a job by an apprentice. To realize this objective in training, it is clear that the practical aspects of training must be emphasized and the content must be job-oriented. [4.47 to 4.51]

6.12 Besides the validation and evaluation of the training courses, the training input and methodology used needs to be reviewed periodically to gear it up to the need of the organization. Review of training programmes should be the shared responsibility of the sponsoring organization and the training institution. Based on the information collected from the Ministries/Departments about their organizational needs, the training objectives of the programme should be laid down clearly. A detailed study of the training objectives of the courses may be conducted. [4.50]

### Training Objectives

6.13 A factor which enhances the learning process and its transfer is the congruence of training objectives between the trainee, his boss and the training institution. To achieve this the institute can evolve questionnaire for the organization/ supervisors asking them about their expectation from the training in view of the stated objectives of training. From the data obtained, the trainers can make sure that training inputs are, by and large, in tune with the requirements of the trainee and his organization. [5.05, 5.10, 5.11, 5.12 and 5.26]

### Preparation of the Trainees for Training

6.14 At present there is no practice of attitudinal stimulation of the trainee's behaviour before they actually land up at ISTM for the foundational programme. The course director should make prior contacts with the trainees to develop better perception of the training programme they are going to attend and what they can expect from it. It would be of advantage to the organization and the trainee, particularly the one who has joined the organization newly and going for a long duration Induction Training, if he was relieved from his desk few days earlier, thus giving him opportunity to get acquainted with the general functioning of the whole department. This will enable him to link the subsequent training input with his own problems. It would be helpful if the trainee made himself familiar with the programme objectives, the design and other information provided by the training institution. [4.33 and 4.36]

## Reaction Feedback

6.15 For long-duration Foundational Programmes, more frequent Reaction Feedback from the participants would help the course coordinator to modify/shape its emphasis keeping in view the needs of a specific group. One feedback at the end of the course help review only the subsequent course on the basis of views of previous group which seldom match. At present, in most of the training institutes and courses the trainer wants to get a feedback on his performance during the session rather than how best the trainees were able to learn about the skill/knowledge through the session. The feedback questionnaire need to be directed towards the training objectives of the session and how far that has been achieved. A revised programme validation questionnaire has been suggested in Appendix 5.4. [5.16 and 5.18]

## Transfer of Training to the Job

6.16 Irrespective of the degree of learning those trainees who expressed the view that the inputs were relevant to their jobs were the ones who were able to transfer maximum learning to the job. This indicates that the opinion of the participants at the end of the course had much to contribute in terms of their motivation to implement what was learnt through training. This was seen and confirmed from the study that a favourable impression about the course promotes transfer of training to the job. To increase the transfer of training to the job, the trainers can find out the factors which help or hinder this transfer in the case of the specific category. Some of these factors have been identified and discussed in para 5.27 above. Of these, two aspects in general are hindering factors viz. the organizational climate and perception of training. Unfavourable organizational climate automatically hinders the transfer of training and wrong perception of training vitiates learning. [5.27]

## Measurement of Learning

6.17 Pre-training tests should be devised to measure the pre-training knowledge, which will help in deciding the input for each course. Post-training test, which should be framed keeping in view of the training objectives, would help in measuring the learning effected by the training. [5.19]

## Follow-up

6.18 The trainer apart from imparting knowledge has to ensure that the knowledge will be of use to the trainee in his job, for at the training session neither the trainee nor the trainer can have an accurate picture of how the training is going to improve the trainee's job performance and thus enhance organizational efficiency. Follow-up of the trainee after a gap of time would give a true picture of the efficacy of the training programme. The follow-up questionnaire in this study were sent a little earlier than it ought to have been; nevertheless the data generated and its analysis in para 5.25 shows sample strength of this technique. The seminars with the past participants being conducted in ISTM only elicit one sided view of the participants. It is necessary to have the bosses' view as well.

## On-the-Job Training

6.19 The trainees as well as their supervisors are heavily in favour of more practical oriented input and also some on-the-job training alongwith classroom training. Particularly in skill to oriented input, at 50 per cent of the session duration should be devoted to exercises, case-studies and discussions. These trainees should also be sent for on-the-job training for one or two weeks in between the course as is presently being done in the case of Section Officers (Probationers). [5.22 and 5.25]

## Design of Courses

6.20 It may be noted that it is the trainer's responsibility, apart from imparting knowledge, to ensure that this knowledge will be of use to the trainee in his job and he has learnt the job. A trainer need to distinguish between what can be learnt in the classroom and what can be done only on the job. By understanding this, the trainer will be able to design programmes better, keeping in view the various aspects that can be covered in the programme.

## Formulation of Training Policy

6.21 In order to survive and operate effectively, all types of organization must adapt and respond to technological, economical and social changes. This requirement becomes imperative as we enter the twentyfirst century and implies that there are particular individual, group, organizational and institutional attitudes and perspectives needed by the nation's manpower. Training is one of the processes by which such needs can be realised. The need of an integrated training system and evolving a need-based training strategy for every Civil Service are the issues intricately linked with the question of an uniform training policy. The two Annual Training Conferences (held in 1981 and 1984 ) made a number of recommendations on innovations in training practices in Government. The National Training Policy formulated by the Government of India has addressed on most of the above issues, and issued guidelines. What is needed now is its implementation by all partners in training initiatives.

In fact, as a policy, the training activity should be an integral part of the personnel policy, which should deal with issues like manpower planning, cadre management, identification of organizational training needs, resource management, enhancing training effectiveness, evaluation and monitoring. The training policy should stress on standardisation of training institutions in terms of infrastructure, design of training courses, quality of trainers and evaluation practices.

# PART—B

# APPENDICES

**APPENDIX 1.1**
(Para 1.39)

# NATIONAL TRAINING POLICY: OPERATIONAL GUIDELINES

## PREAMBLE

Governments have very significant role to play in the developmental process and promotion of appropriate conditions which would lend dynamism to the national effort. In a developing country like India both the Central Government and the State Governments would need to ensure that the administrative machinery is sensitive to the dynamics of development and responsive to the socio-economic aspirations of its citizens. A conscious policy for the development of human resource available to the Governments would require to be fostered for meeting the challenges of development—social, economic and political. Training is one of the effective and tested tools for performance enhancement, as well as upgradation of knowledge and skills of the personnel. Organizational motivation and morale, as reflected in the attitudes and administrative culture, are rendered relevant and sharply focussed through effective training programmes. Sensitivity to emerging political and social concerns, modernity in thinking and re-orientation of administrative systems would require specifically focussed training programmes to enable their diffusion throughout the administrative structure.

## TRAINING OBJECTIVE

2. Training in Government shall strive to achieve the following objectives:
   - (a) Keeping up-to-date and enhancing professional knowledge and skills needed for better performance of individuals and organizations;
   - (b) Promoting better understanding of professional requirements as well as sensitisation to professional, socio-economic and political environment in which work is done; and
   - (c) Bringing about right attitudinal orientation.

## TRAINING CONCERNS

3. Social and political ambience is subject to constant change. The Government machinery would have to be continuously attuned to the changing needs. Training programmes for the Civil Services would, therefore, focus on:
   (a) **Responsiveness**
   - To the challenging democratic needs and expectations of the citizens and organizational and technological developments.

   (b) **Commitment**
   - to democratic values and concept of partnership and participative decision making.

   (c) **Awareness**
   - of technological, economic and social developments.

   (d) **Infusion of scientific temper**

   (e) **Accountibility**
   - to ensure high performance in every professional field and cost—effective methods of delivery.

## TRAINING FOR ALL

4.1 Training would be imparted to all rungs of the Civil Services starting from the lowest and cutting-edge to the highest in policy making.

4.2 For the purpose of appropriate training design, the Civil Services shall be divided into the following three levels:
   (a) The lowest level functionaries, that is operative at the cutting edge, who are mostly members of the Group 'D' services and the lower stages of Group 'C' services;
   (b) The supervisory levels and the middle management/ administrative level; (they are mostly members of the Group 'B' services, but also shade off into higher stages of Group 'C' at one end and the lower stages of Group 'A' at the other); and
   (c) Group 'A' services and All India Services comprising the administration/ management level.

4.3 Training programmes of functionaries at the cutting edge shall address themselves to functional skill and attitudinal orientation. For the middle level, training shall contribute to enhancement of professional knowledge, understanding and skill as also to widening professional outlook. For the higher Civil Services, besides offering stimuli for expansion of the mental horizon and attainment of professional excellence, training shall also endeavour to sharpen perception of inter-relatedness of issues. For the top levels of the higher Civil Services, training shall also be aimed at intellectually and professionally equipping the members for holding positions that involve policy analysis, strategic planning and policy formulation.

## FRAMEWORK FOR TRAINING

5.1 All categories of Civil Servants shall receive:
(a) Induction Training at the time of entry into service; and
(b) in-service training at suitable intervals in their career.

5.2 Attendance in training programmes shall be prescribed as a mandatory exercise with possible linkages with career progression.

5.3 For organized higher Civil Services, career span-specific training programmes in each progressive decade of service shall be imparted to provide scope for competence building.

5.4 In order to improve the effectiveness of personnel at different levels and different sectors, area specific short-term skill upgradation/ sensitisation programmes shall invariably be formulated by Ministries and Departments and specifically targetted to personnel holding specific jobs.

5.5 At the time of movement of personnel from Group 'D' to Group 'C', Group'C' to Group 'B' and Group 'B' to Group 'A', officers shall receive training for specific orientation and competence building. For this purpose, a well-structured detailed programme and Action Plan shall be worked out by each Ministry/Department/Organization.

5.6 Personnel recruited to isolated posts and specialists shall receive training to improve their capabilities of general management outside their chosen area of specialisation.

5.7 The in-service training programme for Group 'C' and 'D' expected at the time of movement to a higher Group may be provided in situ or through distance learning methods.

5.8 Training programmes will be specifically designed to meet the requirements of the target group by the organization in consultation with the institutions/consultants/experts.

5.9 Every organization shall conduct preparatory exercises like analysis of its goals and objectives, training needs analysis, job analysis etc. with a view to determining whether the training intervention needs to be preceded, accompanied by or succeeded by one or more non-training interventions. Such an exercise will also enable development of appropriate criteria for measuring individual and organisational performance, an essential pre-requisite for the launching of an effective training programme.

5.10 As possession of the right attitude plays a pivotal role in improving the performance levels of individuals, by contributing to formation of commitment in them, training programmes aimed at creating self-awareness as well as team building within the organisation shall be given utmost importance by every organisation.

## POLICY FORMULATION AND COORDINATION

6.1 A National Training Council, headed by the Minister-in-charge of Personnel, Public Grievances and Pensions, shall be set up for advising the Government of India on matters related to training policy, training design and programmes as well as issues concerning their implementation.

6.2 The National Training Council shall be assisted by a high powered committee of Directors headed by Secretary (Personnel) in the Ministry of Personnel, Public Grievances and Pensions. This committee shall generally oversee operationalisation of the Training Policy. It shall also ensure that Training Plans are actually drawn up by Cadre Controlling Authorities, syllabi are prepared and proper planning of training activity takes place through preparation of Perspective Plan, Annual Plans and Triennial Reviews.

## NODAL AUTHORITY

7. All organizations will designate training managers at appropriate levels to develop and coordinate training programmes and

monitor them. The Training Manager shall ensure an integrated approach to training with a view to improving overall performance of the organization.

**TRAINING INFRASTRUCTURE**

8.1 All Cadre Controlling Authorities shall endeavour to develop suitable infrastructure for induction and in-service training at the cutting edge and middle levels. Use of distance learning methods and in situ training shall be encouraged. Increasing use shall be made of non-government organisations for training of civil servants at lower levels.

8.2 Training institutions, experts and resource persons shall be increasingly formed into a network for flexibility in the use of human and material resources.

8.3 Training institutions under the government shall be permitted to diversify their training-related activities to cater to the increasing requirements of organizations and functional groups in and outside the government so as to enable them to attain a large measure of self-reliance.

8.4 Utmost care shall be exercised in selecting trainers. Efforts shall be made for evolving systems for identifying trainer-potential.

8.5 Department of Personnel and Training shall set up a workable system for evaluation of training institutions, without impinging adversely upon their professional autonomy.

8.6 Periodic opportunities for development of knowledge and skills in relevant areas shall be provided to trainers through training programmes in institutions of excellence.

8.7 A Trainer Staffing Scheme shall be operationalised, whereby Department of Personnel and Training shall maintain panels of trainers and potential trainers identified on the basis of a scientific system.

8.8 The concept of "once a trainer always a trainer" shall be developed under which expertise developed as a trainer shall be used even after he returns to his line department, either within the organization or by allowing him to go as resource person to outside institutions.

8.9 With a view to promoting harmony between participants, training events and trainers, a system for concurrent monitoring shall be operationalised. Similarly, with a view to avoiding mismatch between organizational objectives and training objectives, comprehensive evaluatory exercises shall be undertaken after a time lag.

## OVERSEAS TRAINING

9.1 Overseas training shall be entirely need-based and shall predominantly aim at drawing lessons from successful cross-country experience. Only institutions which are reservoirs of knowledge and data-base on relevant experiences shall be used.

9.2 The practice of funding most of the overseas training programmes through multilateral aid schemes shall be continued. With a view to maximising gains from overseas training, adequate pre-training preparation and post-training follow-up shall be arranged.

## IN HOUSE EXPERTISE

10.1 There will be a conscious attempt to draw on expertise and insight gained by civil servants in the course of their career. Involvement of civil servants in undertaking specific research and studies with a view to formulating new policy initiatives or evaluation of ongoing projects and programmes would be promoted and necessary facilities for study leave or sabbatical to enable civil servants to engage themselves in such tasks, identified and approved by competent authorities, would be provided.

10.2 Documentation of specific initiatives of Government and analysis of policies would be permitted by encouraging civil servants to take up such assignments at the specific instance of competent authorities.

## FUNDING

11. With a view to providing assured funding for training, each Department shall set apart 1.5 per cent of its salary budget which shall be used solely for the purpose of training and shall not be diverted for use elsewhere. This will be within the overall ceiling of the salary budget. Further, earmarking of funds to the exent of 1.5 per cent of the salary budget may not lead to any increase in the salary budget of the Ministry/ Department.

**APPENDIX 2.1**
(Para 2.9)

# CENTRAL SECRETARIAT SERVICE RULES, 1962

## Introduction

The Central Secretariat Service Rules caters for providing manpower to the various Ministries/Departments of the Central Government except Ministry of External Affairs, Department of Atomic Energy and Ministry of Railways. The Central Secretariat Service is the successor of the Imperial Secretariat Service. The Imperial Secretariat Service was re-organized by Re-organization and Re-enforcement Scheme, 1948. The scheme has been revised and the Central Secretariat Service Rules, 1962 was created w.e.f.1.10.1962.

In the Central Ministries/Departments, the three main services are:—

(a) The Central Secretariat Service (CSS)

(b) The Central Secretariat Clerical Service ( catering for the posts of UDCs and LDCs)(CSCS)

(c) The Central Secretariat Stenographers Service (PPS, PS, SPA and PA)(CSSS).

The officers of CSCS are promoted to the CSS at the level of Assistant and officers of CSSS are inducted in CSS at the level of Section Officer and Grade I officers.

2. Composition of Service and Method of Recruitment

The service consists of four grades:—

(a) Selection Grade (Centralised Cadre): Group 'A' (Gazetted) Rs. 3700-5000:

The posts are filled 100 per cent by promotion on *selection* basis from amongst Grade I officers with five years approved service. Crucial date is July 1, of the year for eligibility for promotion.

(b) Grade I (Centralised Cadre): Group'A' (Gazetted) Rs. 3000-4500:

(i) The posts are filled 100% by promotion from amongst Section Officers/Private Secretaries with eight years "approved service" on selection basis.

(ii) When SC/ST officers are not available to fill reserved vacancies, a Limited Departmental Examination to fill reserved vacancies in Grade I is conducted by UPSC. The eligibility condition for such examination is four years "approved service" in the grade of Section Officer/PS from amongst SC/ST officers only.

(c) Section Officer (De-centralised Cadre): Group 'B' (Gazetted.) Rs. 2000-2120-3500 :

(i) Substantive Posts: 80 per cent from amongst promotees and 20 per cent by direct recruitment through UPSC.

(ii) Temporary Posts:

(a) 50 per cent by seniority from amongst Assistants with eight years "approved service" on non-selection basis; and

(b) 50 per cent by Limited Departmental Examination conducted by UPSC where Assistants/Stenographer Grade 'C' with five years "approved service" or four years service, whichever is later, are eligible to complete.

(d) Assistants Grade (De-centralised): Group 'B' (NG) Rs.1640-2900:

(i) Substantive posts:

(a) 50 per cent by promotees and

(b) 50 per cent by direct recruitment through SSC. In case, sufficient direct recruits are not available, the shortfall quota will be diverted to promotee quota.

(ii) Temporary posts:

100 per cent by promotion from UDCs with five years service on non-selection basis.

3. Appointment to different Ministries/Departments:

After selection to the CSS, the direct recruits to the grade of Assistants and Section Officers are allocated by DoP&T (CS Division) to various Cadres on the basis of vacancies in the respective cadres and overall merit/rank in the competitive examination.

4. Probation: The direct recruits in the grade of Assistants and Section Officers are appointed on probation for a period of two years.

   The promotees to the grade of Assistant and Grade I are appointed on probation for a period of two years Where officers are not found suitable during probation, their services will be discharged or reverted to the grade of CSCS and CSSS as the case may be.
5. Confirmation: The direct recruits in the grade of Assistant and Section Officers are confirmed after completion of their probationary period satisfactorily.
6. Seniority:
   (a) The seniority in the grade of Selection Grade is based on the position in the select list.
   (b) The seniority in the Grade I is based on the position in the select list. In such year where Limited Departmental Examination is conducted, the officers selected through Limited Departmental Examination will be placed at the bottom of such select list for which they have been recruited.
   (c) The seniority in the Section Officers' grade is based on the rotation of substantive quota amongst promotees and direct recruits (in the ratio of 4:1). In case direct recruits or promotees are not available to fill their quota, the unfilled vacancies for particular quota will be carried forward for the next two years. In the last year of carried forward (i.e. second year) if the quota remains unfilled, such quota will be transferred as additional vacancies for the other mode of recruitment. The seniority amongst temporary officers will be on the basis of position in the select list.
   (d) The seniority in the grade of Assistant is based on the rotation of substantive quota amongst promotees and direct recruits (in the ratio of 1:1). In case direct recruits are not available against their quota, the unfilled direct recruits quota will be transferred to promotees. The seniority amongst temporary officers will be on the basis of position in the select list.

7. Inter-cadre transfer: The Department of Personnel and Training (CS Division) may transfer an officer from one cadre to another cadre.
8. Schedules: There are four schedules to the Rules:—
   (a) First Schedule: List of Ministries/Offices to whom the CSS Rules are applicable.
   (b) Second Schedule: The lists of posts and their designation included as "Duty Post" in the service.
   (c) Third Schedule: Authorised strength of Permanent Posts in the various grades of the service.
   (d) Fourth Schedule: Regulations for preparation and maintenance of Select List for the grade of Section Officer and Assistant's Grade and preparation of seniority list.

## APPENDIX 2.2
(Para 2.12)

### CADRE-WISE STRENGTH OF CSS OFFICERS

| *S. No.* | *Name of the Cadre* | *US* | *SO* | *Asstt.* |
|---|---|---|---|---|
| 1. | Agriculture and Cooperation | 30 | 82 | 154 |
| 2. | Civil Aviation | 9 | 31 | 101 |
| 3. | Company Affairs | 7 | 19 | 27 |
| 4. | Commerce | 38 | 131 | 139 |
| 5. | Coal | 5 | 11 | 23 |
| 6. | Civil Supplies | 5 | 13 | 28 |
| 7. | Defence | 88 | 147 | 260 |
| 8. | Education | 21 | 129 | 316 |
| 9. | Environment | 15 | 34 | 72 |
| 10. | Food | 17 | 43 | 88 |
| 11. | Finance (Expenditure) | 67 | 153 | 439 |
| 12. | Fertiliser | 13 | 34 | 52 |
| 13. | Home Affairs | 41 | 278 | 581 |
| 14. | Health and Family Welfare | 38 | 99 | 202 |
| 15. | Information and Broadcasting | 31 | 125 | 300 |
| 16. | Industrial Development | 20 | 105 | 157 |
| 17. | Law (Legal Affairs) | 5 | 21 | 50 |
| 18. | Labour | 16 | 75 | 137 |
| 19. | Mines | 5 | 15 | 40 |
| 20. | Planning Commission | 4 | 23 | 47 |
| 21. | Petroleum and Natural Gas | 9 | 23 | 38 |
| 22. | Power | 12 | 46 | 98 |
| 23. | Posts | 7 | 37 | 102 |
| 24. | Rural Development | 14 | 30 | 73 |
| 25. | Steel | 6 | 21 | 39 |
| 26. | Science and Technology | 8 | 27 | 53 |
| 27. | Surface Transport | 18 | 53 | 106 |
| 28. | Supply | 16 | 65 | 226 |
| 29. | Telecommunication | 7 | 37 | 102 |
| 30. | Urban Development | 27 | 146 | 278 |
| 31. | UPSC | 45 | 106 | 281 |
| 32. | Welfare | 10 | 31 | 58 |
| 33. | Water Resources | 14 | 53 | 122 |
| | Total | 668 | 2243 | 4789 |

**APPENDIX 3.1**

(Paras 3.30 and 5.05)

## INSTITUTE OF SECRETARIAT TRAINING AND MANAGEMENT

Dear faculty colleague,

As part of my Ph.D work an exercise has been undertaken to analyse and study the "Structure and Organization of ISTM" with a view to identifying the various factors which influence the functioning of ISTM as a training institute of public administration.

2. Your views, as a faculty member of ISTM will be of great value to this study. I shall be grateful to have your response in the enclosed questionnaire. Kindly devote adequate time and thought to various questions before recording your answer.

3. Your views and the information furnished by you will neither be used for any other purpose nor shall be quoted in any other context than for the data analysis purpose of the study mentioned above.

Thanking you,

(A.N. CHAKRAVARTY)

**APPENDIX 3.1**
(Paras 3.30 and 5.05)

Code : 2.2

## INSTITUTE OF SECRETARIAT TRAINING AND MANAGEMENT

## ISTM FACULTY PROFILE—QUESTIONNAIRE

**PART-A: PERSONAL DATA**

1. NAME (Optional):
2. DESIGNATION:
3. DATE OF JOINING GOVT. SERVICE: / /
4. SERVICE TO WHICH BELONGS:
5. DATE OF JOINING ISTM (Present term):
6. LAST APPOINTMENT BEFORE JOINING ISTM:
7. QUALIFICATIONS: *Subject*

   Graduation [ ] ____________________

   Post Graduation [ ] ____________________

   Doctoral [ ] ____________________

   Others [ ] Specify____________________

8. TRAININGS (Specify courses attended during the last five years)

   S.No. Name of the Course Institute Dates

9. WORK EXPERIENCE:

10. EXPERIENCE WHICH YOU THINK IS RELEVANT TO YOUR POST IN ISTM:

11. EARLIER TERM (S), IF ANY, IN ISTM:

| *Post* | *From* | *to* | *Subject Areas* |
|---|---|---|---|
| ____________ | / / | / / | |
| ____________ | / / | / / | |

12. Indicate *one best* reason, of the following, for your joining ISTM:
   (a) A change from the previous job [ ]
   (b) Highers emoluments/remuneration [ ]
   (c) Liking for teaching/training [ ]
   (d) Lıking for organ. environ. of ISTM [ ]
   (e) any other, specify ____________________ [ ]

**PART-B: TRAINING FUNCTIONS**

**I. As a Direct Trainer**

1. Average No. of sessions per week you have taken during the current year: No.________ Areas________________

| | *Yes* | *Some times* | *No* |
|---|---|---|---|
| 2. Do you require preparation before the session? | [ ] | [ ] | [ ] |
| 3. Do you prepare your lesson plan for each session? | [ ] | [ ] | [ ] |
| 4. Do you feel satisfied with your session? | [ ] | [ ] | [ ] |
| 5. Do you test the learning ot your trainees at the end of each session? If yes, how?________________ ____________________ | [ ] | [ ] | [ ] |

**II. As a Course Coordinator**

6. No. of courses you have conducted during the current year

*Year* *Name of the course* *Duration*

| | Fully | Partly | Not at all |
|---|---|---|---|
| 7. Do you think that the courses met the need of the trainees? | [ ] | [ ] | [ ] |
| 8. Do you receive adequate support/ cooperation in conducting the course effectively? | | | |
| (a) From your superior | [ ] | [ ] | [ ] |
| (b) From course faculty | [ ] | [ ] | [ ] |
| (c) From the trainees | [ ] | [ ] | [ ] |
| 9. Do you agree that success of the course mainly depends on effective coordination by the Course Coordinator | [ ] | [ ] | [ ] |

If 'partly' or 'not at all', what do you think are the other factors for the success of a course?

________________________________

________________________________

| | Yes | Some-times | No |
|---|---|---|---|
| 10. Do you think that the trainees mostly come to the course with a clear objective of learning new things? | [ ] | [ ] | [ ] |

11. What do you think are the other possible objectives they come with?

________________________________

________________________________

## III. On Training/Reading Material

12. Please furnish details of the handouts/exercises/case-studies prepared/updated by you during the last three years:

| *S.No.* | *Description* | *Whether Original or Updated* | *Approx. time devoted* |
|---|---|---|---|

(Use separate sheet if not sufficient)

| | Yes | Some-time | No |
|---|---|---|---|
| 13. Do you think the training material available on your subject area are sufficient and up-to-date? | [ ] | [ ] | [ ] |
| 14. Do you make use of the training material prepared by ex-faculty? | [ ] | [ ] | [ ] |
| Are they readily available for use? | [ ] | [ ] | [ ] |
| 15. Do you agree that faculty should always use his own training handouts/materials? | [ ] | [ ] | [ ] |
| Please give reasons for your answer: | | | |
| 16. Do you get encouragement from your superiors for preparing more original material? | [ ] | [ ] | [ ] |
| 17. Do you get matching administrative support in the matter of preparing them? | [ ] | [ ] | [ ] |
| If no, what more do you require? | | | |

**PART-C: MOTIVATION AND DEVELOPMENT**

| | Yes | No |
|---|---|---|
| 1. Do you think, your experience in the Secretariat was adequate for performance of your job as a trainer? | [ ] | [ ] |

2. After joining ISTM, what helped you becoming
   (i) an effective trainer : ______________________________
   (ii) a specialist in your subject area: ______________________________

| | Yes | Some-times | No |
|---|---|---|---|
| 3. Do you value the feedback given by your trainees about your session? | [ ] | [ ] | [ ] |
| 4. Do you expect feedback from your | | | |
| (i) colleagues | [ ] | [ ] | [ ] |
| (ii) superiors | [ ] | [ ] | [ ] |
| If yes, do you receive them in time? | [ ] | [ ] | [ ] |

| | | | |
|---|---|---|---|
| 5. Do you think that efficiency and hardwork is adequately and timely rewarded in ISTM? | [ ] | [ ] | [ ] |
| 6. Do you think you have had adequate opportunities for your development as an effective trainer in ISTM? | [ ] | | [ ] |
| If 'no', what opportunities are you looking forward to? | | | |
| 7. Do you think, the present feedback form in ISTM is adequately useful for improving trainers' performance, if any? | [ ] | [ ] | [ ] |
| If 'no', what are your suggestions: | | | |
| 8. Do you think, your superior is always kept informed about your performance as a trainer and coordinator? | [ ] | [ ] | [ ] |
| Do you value it? | [ ] | [ ] | [ ] |

## PART-D: EVALUATION OF TRAINING

### I. Pre-training Evaluation

| | *Yes* | *Some-times* | *No* |
|---|---|---|---|
| 1. As coordinator do you match the trainees' and their Orgnization's need with the course objectives? | [ ] | [ ] | [ ] |
| 2. Do you test the trainees' pre-training knowledge, skill and attitude? | [ ] | [ ] | [ ] |
| 3. If 'yes' or 'sometimes', do you modify the input and context of the course suitably? | [ ] | [ ] | [ ] |

### II. Post-training Evaluation

| | | | |
|---|---|---|---|
| 4. Do you use an Immediate Reaction Questionnaire at the end of | | | |
| (a) each session/learning unit | [ ] | [ ] | [ ] |
| (b) each Module (group of related units) | [ ] | [ ] | [ ] |
| (c) the course | [ ] | [ ] | [ ] |
| (d) any other way, specify ______________________ | | | |

5. Are the feedbacks used for necessary improvement of the

| | | | |
|---|---|---|---|
| (a) course input | [ ] | [ ] | [ ] |
| (b) training methods | [ ] | [ ] | [ ] |
| (c) presentation | [ ] | [ ] | [ ] |
| (d) training material | [ ] | [ ] | [ ] |
| (e) physical facilities | [ ] | [ ] | [ ] |
| (f) others ________________ | | | |

Give some recent instance with results:

| | | | |
|---|---|---|---|
| 6. As a direct trainer do you include measurement of learning as a part of your session? | [ ] | [ ] | [ ] |

What instrument/method do you use? ____________________

**III. Follow up of Trainees**

| | *Yes* | *No* | *Not known* |
|---|---|---|---|
| 7. Do you think, there is need of systematic follow up of the trainees after they return to their jobs? | [ ] | [ ] | [ ] |

If yes, what benefits would you derive from such an exercise ____________________

____________________________________________

8. Do you think, if planned, such systematic follow up could be possible for

| | | | |
|---|---|---|---|
| (a) ISTM | [ ] | [ ] | [ ] |
| (b) Ministries/Departments | [ ] | [ ] | [ ] |

Please give your suggestions, if any, in this regard:

**Part-E: PHYSICAL FACILITIES**

| | | | |
|---|---|---|---|
| 1. Do you think that facilities available to the trainees are adequate for providing effective learning conditions? | [ ] | | [ ] |

If 'no', your suggestions for improvement:

2. Are the physical and administrative facilities available to the faculty in ISTM helpful in providing effective training environment? [ ] [ ]

   If 'no', mention hindrances

   ______________________________

3. Are the faculty members actively involved in deciding on training facilities to be provided to the trainees? [ ] [ ]

| | *Yes* | *Some times* | *No* |
|---|---|---|---|
| 4. Do you make use of a computer for: | | | |
| (i) issuing training circulars | [ ] | [ ] | [ ] |
| (ii) processing nominations | [ ] | [ ] | [ ] |
| (iii) processing examination results | [ ] | [ ] | [ ] |
| (iv) printing examination results | [ ] | [ ] | [ ] |
| (v) preparing training material | [ ] | [ ] | [ ] |
| (vi) any other, specify ________ | | | |
| 5. Do you think the existing Computer facilities in ISTM for faculty use is adequate? | [ ] | [ ] | [ ] |

If 'no', what are your suggestions

______________________________

| | *Exten-sively* | *Some times* | *Don't know their avail-ability/ utility* | *Didn't have occa-sion to use* |
|---|---|---|---|---|
| 6. How frequently do you use the following facilities available in ISTM: | | | | |
| (a) Desk Top Publishing | [ ] | [ ] | [ ] | [ ] |
| (b) Video Projection System | [ ] | [ ] | [ ] | [ ] |
| (c) Video camera | [ ] | [ ] | [ ] | [ ] |
| (d) Video films | [ ] | [ ] | [ ] | [ ] |
| (e) Rota Print | [ ] | [ ] | [ ] | [ ] |

| | | | | |
|---|---|---|---|---|
| (f) Risograph | [ ] | [ ] | [ ] | [ ] |
| (g) Photocopier | [ ] | [ ] | [ ] | [ ] |
| (h) Spiral binding | [ ] | [ ] | [ ] | [ ] |
| (i) Staple binding | [ ] | [ ] | [ ] | [ ] |
| (j) Lamination machine | [ ] | [ ] | [ ] | [ ] |

| | *Yes* | *No* |
|---|---|---|
| 7. Do you make use of the ISTM Library? | [ ] | [ ] |

If yes, (a) for what purpose
(b) how frequently

| | *Fully* | *Partly* | *Not at all* |
|---|---|---|---|
| 8. Is the ISTM Library adequate for meeting the needs of trainees and faculty? | [ ] | [ ] | [ ] |

| | *Strongly* | *Not so sure* | *Not at all* |
|---|---|---|---|
| 9. Do you feel the need of a regular house-journal of ISTM ? | [ ] | [ ] | [ ] |

| | *Yes* | *No* |
|---|---|---|
| 10. Are you satisfied with the present system of hierarchy in the ISTM faculty? | [ ] | [ ] |

If 'no', please give reasons and your suggestions for improvement:

11. Any other suggestion for improvement of ISTM as a better training institution:

Thank you, for completing the questionnaire!

## APPENDIX 3.2

(Para 3.31)

List of Publications of Secretariat Training School (STS) and Institute of Secretariat Training and Management (ISTM)

| | *Title* | *Year of First issue* | *Last Revised in* |
|---|---|---|---|
| 1. | Organizational set-up and functions of the Ministries and Department of the Government of India | 1957 | |
| 2. | Notes on Office Procedure | 1960 | |
| 3. | Notes on Financial Rules | 1960 | |
| 4. | Handbook of Typewriting | 1962 | |
| 5. | Hindi Typewriting Prashikshak | 1963 | |
| 6. | Work Study—Part I Administrative Research | 1966 | |
| 7. | Work Study—Part II Method Study | -do- | |
| 8. | Work Study—Part III Work Measurement and associated techniques | -do- | |
| 9. | Work Study—Part IV Report Writing and Oral Presentation | -do- | |
| 10. | Notes on CCS (Conduct) Rules, 1964 | 1969 | |
| 11. | Manak Ashulipi | 1969 | |
| Important training monographs: | | | |
| 1. | Desk Officer System | 1974 | |
| 2. | Records Management | 1974 | 1986 |
| 3. | A Guide for various levels working in the Desk Officer System | 1975 | |
| 4. | A Guide for civilian officers in Armed Forces Headquaters and officers in the Ministry of Defence | 1975 | |
| 5. | Behavioural Patterns in Central Secretariat and Armed Forces Hqrs. | 1975 | |
| 6. | Manual for LDCs Trainers | 1975 | |

| | | | |
|---|---|---|---|
| 7. | Constitution as an Ethical Synthesis of all Indian Religions | 1975 | |
| 8. | Central Secretariat Service-Genesis, Objectives and Culture | 1975 | |
| 9. | Summary of Case Laws in Disciplinary Matters | 1976 | 1981 |
| 10. | The Role of a Private Secretary/Personal Assistant | 1976 | |
| 11. | Fundamental Duties in the Constitution of India—a Survey | 1976 | |
| 12. | Physical Facilities for Training Institutions | 1977 | |
| 13. | Anti-Corruption Laws | 1977 | 1983 |
| 14. | Aspects of Indian Constitution | 1980 | |
| 15. | Reservation in Services for SCs/STs | 1981 | 1986 |
| 16. | Administrative Work Study | 1981 | |
| 17. | Performance Budgeting | 1982 | |
| 18. | Evaluation of Training—a Study | 1988 | |
| 19. | Computer Primer | 1991 | |
| 20. | Database Management System | 1991 | |

**APPENDIX 3.3**
(Para 3.44)

## Existing Sanction Strength of Administrative Staff of ISTM

As on 1 March 1995

| *Sl. No.* | *Name of the Post* | *Scale of Pay* | *No. of Posts* | | |
|---|---|---|---|---|---|
| | | | *Perma-nent* | *Tempo-rary* | *Total* |
| **Group B Gazetted** | | | | | |
| 1. | Section Officer | 2000-3500 | 1 | - | 1 |
| 2. | Steno Grade B | 2000-3500 | 2 | 1 | 3 |
| **Group B Non-gazetted** | | | | | |
| 3. | Assistant | 1640-2900 | 4 | - | 4 |
| 4. | Steno Grade C | 1640-2900 | 7 | - | 7 |
| **Group C** | | | | | |
| 5. | Librarian | | 1 | - | 1 |
| 6. | Draftsman | | | | |
| 7. | UDC | | 4 | - | 5 |
| 8. | Steno Grade D | | 7 | - | 7 |
| 9. | LDC | | 4 | - | 4 |
| 10. | Library Attendant | | 1 | - | 1 |
| 11. | Projector Operator | | 1 | - | 1 |
| 12. | Telex Operator | | - | 1 | 1 |
| 13. | Staff Car Driver | | 1 | 1 | 2 |
| 14. | Mini Bus Driver | | - | 1 | 1 |
| **Group D** | | | | | |
| 15. | Jr. Gestetner Operator | | 1 | | |
| 16. | Daftry | | 1 | | |
| 17. | Peon | | 12 | | |
| 18. | Farash | | 4 | | |
| 19. | Chowkidar | | 5 | | |
| 20. | Sweeper | | 6 | | |
| **Hindi** | | | | | |
| 21. | Assistant Director | | - | 1 | 1 |
| 22. | Sr. Hindi Translator | | - | 1 | 1 |
| 23. | Jr. Hindi Translator | | 1 | - | 1 |

**APPENDIX 3.4**
(Para 3.50)

## ORGANIZATION CHART OF ISTM
As on 1.7.95

Director

- General Management and Office Administration
  - JD(MS)
    - DD(MS)-4
    - DD(OM)-2
    - AD(OM)-1
- Behavioural Sciences and Training Research
  - JD(BT)
    - DD(BT)-1
    - AD(ES&T)-4
- Financial Administration and Management
  - JD(FM)
    - DD(A/c)-2
    - DD(FM) -1
    - DD(EDP)-1
    - AD(A/C)-1
    - AD(OM) -3
- Personal Management and Training Methods
  - JD(TRG)
    - DD(OM)-1
    - DD(PT)-2
    - DD(FC)-2
    - DD(V) -1
    - AD(OM)-1

Legends:

MS = Management Services
OM = Office Management
BT = Behavioural Training
ES&T = English Shorthand and Typewriting
FM = Financial Management
A/C = Accounts
EPD = Economic Development and Planning
TRG = Training
PT = Peripatetic Training
FC = Foundational Course
V = Vigilance

**APPENDIX 3.5**
(Para 3.55)

## Existing Strength of Training Faculty and Staff in ISTM
As on 1 March 1995

| Sl. No. | Name of the Post | Scale of Pay | No. of Posts | | |
|---|---|---|---|---|---|
| | | | Permanent | Temporary | Total |
| 1. | Director | 5900-6700 | 1 | - | 1 |
| 2. | Joint Director | 3700-5000 | 1 | 3 | 4 |
| 3. | Deputy Director | 3000-4500 | 11 | 5 | 16 |
| 4. | Asstt. Director (Accounts) | 2300-3500 | 1 | - | 1 |
| 5. | Asstt. Director (Office Management) | 2000-3500 | 5 | - | 5 |
| 6. | Asstt. Director (English Shorthand and Typewriting) | 2000-3500 | - | 4 | 4 |
| 7. | Training Associate | 1640-2900 | - | 3 | 3 |

**APPENDIX 3.6**
(Para 3.56)

## PROFORMA INDICATING VARIOUS ACTIVITIES PERFORMED BY ISTM FACULTY

### PART I

### Training Courses

1. *Sessions in Training Courses*

(A) In ISTM — *Course Code* — *Date* — *No. of sessions*
- (i) Scheduled
- (ii) Unscheduled

Total =

(B) Peripatetic and Faculty Assistance
- (i) In Delhi
- (ii) Outside Delhi

Total =

2. *Preparation for Lectures*
- (i) Original Lectures
- (ii) Repeat Lectures
- (iii) Updating Lectures (additions/alterations)

3. *Course Coordination*
- (i) Finalising syllabus
- (ii) Scheduling sessions
- (iii) Inviting nominations
- (iv) Scrutiny of nominations
- (v) Follow up of (iv)
- (vi) Setting up of Test papers
  - (a) Weekly Tests
  - (b) Terminal Tests
- (vii) Conducting Tests
- (viii) Evaluation of answer papers and tabulation of result
- (ix) Compilation of results and preparation of certificates
- (x) Arranging/Fixing up project work
- (xi) As faculty guide for project
- (xii) Any other item

4. *Tours* *No. of days*
   - (i) Peripatetic Courses
     - (a) Journey time
     - (b) On course
   - (ii) Project Work
     - (a) Journey time
     - (b) On project
   - (iii) Study Tour
     - (a) Journey Time
     - (b) At destination
   - (iv) Other tours

   Total =

5. Any other item with the course and post-course action e.g. evaluation of course, release of trainees etc.

**PART II**

(Meetings/Discussions/Administrative work of ISTM)

| | *No. of sessions* | *Time (Hrs./Mnts)* |
|---|---|---|
| (i) Faculty Meetings | | |
| (ii) PAC Meetings | | |
| (iii) Other Meetings | | |
| (iv) Discussions | | |
| (v) Administrative Work | | |
| | Total = | |

**PART III**

(Training Course/Seminars/Conference/Workshops/ other lectures attended)

| | *Dates* | *No. of Days* |
|---|---|---|
| (a) Course | | |
| (b) Seminars | | |
| (c) Conference | | |
| (d) Workshop | | |
| (e) Other lectures | | |

Total =

## APPENDIX 3.7
(Para 3.56)

### WORK LOAD OF TRAINING FACULTY IN ISTM

| Year | International | Foundation | Refresher | General Administration | Training Technique | Financial Management | Management Services | Organizational Behaviour | Computer | Total In-house | PT Courses | Grand Total | Faculty Required | Faculty Available | Excess Faculty |
|---|---|---|---|---|---|---|---|---|---|---|---|---|---|---|---|
| (1) | (2) | (3) | (4) | (5) | (6) | (7) | (8) | (9) | (10) | (11) | (12) | (13) | (14) | (15) | (16) |
| | | | | | | | No. of Course Weeks | | | | | | | | |
| 1988-89 | 13.00 | 104.00 | 38.00 | 41.00 | 8.00 | 51.00 | 45.00 | 6.00 | 0.00 | 306.00 | 29.00 | 335.00 | 17.63 | 26.00 | 8.37 |
| 1989-90 | 13.00 | 90.00 | 32.00 | 38.00 | 12.00 | 53.00 | 52.00 | 6.00 | 0.00 | 296.00 | 15.00 | 311.00 | 16.37 | 25.00 | 8.63 |
| 1990-91 | 15.00 | 68.00 | 32.00 | 37.00 | 8.00 | 49.00 | 52.00 | 6.00 | 4.00 | 271.00 | 17.00 | 288.00 | 15.16 | 23.00 | 7.84 |
| 1991-92 | 7.00 | 68.00 | 38.00 | 18.00 | 11.00 | 47.00 | 56.00 | 7.00 | 8.00 | 260.00 | 21.00 | 281.00 | 14.79 | 24.00 | 9.21 |
| 1992-93 | 15.00 | 68.00 | 33.00 | 19.00 | 11.00 | 45.00 | 53.00 | 5.00 | 10.00 | 259.00 | 18.00 | 277.00 | 14.58 | 27.00 | 12.42 |
| 1993-94 | 0.00 | 92.00 | 44.00 | 19.00 | 6.00 | 53.00 | 54.00 | 6.00 | 7.00 | 281.00 | 14.00 | 295.00 | 15.53 | 24.00 | 8.47 |
| 1994-95 | 0.00 | 94.00 | 48.00 | 19.00 | 8.00 | 51.00 | 40.00 | 7.00 | 7.00 | 274.00 | 5.00 | 279.00 | 14.68 | 17.00 | 2.32 |

**APPENDIX 4.1 (a)**

(Paras 4.05,4.06 and 4.07)

APPENDIX 4.1 (a)

## SYLLABUS FOR DIRECT RECRUITS TO THE SECTION OFFICERS' GRADE OF THE CENTRAL SECRETARIAT SERVICE

A Initial training at the Secretariat Training School (Three and a half months)

I. Organization of machinery of Government

(1) Principal Wings—Legislature, Executive and Judiciary in Union and States.

(2) Distribution of legislative functions between the Union and the States.

(3) Union Government—Ministries, Departments and Boards, Attached and Subordinate Offices.

(4) Subject dealt with in the different Ministries/Departments.

(5) Public Undertakings, semi-Government Organizations.

(6) System of financial control and audit.

(7) Safeguards against conflicts and for coordination in framing and execution of policies and decisions.

(8) Planning and economic development.

II. General Survey of Rules and Regulations

(1) Salient provisions of the Constitution relating to Services.

(2) Central Civil Services (Classification, Control and Appeal) Rules, 1957.

(3) UPSC (Exemption from Consultation) Regulations, 1958.

(4) Central Civil Services (Temporary Service) Rules, 1949.

(5) Central Civil Service (Conduct) Rules, 1964.

(6) Fundamental and Supplementary Rules.

(7) Civil Service Regulations (Pension portion only) and Liberalised Pension Rules.

(8) General Provident Fund (Central Services) Rules, 1960.

(9) General Financial Rules (Revised and Enlarged) 1963.

(10) Compilation of the Delegation of Financial Power Rules, 1958.

(11) Treasury Rules (Vol.I and II).
(12) Official Secrets Act.
(13) Rules for printing and binding.
(14) Rules for the supply of stationery stores.
(15) Budget and Control of Expenditure (including Foreign Exchange control and Budgeting )
(16) Central Government Health Scheme.
(17) Machinery for redress of grievances—Staff Councils and Joint Consultation and Arbitration, etc.

III. Office Procedure

(1) Full grounding and practice in the office procedure laid down in the Manual and of functions assigned to LDCs, UDCs and Assistants.
(2) Preliminary talks on duties and functions of a Section Officer—his place in the organization and role he is expected to play.

IV. Typewriting

B. On the Job Training in a Ministry (three months)

(1) General briefing regarding the organization of the Ministry, its attached and subordinate offices, distribution of work among sections. 1 day
(2) Attached to Central Registry. 1 day
(3) Attached to Typing and Issue Section 1 day
(4) Attached to Administration and Cash Section 1 week (6 days)
(5) Attached to a regular section in the Ministry
( The section selection should not be a routine section but such as will offer a good scope for examination of problems, noting, drafting etc. The Director of School should satisfy himself on this point).
Briefing about the organization and functioning of the section; distribution of work among the staff, registers and records, etc.
Working as a Diarist (Diarising of receipts, movement of files, file register, indexing, arrear statements and other items of work done by the Diarist of the section). 1 week

(6) Working as a regular Assistant with normal allotment of work under the systematic guidance of S.O. of the section. 6 weeks

(7) Attachment as Section Officer (in the same section)
To work as attache under the guidance of the S.O. doing a certain number of cases—watching and learning how the S.O. performs his duties as supervisor and guides his staff and the kind of files and papers he deals with himself. 1 week

(8) Working in full charge of the same section. 3 weeks

NOTES: (i) The Under Secretaries in charge of Administration/ Establishment will—

(a) personally ensure that the trainees are given proper and systematic training based on this programme; and

(b) follow their progress in training.

(ii) The trainees are requested to send weekly Progress Report showing the work done by them during the week.

(iii) The Instructors of the Secretariat Training School will continue to keep in touch with the trainees from time to time.

C. Further training at the STS (two months)

I. General brushing up in Office Procedure in the light of the practical experience.

II. Full grounding in and elaboration in respect of duties and functions of a Section Officer, particularly in respect of —

(1) Standard Heads
(2) Indexing and Recording
(3) Editing and Printing of Files
(4) Checks on Delays
(5) Reports and Returns
(6) Inspection of registers and tables
(7) Security requirements
(8) Reference Books
(9) Distribution of work among staff
(10) Watch over progress of urgent and important files and papers

(11) Sectional Note Book
(12) Standing Guard Files

III. Special procedures regarding disposal of certain types of matters —

(1) Procedure for submission of cases to the Cabinet/ Committees of Cabinet.
(2) Matters in which consultation with UPSC is necessary and procedure for making reference to UPSC.
(3) Questions, resolutions in Parliament and other Parliamentary business.
(4) Publicity in the press.
(5) Court cases (e.g. civil suits, writ petitions, etc.).

IV. Office Management

(1) Attendance
(2) Attendance on holidays
(3) Casual Leave and other absence from duty
(4) Charge reports, and
(5) Tidiness, cleanliness and orderliness in office.

V. Supervisory Training

(1) Maintenance of discipline
(2) Guidance and training to staff
(3) Human relations, and
(4) Writing of Confidential Reports.

VI. Work Simplification and Work Study

(1) Work Simplification
(2) Work Measurement
(3) Case studies—procedure
(4) Development of standard forms, skeleton drafts etc.

D. Further Practical Training in Ministries/Departments etc. (Three and a half months).

During this period, the trainees will be first attached to the O&M Section for practical training in Work and Methods studies for one month and, thereafter, to an experienced Section Officer, as far as possible, and encouraged to perform all the duties of a Section Officer under his guidance.

E. Independent charge of light sections in the Ministry/ Department (to test the trainees' suitability for permanent appointment as Section Officer. (One year).

**Note:** After the trainee has held independent charge of a section for about six months, he should be required to conduct at least two work studies independently.

F. Examinations

The trainees will be required to pass a Preliminary as well as the Final Examination as per Annexure I.

**Notes:** (i) A minimum of 50 per cent marks will be required for a pass in each of the written papers. Obtaining 50 per cent or more marks in any paper will entitle the trainee to exemption from re-examination in that paper.

(ii) A trainee who fails to secure the prescribed minimum marks in the written part of the Final Examination will be allowed two more chances to pass the examination, normally within the next six months. If he fails to pass the examination even after availing these two additional chances, he will be liable to appropriate actions under rule 17 of the CSS Rules, 1962.

(iii) If a trainee absents himself from the Final Examination or a re-examination, he will normally be regarded as having utilised a chance and failed in the examination.

(iv) An extract from the result sheet, showing the marks obtained by the trainee in the Final Examination will be added to his Confidential Record. If he fails to appear in the examination or to avail of a chance, an entry in this regard will also be made in the Confidential Record. Rule 17 of the CSS Rules, 1962.

17. Discharge or reversion of probationers

(1) A probationer who has no lien on any post under the Central Government or any State Government shall be liable to be discharged from the service at any time without notice if—

(i) on the basis of his performance or conduct during probation, he is considered unfit for further retention in the service; or

(ii) if on the receipt of any information relating to his nationality, age, health, or antecedents, the appointing authority is satisfied that he is ineligible or otherwise unfit for being a member of the Service.

(2) A probationer who holds a lien on a post under the Central Government or any State Government may be reverted to such post at any time in any of the circumstances specified in sub-rule (1).

(3) A probationer who is not considered suitable for confirmation at the end of the period of probation prescribed in sub-rule (1) of rule 15 or at the end of the extended period of probation, if any, under sub-rule (3) of that rule, shall be discharged or reverted in accordance with sub-rule (1) of sub-rule (2), as the case may be.

ANNEXURE I

## SCHEME OF EXAMINATIONS FOR DIRECT RECRUITS TO THE SECTION OFFICERS' GRADE OF CENTRAL SECTT. SERVICE

*Preliminary Examination*—A preliminary examination will be held towards the end of the two months' training in the School. This will cover the portions taught up to that date.

*Final Examination*—On the completion of the training in the School and prior to their final posting to the Ministries / Departments the trainees will be required to appear at the Final Examination. The subjects and the maximum marks for each paper are as shown below:

(1) 1st Paper—Office Procedure — 100 marks

- (a) Office Procedure.
- (b) Noting and Drafting.
- (c) Rules of Procedure and Conduct of Business in Parliament.
- (d) Procedure for submission of cases to the Cabinet.

(2) 2nd Paper—General Rules — 100 marks

- (a) Organization of the Government of India and subject for which each Ministry or Department of the Government of India is reponsible.
- (b) Constitution of India—Parts V and XIV.
- (c) UPSC (Exemption from Consultation) Regulations, 1958.
- (d) Central Civil Services (Conduct) Rules, 1964
- (e) Central Civil Services (Classification, Contro and Appeal) Rules, 1957.
- (f) Central Civil Services (Temporary Service) Rules.
- (g) Rules for Printing and Binding; Procurement of Stationery and Forms.
- (h) Other important general instructions issued by the Government of India from time to time.

(3) 3rd Paper—Fundamental Rules & Supplementary Rules; Pension Rules — 100 marks

- (a) Fundamental Rules and Supplementary Rules.
- (b) Civil Service Regulations—Pension part only and the Liberalised Pension Rules.

(4) 4th Paper—General Financial Rules, Planning and Economic Development 100 marks

- (a) General Provident Fund (Central Services) Rules, 1960.
- (b) General Financial Rules (Revised and Enlarged) 1963 and Delegation of Financial Powers Rules, 1958.
- (c) Budget and Control of Expenditure.
- (d) Treasury Rules.
- (e) Planning and Economic Development.
- (f) Foreign Exchange Budgeting and Control.

(5) In addition to the written examination in the above subjects, the trainee will be awarded a maximum of 100 marks on the basis of his behaviour and conduct and the progress shown by him in practical work during the period of training at the School. The allotment of marks will be as shown below:

| | Marks |
|---|---|
| (a) Punctuality and regularity in attending classes. | 20 |
| (b) Practical work done in the classes ( each trainee will maintain a separate file for class work in respect of the work handled by each Instructor) | 50 |
| (c) Discipline, behaviour, conduct, intelligence and capacity for self-expression. | 30 |

**N.B.** Use of reference books during the written examination is not allowed except in the case of Fundamental Rules and Supplementary Rules.

APPENDIX 4.1.b

## SYLLABUS FOR DIRECT RECRUITS TO THE ASSISTANTS' GRADE OF THE CENTRAL SECRETARIAT SERVICE

A. Initial training at the Secretariat Training School
(Three and a half months)

I. Organization of machinery of Government

(1) Principal Wings—Legislature, Executive and Judiciary in Union and States.
(2) Distribution of legislative functions between the Union and the States.
(3) Union Government—Ministries, Departments and Boards, Attached and Subordinate Offices.
(4) Subject dealt with in the different Ministries/Departments.
(5) Public Undertakings, semi-Government Organizations.
(6) System of financial control and audit.
(7) Safeguards against conflicts and for coordination in framing and execution of policies and decisions.
(8) Planning and economic development.

II. General Survey of Rules and Regulations

(1) Salient provisions of the Constitution relating to Services.
(2) Central Civil Services (Classification, Control and Appeal) Rules, 1957.
(3) UPSC (Exemption from Consultation) Regulations, 1958.
(4) Central Civil Services (Temporary Service) Rules, 1949.
(5) Central Civil Service (Conduct) Rules, 1964.
(6) Fundamental and Supplementary Rules.
(7) Civil Service Regulations (Pension portion only) and Liberalised Pension Rules.
(8) General Provident Fund (Central Services) Rules, 1960.
(9) General Financial Rules (Revised and Enlarged) 1963.
(10) Compilation of the Delegation of Financial Power Rules,1958.
(11) Treasury Rules (Vol.I and II).
(12) Official Secrets Act.
(13) Rules for printing and binding.
(14) Rules for the supply of stationery stores.

(15) Budget and Control of Expenditure (including Foreign Exchange control and Budgeting ).

(16) Central Government Health Scheme.

(17) Machinery for redress of grievances—Staff Councils and Joint Consultation and Arbitration, etc.

III. Office Procedure

(1) Full grounding and practice in the office procedure laid down in the Manual and practice regarding :

(a) Standard Heads.

(b) Indexing and Recording.

(c) Editing and Printing of Files.

(d) Checks on Delays.

(e) Reports and Returns.

(f) Security requirements.

(g) Reference Books.

(h) Watch over progress of urgent and important files and papers.

(i) Sectional Note Book.

(j) Standing Guard Files.

(2) Functions assigned to LDCs and UDCs.

(3) Duties and functions of an Assistant—his place in the organization and the role he is expected to play.

(4) Special procedures regarding disposal of certain types of matters—

(a) Procedure for submission of cases to the Cabinet.

(b) Matters in which consultation with UPSC is necessary and procedure for making reference to UPSC.

(c) Questions, resolutions etc. in Parliament.

(d) Court cases (e.g. civil suits, writ petitions, etc.).

IV. Typewriting

B. On the Job Training in a Ministry (Three months)

(1) General briefing regarding the organization of the Ministry, its Attached and Subordinate Offices, distribution of work among sections. 1 day

(2) Attached to Central Registry. 3 days

(3) Attached to Typing and Issue Section. 2 days

(4) Attached to Administration and Cash Section. 1 week 6 days

(5) Attached to a regular section in the Ministry
( The section selection should not be a routine section but such as will offer a good scope for examination of problems, noting, drafting etc. The Director of School should satisfy himself on this point).
Briefing about the organization and functioning of the section; distribution of work among the staff, registers and records etc.
Working as a Diarist ( diarising of receipts, movement of files, File Register, indexing, arrear statements and other items of work done by the Diarist of the section). 1 week

(6) Working as a regular Assistant with normal allotment of work under the systematic guidance of S.O. of the section. 6 weeks

(7) Attachment as Section Officer (in the same section)
To work as attache under the guidance of the S O. doing a certain number of cases. Watching and learning how the S.O. performs his duties as supervisor and guides his staff and the kind of files and papers he deals with himself. 1 week

(8) Working in full charge of the same section. 3 weeks

NOTES: (i) The Under Secretaries in charge of Administration/ Establishment will—

(a) personally ensure that the trainees are given proper and systematic training based on this programme; and

(b) follow their progress in training.

(ii) The trainees are requested to send weekly Progress Report showing the work done by them during the week.

(iii) The Instructors of the Secretariat Training School will continue to keep in touch with the trainees from time to time.

C Further Practical Training in the Ministries/Departments etc (Five and a half months.)

During this period, the trainees will be first attached to an experienced Section Officer, as far as possible, and encouraged to perform all the duties of an Assistant under his guidance. Towards the end of this period, he will be attached to O&M Section for practical training in work and method studies for about one month.

D Examinations

The trainees will be required to pass a Preliminary as well as Final Examinations as per Annexure II. A list of prescribed books is at Annexure.

NOTES: (1) A minimum of 50% of marks will be required for a pass in each of the written papers. Obtaining 50% or more marks in any paper will entitled the trainee to exemption from re-examination in that paper.

(2) A trainee who fails to secure the prescribed minimum marks in the written part of the Final Examination will be allowed two more chances to pass the examination, normally within the next six months. If he fails to pass the examination even after availing these two additional chances, he will be liable to appropriate actions under rule 17 of the CSS Rules, 1962.

(3) If a trainee absents hemself from the Final Examination or a re-examination, he will normally be regarded as having utilised a chance and failed in the examination.

(4) An extract from the result sheet, showing the marks obtained by the trainee in the Final Examination will be added to his Confidential Record. If he fails to appear in the examination or to avail of a chance, an entry in this regard will also be made in the Confidential Record.

ANNEXURE II

## SCHEME OF EXAMINATION FOR DIRECT RECRUITS TO ASSISTANTS' GRADE

Preliminary Examinations—A Preliminary Examination will be held after about six weeks, from the date of commencement of the training. This will cover the portions taught upto that date.

Final Examination—Towards the end of the period of training in the School and prior to posting to the Ministry/Department for practical training, the trainees will be required to appear at a Final Examination. The subjects and the maximum marks for each paper will be as shown below:

(1) 1st Paper—Office Procedure 100 marks
- (a) Office Procedure
- (b) Noting and Drafting
- (c) Rules of procedure and conduct of business in Parliament
- (d) Procedure of submission of cases to the Cabinet.

(2) 2nd Paper—General Rules
- (a) Organization of the Government of India and subjects for which each Ministry or Department of the Government of India is responsible.
- (b) Constitution of India—Parts V and XIV.
- (c) UPSC (Exemption from Consultation) Regulations, 1958.
- (d) Central Civil Services (Conduct) Rules, 1964.
- (e) Central Civil Services (Classification, Control and Appeal) Rules, 1957.
- (f) Central Civil Services (Temporary Service) Rules.
- (g) Other important general instructions issued by the Government of India from time to time.

(3) 3rd Paper—Fundamental Rules & Supplementary Rules ; Pension Rules 100 marks
- (a) Fundamental Rules and Supplementary Rules.
- (b) Civil Service Regulations—Pension part only and the Liberalised Pension Rules.

(4) 4th Paper—General Financial Rules, Planning and Economic Development 100 marks
  (a) General Provident Fund (Central Services) Rules, 1960.
  (b) General Financial Rules (Revised and Enlarged) 1963 and Delegation of Financial Powers Rules, 1958.
  (c) Budget and Control of Expenditure.
  (d) Treasury Rules.
  (e) Planning and Economic Development.
  (f) Foreign Exchange Budgeting and Control.

(5) In addition to the written examination in the above subjects, the trainee will be awarded a maximum of 100 marks on the basis of his behaviour and conduct and the progress shown by him in practical work during the period of training at the School. The allotment of marks will be as shown below:

| | | Marks |
|---|---|---|
| (a) | Punctuality and regularity in attending classes. | 20 |
| (b) | Practical work done in the classes ( each trainee will maintain a separate file for class work in respect of the work handled by each Instructor). | 50 |
| (c) | Discipline, behaviour, conduct, intelligence and capacity for self-expression. | 30 |

**N.B.** Use of reference books during the written examination is not allowed except in the case of Fundamental Rules and Supplementary Rules.

ANNEXURE III

## LIST OF BOOKS PRESCRIBED FOR SECTION OFFICERS AND ASSISTANTS

(1) Organizational set up and functions of the Ministries/ Departments of the Government of India.
(2) Manual of Office Procedure.
(3) Notes on Office Procedure.
(4) Constitution of India.
(5) Central Civil Services (Classification, Control & Appeal) Rules, 1957.
(6) Central Civil Services (Temporary Service) Rules, 1949.
(7) Central Civil Services (Conduct) Rules, 1964.
(8) Fundamental Rules & Supplementary Rules, Vols I & II.
(9) Civil Service Regulations.
(10) General Financial Rules (Revised and Enlarged), 1963.
(11) Delegation of Financial Power Rules, 1958.
(12) Financial and Cognate Powers Delegated to Ministries and Heads of Departments.
(13) Treasury Rules, Vols I & II.
(14) Notes on Financial Rules.
(15) General Provident Fund (Central Services) Rules, 1960.
(16) Handbook for Establishment Officers.
(17) Five Year Plan Summary.

**APPENDIX 4.1.c**

## SYLLABUS FOR REFRESHER COURSE TRAINING OF SECTION OFFICERS

(Duration: Two months)

The course of study will cover the following subjects:—

(1) Office Procedure
- (a) Manual of Office Procedure (important provisions).
- (b) Notes on Office Procedure—Office Management, functions of different grades of officers in Ministries, writing of confidential reports, the editing of files, submission of cases to the Cabinet, etc.
- (c) Rules of Procedure and Conduct of Business in Parliament.
- (d) Noting and Drafting.
- (e) Departmental Security Instructions.

(2) Financial Rules
- (a) Fundamental and Supplementary Rules.
- (b) Pension portion of the Civil Service Regulations and Liberalised Pension Rules.
- (c) General Provident Fund (Central Services) Rules, 1960.
- (d) General Financial Rules.
- (e) Delegation of Financial Power Rules, 1958.
- (f) Treasury Rules.
- (g) Estimates Committee, Public Accounts Committee etc.
- (h) Constitution of India—Part XII.

(3) General
- (a) Organization of the Government of India Secretariat including subjects dealt with in the different Ministries and Attached Offices.
- (b) Constitution of India—Parts V and XIV.
- (c) UPSC (Exemption from Consultation) Regulations, 1958.
- (d) Departmental Promotion Committee Procedure.
- (e) Central Civil Services (Conduct) Rules, 1964.
- (f) Central Civil Services (Classification, Control and Appeal) Rules, 1957.
- (g) Central Civil Services (Temporary Service) Rules.
- (h) Planning and Economic Development.

(i) Foreign Exchange Budgeting and Control.
(j) Duties and Responsibilities of Section Officers
(k) Staff Relationship.
(l) Training of staff.
(m) Office discipline, attendance, cleanliness, orderliness etc.
(n) Work Study.
(o) Case study.
(p) Supervisory Training—
    (i) Instruction Programme.
    (ii) Methods Programme.
    (iii) Relation Programme.

**APPENDIX 4.1.d**

## SYLLABUS FOR REFRESHER COURSE TRAINING OF ASSISTANT

(Duration: Two months)

The course of study will cover the following subjects:—

(1) Office Procedure
   (a) Manual of Office Procedure (important provisions).
   (b) Rules of Procedure and Conduct of Business in Parliament.
   (d) Noting and Drafting.

(2) Financial Rules
   (a) Fundamental and Supplementary Rules.
   (b) General Provident Fund (Central Services) Rules, 1960.
   (c) General Financial Rules.
   (d) Foreign Exchange Budgeting and Control.
   (e) Delegation of Financial Power Rules, 1958.
   (f) Treasury Rules.
   (g) Estimates Committee, Public Accounts Committee etc.
   (h) Constitution of India—Part XII.

(3) General
   (a) Organization of the Government of India Secretariat including subjects dealt with in the different Ministries and Attached Offices.
   (b) Constitution of India—Parts V and XIV.
   (c) UPSC (Exemption from Consultation) Regulations,1958.
   (d) Departmental Promotion Committee Procedure.
   (e) Central Civil Services (Conduct) Rules, 1964.
   (f) Central Civil Services (Classification, Control and Appeal) Rules, 1957.
   (g) Planning and Economic Development.
   (h) Duties and Responsibilities of Assistants.
   (i) Staff Relationship.
   (j) Methods Improvement.

APPENDIX 4.2

(Para 4.08)

## REVISED LIST OF SUBJECTS TAUGHT IN SECRETARIAT TRAINING SCHOOL

1. Public Administration.
2. Public Servants and the Law.
3. Modern History.
4. Political Theory and Constitution of India.
5. Organization of the Machinery of Government.
6. Planning and Economic Development.
7. Office Procedure and Office Management.
8. Parliamentary Procedure.
9. Vigilance Procedure and Methods.
10. Departmental Security Instructions.
11. Supervisory Training (for S.O.s).
12. Work Study and O&M Techniques.
13. General Survey of Rules and Regulations.
    - (a) Rules of Conduct and Discipline.
    - (b) Fundamental Rules and Supplementary Rules.
    - (c) General Financial Rules.
    - (d) Delegation of Financial Power Rules.
    - (e) Treasury Rules.
    - (f) Pension Rules.

**APPENDIX 4.3**

(Para 4.15)

## CADRE TRAINING PLAN FOR THE CENTRAL SECRETARIAT SERVICE

### SCOPE

1. This plan deals with the Cadre Training for CSS Officers at various levels. The details viz. frequency, duration and the content of training at each stage have been worked out, which are given as under:—

### TRAINING PROGRAMMES

2. **DIRECTLY RECRUITED SECTION OFFICERS**

2.1 There shall be a foundational training programme for the directly recruited Section Officers. This programme shall be conducted by ISTM each year.

2.2 The foundational training programme shall be of 24 weeks duration. The course content shall comprise of four Modules and on-the Job Training (OJT) as indicated below:—

| | | |
|---|---|---|
| Module I | - | 4 weeks |
| Module II | - | 4 weeks |
| Module III | - | 4 weeks |
| On the Job Training (OJT) | - | 7 weeks |
| Module IV | - | 2 weeks |

Module-I will be followed by one week study tour to a voluntary agency/village in a remote and backward area.

Module-II will be followed by two weeks study tour to a state capital to visit the secretariat, a nearby Public Sector Undertaking and Rural Development Project.

2.3 The session-wise details for each Module are given at Annexe-I. The curriculum for OJT shall be as detailed in Annexe-II. These have been designed in a manner that the training provides sufficient exposure to the directly recruited Section Officers regarding their duties and responsibilities and make them competent to discharge their functions efficiently, on taking up the new assignment.

2.4 The training methodology for the foundational programme shall be substantially participative. It shall comprise of group discussions, exercises, field visits, project work, seminars, book reviews, syndicate discussion and increased use of audio-visual aids. In addition the faculty members shall set apart 25% of their input for practical exercises and shall follow the 'broken' lecture method so as to encourage the participants to take active participation in discussion on the subject. Lecture notes shall be circulated in advance so that the participants by way of going through these lecture notes shall have the theoretical background and the session then becomes discussion oriented.

2.5 There shall be a written examination at the end of each Module.The examination at the end of Module IV shall also test experience gained by the probationers in OJT.

2.6 The Foundational Training Programme shall be governed by the scheme as detailed in Annexe-III.

3. **PROMOTEE SECTION OFFICERS**

3.1 Regular training programmes for promotee Section Officers shall be conducted by ISTM. These programmes shall be of 4 weeks' duration.

3.2 The course content, methodology and session-wise break up shall be as detailed in Annexe-IV.

3.3 There shall be six programmes run every year. These programmes will be announced by ISTM in the last quarter of the preceding year.

3.4 All promotee Section Officers shall be required to undergo this training programme within one year of their promotion. They shall earn their next increment only on successful completion of the programme.

3.5 Ministries/Departments shall nominate promotee Section Officers in consultation with ISTM with a view to ensuring that these officers successfully complete the training programme within one year of their promotion positively.

4. **UNDER SECRETARIES**

4.1 The training would be in the nature of professional course. Regular training programmes for empanelled Under Secretaries shall be conducted in ISTM. These programmes shall be for four weeks duration.

4.2 The course content and the session-wise details of the Professional Programme for Under Secretaries shall be as detailed in Annexe-V.

4.3 There shall be four programmes run every year. This will be announced by ISTM in the last quarter of the preceding year.

4.4 All officers promoted as Under Secretary shall be required to undergo training within one year of their promotion. They shall earn their next increment only on successful completion of the professional course.

4.5 Ministries/Departments shall nominate promotee Under Secretaries in consultation with ISTM with a view to ensuring that these officers successfully complete the training programme within one year of their promotion, positively.

## 5. DEPUTY SECRETARIES

5.1 The training would be in the nature of a Professional Course for Deputy Secretaries. This programme for empanelled Deputy Secretaries shall be conducted by IIPA. The programme shall be of four weeks duration.

5.2 The course content and the session-wise details shall be as detailed in Annexe-VI.

5.3 Considering the number of officers involved, normally one or two programmes shall be scheduled in a year. The dates for these programmes shall be announced in the last quarter of the preceding year in consultation with IIPA.

5.4 All officers promoted as Deputy Secretary shall be required to undergo the training programme within one year of their appointment as Deputy Secretary. They shall earn their next increment only on successful completion of the programme.

5.5. Ministries/Departments shall nominate promotee Deputy Secretaries in consultation with IIPA with a view to ensuring that these officers successfully complete the training programme within one year of their promotion, positively.

## EVALUATION OF PARTICIPANTS

6. There shall be an evaluation of participants attending the four weeks professional programmes at various levels. The format for evaluation of CSS officers at the Section Officer (promotee)

and Under Secretary's level shall be as detailed at Annexe-VII. For Deputy Secretary undergoing professional programme, the evaluation proforma shall be as at Annexe-VIII.

## EVALUATION AND CORRECTIVE MEASURES

7. Each training programme conducted by ISTM/IIPA shall also be evaluated. This evaluation shall be done by the Institute at the end of programme taking into account feedback received from the participants.
8. The programme design shall be reviewed once in six months, by a Committee consisting of Director (ISTM), JS(CS) and JS(T).

## PROGRAMME DESIGN AND WORK SCHEDULE

9. The Institutes shall prepare a standard package giving a model work schedule, list of faculty, a compendium of background readings, the list of case studies, exercises etc. so that the Course Director does not have to restructure the course afresh every time but only modify it in the light of evaluation referred in para 8 above.

## REFRESHER COURSES

10. The question of organizing Refresher Courses for CSS officers shall be considered after foundational and promotional courses referred above, have been institutionalised. In the meantime, CSS officers will make use of the "Subject Specific" course which are being arranged by the Training Division.
    - Financial Management,
    - Behavioural Sciences,
    - Management Techniques,
    - General Administration,
    - Computers.

ANNEXURE - I

## FOUNDATIONAL TRAINING PROGRAMME FOR DIRECTLY RECRUITED SECTION OFFICERS

## COURSE DESIGN

A. **MODULE - I**

| | | | |
|---|---|---|---|
| Duration | : | 4 weeks | |
| No. of Sessions | : | 90 | |
| **Session-wise break-up** | | | |
| Registration, Introduction, Issue of Books, etc. | : | 3 | |
| Public Administration | : | 7 | |
| Basic Economics & Statistics | : | 8 | |
| Typing | : | 20 | |
| Constitution of India | : | 5 | |
| Anti-poverty Programme | : | 4 | |
| Office Procedure | : | 10 | |
| Discussions on gist of transactions of business of Government | : | 2 | |
| Official Language Policy | : | 2 | |
| Anti-corruption Law | : | 8 | (This would include ethics in Admn. which could be covered by an eminent Guest speaker). |
| CSS Rules | : | 2 | |
| Organizational Behaviour | : | 6 | |
| History and Culture | : | 4 | (Films will be used extensively) |
| Guest Lectures | : | 4 | |
| Examination | : | 5 | |
| **Total** | : | **90** | |

This would be followed by a week's study tour to a voluntary agency/ village in a remote and backward area.

B. **MODULE - II**

| | | |
|---|---|---|
| Duration | : | 4 weeks |
| No. of Sessions | : | 90 |
| **Session-wise break-up** | | |
| Office Procedure | : | 10 |
| Parliamentary Procedure | : | 10 |
| Hands on Experience on Micro-Computers | : | 15 |
| Security Instructions | : | 2 |
| Establishment Rules | : | 8 |
| Organizational Behaviour | : | 6 |
| Desk Office System | : | 2 |
| Reservation in Services | : | 4 |
| Effective Speaking/ Book Review | : | 5 |
| Purchase Procedures for Stationery, furniture etc. DGS&D Purchase, Inventory, Management, Printing and Publication, House Keeping functions etc. | : | 8 |
| Visit to Parliament and BPST | : | 5 |
| Village Visit Seminar | : | 5 |
| Guest speakers | : | 5 |
| Examination | : | 5 |
| **Total** | **:** | **90** |

At the end of this Module, the group shall undertake two weeks tour to a State Capital, and visit the Secretariat, a nearby Public Sector Undertaking and a Rural Development Project.

C **MODULE -III**

| | | |
|---|---|---|
| Duration | : | 4 weeks |
| No. of Sessions | : | 90 |
| **Session-wise break-up** | | |
| CCA Rules | : | 8 |
| Conduct Rules | : | 5 |
| Leave Rules | : | 4 |

| | | |
|---|---|---|
| Organisational Behaviour | : | 6 |
| Pension Rules | : | 4 |
| Records Management | : | 5 |
| Personnel Management | : | 6 |
| Economic Planning and Development | : | 10 |
| FRs/SRs | : | 11 |
| Guest Speakers | : | 4 |
| TA/LTC | : | 4 |
| DPFRs | : | 6 |
| GPF | : | 2 |
| Noting and Drafting | : | 10 |
| Examination | : | 5 |
| **Total** | **:** | **90** |

At the end of this module, the group shall undergo seven week's On the Job Training as detailed in Annexe-II.

D. **MODULE - IV**

| | | |
|---|---|---|
| Duration | : | 2 weeks |
| No. of Sessions | : | 48 |

**Session-wise break-up**

| | | |
|---|---|---|
| Syndicates based on OJT | : | 12 (5 specific topics will be taken up, including noting and drafting) |
| Organizational Behaviour | : | 6 |
| Financial Management | : | 6 |
| Economic Planning and Development | : | 5 |
| Meeting participants/ preparation of minutes | : | 4 |
| Report Writing | : | 4 |
| Noting and Drafting | : | 6 |
| Management Techniques, Effective Listening and Counselling | : | 5 |
| **Total** | **:** | **48** |

ANNEXURE-II

## ON THE JOB TRAINING (OJT)

The On the Job Training (OJT) shall be of two months duration. The curriculum for OJT and the broad time-table to be followed by participants is indicated below. This may be modified by Ministries/ Departments, but the total duration shall be restricted to two months.

1st Day Meeting with the Secretary/JS (Admn) and briefing about the overall functions of the Ministry/Department from selected Head of Divisions.

2nd Day The probationer shall work in the Central Registry Section to understand the procedures of Receipt and Despatches and perform functions such as:

- Receipt and acknowledgement of dak;
- Registration of dak; and
- Distribution of dak, etc.

as detailed in Chapter-III of the Manual of Office Procedure (hereinafter called the Manual).

3-4 Day He shall hold independent charge as Diarist and perform duties relating to:

- Perusal and marking of receipts;
- Diarising of receipts;
- Movement of receipts;
- Allocation of disputed receipts etc.

As detailed in Chapter IV of the Manual

5-7 Day The probationer shall hold independent charge as LDC and perform all the duties assigned to him by the Section Officer, including:

- Noting on files received from other departments;
- Filing of papers;
- Arrangement of papers in a case;
- Referencing;
- Linking of files;
- Use of urgency gradings;
- Forms of written communications;
- Acknowledgement and interim replies; and
- Target date for replies.

As detailed in Chapter V and VI of the Manual.

8-12 Day He shall hold independent charge as an Upper Division Clerk and perform duties such as:

- Drafting of communications;
- Issue of drafts;
- Filing system; and
- Indexing and recording; etc.

  As detailed in Chapters VII,VIII,IX and X of the Manual.

13-27 Day He shall hold independent charge as an Assistant and handle duties pertaining to:

- Security of official information and documents;
- Checks and delays through weekly/monthly statements, call book, reminder diary;
- Exercise inspection; and
- The work relating to official language for the purpose of Government work, departmental instructions, maintenance of reference book etc.

  As detailed in Chapter XI,XII,XIII and XIV of the Manual.

28-42 Day The probationer shall function independently as Section Officer and understand the working of the Desk/ Section assigned.

ANNEXURE-III

## FOUNDATIONAL TRAINING PROGRAMME FOR DIRECTLY RECRUITED SECTION OFFICERS

| | |
|---|---|
| Foundational Course—Date of commencement | 1. The Foundational Training Course shall commence at ISTM either on May 1, or on June 1, every year, depending upon finalisation of allocations to Group 'B' services by AIS Division. |
| Probation period completion of Foundational Training Course | 2. Directly recruited Section Officers shall initially be appointed on probation for a period of two years. They shall first be directed to attend the Foundational Training Course at ISTM by the DOP, pending finalisation of allocation of Ministries and Deptts. Their appointment as Section Officers shall be subject to successful completion of the Foundational Training Courses and the two year probation. |
| Permission to appear in Group 'A' Exam. | 3. Directly recruited Section Officers, who wish to appear for Group 'A' Service Examination and are so permitted by the Government, shall not be permitted to join the Foundational Course along with their batchmates. They shall attend the Foundational Course only the next year, alongwith the next batch. They shall, however, be given seniority in their own batch, below all those who have already successfully completed the Foundational Course. |
| Joining Instructions | 4. Directly recruited Section Officers shall report for the Foundational Training Course at ISTM on the due date. Specific cases where candidates are not in a position to join the course on the due date shall be considered by the Government (separately) on merits. Those who fail to report on the due date, without specific approval of the Government, shall undergo the Foundational Course the next year. |
| Allocation to Ministries/ Deptt. | 5. While tentative allocation to respective Ministries/Deptts. shall be advised to the candidates at the time of directing them to |

report for Foundational Training Course at ISTM; these allocations shall be finalised and communicated to them before completion of Foundational Course.

System of Examination

6. The following shall be the Schedule of Examination in the Foundational Training Programme:-

| *Time Schedule* | *No. of Papers* | *Subjects for Examination* | | *Max. Marks* |
|---|---|---|---|---|
| At the end of Module I | 2 | Public Administration | I | 50 |
| | | Office Management and Procedures | I | 50 |
| At the end of Module II | 2 | Public Administration | II | 50 |
| | | Office Management and Procedures | II | 50 |
| At the end of Module III | 2 | Public Administration | III | 50 |
| | | Office Management and Procedures | III | 50 |
| At the end of Module IV | 2 | Public Administration | IV | 50 |
| | | Term Paper | | 25 |
| | | Syndicate | | 25 |
| | | | | 400 |
| Internal Assessment (based on probation's performance, attendance, discipline, attentiveness and participation in class) | | | | 50 |
| | | | | 450 |

Supplementary examination—Number of chances

7. Directly recruited Section Officers who fail to successfully complete the Foundational Training course shall be permitted to appear in the supplementary examination. If they fail to qualify the supplementary examination also, they shall be liable to be discharged from service.

Seniority

8. The seniority of directly recruited Section Officers shall be determined on similar lines as in the case of IAS, in accordance with the aggregate marks obtained by the probationer:
   (a) at the Competitive Examination; and
   (b) at the Foundational Examination conducted by ISTM.

# TRAINING PROGRAMME FOR PROMOTEE SECTION OFFICERS

## INTRODUCTION

In this programme, the participants come from two broad streams, those who are promoted in the normal course from the cadre of Assistants, and those who enter through a Special Limited Departmental Examination, from the posts of Assistants or Stenographers Grade II. Both categories of officers would have had a basic grounding of rules and procedures in their foundational programme or through experience and the "examinee recruits" would have refreshed their knowledge in the L.D. Exam. It was, therefore, decided to have a unified training programme for these two categories, of promotees as the levels of knowledge are comparable.

## PROGRAMME CONTENT

As the participants in this programme are moving up to the supervisory level, they too could be given a general overview of the framework within which they have to operate. The largest single input would be on computer skills, a subject to which they would be exposed for the first time. This would help keep them abreast of their changing work situation.

Another sizeable input would be in behavioural skills. This, in the view of the Committee, is vital, as the participants are now moving up to a level where they would be more concerned with man-management.

The other inputs would concentrate on the application of various rules and procedures.

## METHODOLOGY

These sessions would be much more participative and related to work experience. ISTM will run more case studies and prepare group exercises, so that undue emphasis in not paid to the theoretical aspects of the rules and procedures. In such a programme, there may be different levels of knowledge among the participants. ISTM will, therefore, provide hand-outs and motivate those not familiar with certain subjects to read these. They would consequently conduct this course at a higher level than at present.

## SESSION-WISE BREAK-UP

The proposed break-up of sessions may be as indicated below:—

| | *Subject* | *No. of Sessions* |
|---|---|---|
| 1. | Behavioural Sciences | 12 |
| 2. | Constitution of India | 6 |
| 3. | Establishment Rules | 6 |
| 4. | Public Administration | 6 |
| 5. | Security Instructions | 2 |
| 6. | Machinery of Government | 4 |
| 7. | Office Procedure and Effective Writing | 6 |
| 8. | Office Language Policy | 2 |
| 9. | Parliamentary Procedure | 6 |
| 10. | Records Management—Desk Officer System | 2 |
| 11. | FRs/SRs | 6 |
| 12. | Computer | 16 |
| 13. | Budget | 2 |
| 14. | Reservation in Services | 4 |
| 15. | Office Lay-out | 2 |
| 16. | Work Simplification | 2 |
| 17. | Conduct Rules | 4 |
| 18. | CCA Rules | 5 |
| 19. | Planning Process | 2 |
| 20. | Time Management | 2 |
| 21. | Leave Rules | 2 |
| 22. | Pension Rules | 2 |
| 23. | TA/LTC | 2 |
| 24. | GPF | 2 |
| 25. | DFPR | 3 |
| | | 108 |

ANNEXURE-V

## TRAINING PROGRAMME FOR UNDER SECRETARIES

### PROGRAMME OBJECTIVES

A Branch Officer is a second-line supervisor, and can also be considered as the lowest rung in the middle management set-up. He is directly responsible for the working of the Section/Desks under his charge and is the final authority as far as procedural matters are concerned. In addition, certain basic conceptual skills have to be developed as he can and should provide work improvement inputs. He should also develop a capacity to lead, an ability to sort the grain from the chaff and identify the important issues which are to be examined in detail by the senior officers. He is also the ultimate authority as far as precedents are concerned and is also required to perform many inspection functions. It is for this reason that inputs in office management and procedure and Parliamentary Procedure are being provided, but the emphasis would be on the actual work situation.

### METHODOLOGY

ISTM is running some case studies, but a more liberal use of this methodology could be reported to. If necessary, the coverage could be reduced in terms of width and increased in depth by highlighting a few common issues i.e. the pitfalls to be avoided in preparing answers and notes for supplementaries in Starred Parliament Questions, the preparation of notes for the Cabinet, the examination of matters involving judgments of different courts and the evaluation of projects prepared by certain public sector undertakings.

During the course some group and individual exercises could be run to test the understanding of the participants, ascertain their weak areas, take steps to remedy these and check whether they have fully benefited from the course. This is linked with another issue, the evaluation of participants. The Course Co-ordinator, in addition to reporting on the attendance, punctuality and attentiveness of the participants is required, as per a Government decision, to reflect on the quality of their participation both written and oral and aspects of creative and constructive thinking as manifested in the course. The draft evaluation proforma is as Annexure VA.

## ORGANIZATIONAL BEHAVIOUR

Another major subject in the professional programme for Under Secretaries would be Organizational Behaviour. Their previous exposure to the subject would have been at least eight years earlier and they require greater skills in handling people in their new positions.

## SYNDICATE STUDIES/BOOK REVIEWS

12 persons are proposed to be devoted to syndicate studies where topical and relevant subjects would be taken up for discussion and where the participants' written and oral presentation skills would be reviewed. In addition, an effective writing capsule is proposed to be provided. ISTM have introduced a 12 session capsule in their current programme. ISTM's trainers have recently filmed syndicate sessions/book review presentations and played them back to the participants after office hours. This was followed by a discussion on the common pitfalls of oral presentations.

## DECISION-MAKING PROCESS

Another key requirement for a branch officer is a thorough understanding of the decision making process. 12 sessions are proposed to be devoted to Financial Management, including general inputs on Economics and Planning and some sessions will be devoted to Management Techniques, including Management Information Systems and Work Study, Public Administration (including; Policy inputs) and Outdoor Management Programme.

## FIELD VISITS

A day visit to Rural Development Projects etc.is proposed to be retained, but the decision to abolish the study tour should stand as this was not found to be cost-effective in a Refresher programme.

## SESSION-WISE BREAK-UP

| | | | |
|---|---|---|---|
| 1. | Financial Management including Economics and Planning | : | 12 |
| 2. | Behavioural Science | : | 19 |
| 3. | Office Management and Procedure including Parliamentary Procedure and Case Studies | : | 22 |
| 4. | Syndicate Group Meeting | : | 12 |
| 5. | Outdoor Management Programme | : | 5 |
| 6. | Management Techniques including MIS and Work Study | : | 8 |
| 7. | Public Administration (including policy inputs) | : | 6 |
| 8. | Registration/Introduction | : | 1 |
| 9. | Action Plan | : | 1 |
| 10. | Day Visit | : | 5 |
| 11. | Evaluation | : | 1 |
| | | | 92 |

ANNEXEURE-VI

## PROFESSIONAL PROGRAMME FOR EMPANELLED DEPUTY SECRETARIES

| | |
|---|---|
| Duration | : 4 weeks |
| No. of session | : 100 |

**Session-wise break-up**
**Programme coverage**

| | |
|---|---|
| A. Imparting skills | |
| (i) Computer/Management Information/ skill upgradation | : 10 sessions |
| (ii) Time Management | : 5 sessions |
| (iii) Rapid Reading | : 5 sessions |
| B. Behavioural Science | : 20 sessions |
| C. New concepts in the field of (i) Development Administration (ii) Administrative, Law and Regulatory Administration (iii) Welfare Administration (iv) Economic Administration (v) Financial Management and Budgetary Procedure (vi) Techniques in problem solving | : 20 sessions |
| D. Electives—in the nature of Tutorials/Syndicate Work | : 20 sessions |
| E. Experience sharing | : 10 sessions |
| F. Filed Visits | : 10 sessions |
| **Total** | **: 100 sessions** |

The programme shall be structured in a manner that the participants acquire real professional skill and are better equipped to discharge the functions of their new assignment as Deputy Secretaries. The programme shall provide practical bias relating to the subjects/topics outlined.

ANNEXURE- VII

## PROFESSIONAL DEVELOPMENT PROGRAMME EMPANELLED UNDER SECRETARIES AND PROMOTEE SECTION OFFICERS

Resume on participants to be submitted by the Programme Director to the CS Division, Department of Personnel.

| *Name of the participant* | *Year of select* | *Min./Department where employed* | *Date From* | *To* |
|---|---|---|---|---|
| | | | | |

The Course Director should give a brief resume about the performance of the participants, covering, inter-alia, the following points:

1. Attendance and Punctuality
2. Attentiveness
3. Quality of participation (both oral and written)
5. Creative and Constructive thinking
6. Anything exceptional, which the co-ordinator would like to highlight–like special initiative shown or erratic behaviour.

The entire matter in column 3 and 4 could be based not only in the observed classroom behaviour, but also on the syndicate sessions, written assignments, case studies, book reviews and individual and group exercises.

ANNEXURE- VIII

## PROFESSIONAL PROGRAMME FOR EMPANELLED DEPUTY SECRETARIES

## EVALUATION SHEET

Name of participant

Year of Select List

Ministry/Department
where employed

Venue

Date From To

**I. ATTENDANCE**

Did he report on time?

Did he attend all lectures?

Was he absent on any day?

**II. QUALITY OF PARTICIPATION**

Alertness in listening to lectures?

Participation in discussion.

**III. INTERACTION**

How did he interact with the faculty?

How did he interact with guest lecturers?

How did he interact with other participants?

How did he interact with the administration?

**IV. CREATIVITY**

Was he able to analyse his experience?

Was he open to new ideas or had a closed mind?

Did he throw out any original ideas?

Did he make any creative contribution to the group work?

## V. ABILITY TO APPLY CONCEPTS

Could he understand theoretical concepts?
Could he relate them to practice?
Could he analyse practical experience and formulate it in terms of some concepts?
Did he express or exhibit any conceptual skill or capacity for conceptualisation?

## VI. WRITTEN ASSIGNMENT/GROUP STUDY

Was he able to make a presentation clear and forcefully?
How was the content of his presentation?
What is your assessment of his capacity to verbalise?
Was he able to take a systems views in his approach?
Did his work show evidence of any scholarship?

**APPENDIX 4.4.a**
(Para 4.16)

## SUMMARY OF THE SESSION PLAN FOR ASSISTANTS (DR) COURSE

### COURSE OBJECTIVES

On completion of the training course, the trainees will be able to:

(i) describe the organization of a Government machinery and the constitutional basis of that organization;

(ii) identify his/her role in the Government in terms of both functions and hierarchy;

(iii) apply the provisions of Office Procedure;

(iv) state the provisions of Establishment Rules including Reservation in Service (SC/ST/OBC), Pay Fixation Rules, GFRs, DFPRs, Budgetary Procedure, Conduct Rules, CCA Rules, Leave Rules, TA/LTC Rules, Official Language Policy, CAT Procedures, Income Tax, Pension Rules;

(v) prepare notes and draft communications and replies to Parliament questions in accordance with prescribed procedures;

(vi) work on computer (on Wordstar Packages);

(vii) state the principle to be adopted for fruitful human relations; and

(viii) explain the principles and the activities involved in Records Management.

| *S. No.* | *Topics* | *Sessions* | *Marks* | *Faculty* |
|---|---|---|---|---|
| I. | BEHAVIOURAL SCIENCES | 4 | - | |
| II. | GENERAL ADMINISTRATION | 34 | 100 | |
| 1. | *Government Machinery*<br>- Constitutional Provisions and Organizational Structure<br>- Constitutional provisions on executive, judiciary and Parliament<br>- Role and functions of Executive vis-a-vis Judiciary and the Legislature<br>- Organizational structure of the Government<br>- Constitutional authorities and their functions<br>- Planning Commission, National Development Council, Chief Vigilance Commissioner | 5 | 20 | |

| *S. No.* | *Topics* | *Sessions* | *Marks* | *Faculty* |
|---|---|---|---|---|
| | - Allocation of Business Rules and Transaction of Business Rules<br>- References to Cabinet and Cabinet Committees. | | | |
| 2. | *Office Procedure*<br>- Dak—Receipt, Registration and Distribution<br>- Receipts—submission and diarisation<br>- Action on Receipts and aids to processing<br>- Filing System<br>- Check on Delays and Inspection<br>- Action Plan and Monitoring<br>- Use of Mechanical aids | 11 | 30 | |
| 3. | *Noting and Drafting*<br>- General instructions regarding Noting<br>- Hints for preparation of summary or statement of cases for Secretary or Minister<br>- Forms of Communication<br>- General Instructions regarding drafting | 8 | 25 | |
| 4. | *Departmental Security Instructions* | 2 | 5 | |
| 5. | *Records Management*<br>- Objectives and principles of Records Management<br>- Principal activities in Records Management<br>- Creation, Classification, Custody and requisitioning of records<br>- Recording, Indexing, Review and Weeding of Records/Files<br>- Retrieval and aids to be maintained for retrieval of records<br>- Record reduction | 4 | 10 | |
| 6. | *Parliamentary Procedure*<br>- Parliament Questions<br>- Procedure in Ministries/Departments<br>- Parliamentary Debates: Half an hour Discussion, Calling Attention, Adjournment Motion | 4 | 10 | |

- Parliamentary Committees: Powers and Privileges
- Visit to Parliament(session included under General Assessment)

| | | | |
|---|---|---|---|
| III. | PERSONNEL ADMINISTRATION | 46 | 100 |
| 1. | *Constitution of India*<br>- Fundamental Rights<br>- Directive Principles<br>- Fundamental Duties | 4 | 10 |
| 2. | *Conduct Rules*<br>- Fundamental Rights and Conduct Rules<br>- Various provisions of Conduct Rules | 4 | 10 |
| 3. | *Establishment Rules*<br>- Direct Recruitment Procedure<br>- Framing of Recruitment Rules<br>- Probation and Confirmation<br>- Seniority Rules<br>- DPC/Promotion Procedures | 7 | 15 |
| 4. | *CCS (CCA) Rules*<br>- Classification of Posts<br>- Suspension<br>- Penalties<br>- Procedure for imposition of Major/Minor Penalties<br>- Action on Inquiry Reports<br>- Appeal, Revision and Review | 4 | 10 |
| 5. | *FR/SRs*<br>- Medical Examination<br>- Fees and Honorarium<br>- Joining Time<br>- Maintenance of Service Book | 4 | 10 |
| 6. | *Reservation in Services*<br>- Constitutional Provisions<br>- Verification of Claims<br>- Scope and Applicability<br>- Exemptions and Exclusion<br>- Maintenance of Roster<br>- Dereservation/Carry Forward/ Exchange | 6 | 10 |

| | | | |
|---|---|---|---|
| 7. | *Leave Rules*<br>- General conditions<br>- Detailed provisions regarding grant of Earned Leave, Half Pay Leave, Commuted Leave, Leave Not Due, Extra-Ordinary Leave, Maternity Leave and Study Leave | 4 | 10 |
| 8. | *Leave Travel Concession* | 2 | 5 |
| 9. | *Official Language Policy*<br>- Constitutional Provisions, Official Language Act, 1963.<br>- Government of India Resolution, 1968<br>- Official Language (use for Official purpose of Union) Rules, 1976. | 2 | 5 |
| 10. | *Central Administrative Tribunal*<br>- Constitutional Provisions<br>- Administrative Tribunal Act, 1985<br>- Central Administrative Tribunal - Rules and Procedure | 2 | 4 |
| 11. | *Handling Court Cases* | 2 | 4 |
| 12. | *Central Secretariat Service Rules* | 2 | 5 |
| 13. | *Joint Consultative Machinery*<br>- National Council, Departmental Councils, Office Councils, Constitution, Scope and Membership | 1 | 2 |
| III. | FINANCIAL ADMINISTRATION | 43 | 100 |
| 1. | *Economic Development and Planning*<br>- Dimensions/Indicators of Development<br>- Role of Economic Planning in Devt., etc.<br>Planning Process in India<br>- Concept of Perspective, Medium and Annual Plans<br>- Role of NDC, Planning Commission, Ministries/Departments, Working Groups etc. in Plan Process<br>- Financing of the Plans<br>- Central, State and Centrally Sponsored Schemes | 5 | 10 |

- Link between Budget and Plan, etc.

Sectoral Development in India

- Primary Sector—Agriculture, Mining and allied activities
- Agriculture/Rural Development Policies
- Industrial Policies/Industrial Development
- Ministries involved in the task, etc.

National Income Concept

- GDP, GNP, NDP, NNP
- Sectoral Constituents of N.I.
- Savings and Capital Formation
- Balance of Payments/Balance of Trade and Foreign Exchange Budgeting, etc.

2. *Project Planning* 4 10
   - Projects and Planning
   - Project Formulation
   - Project Appraisal etc.
3. *Budget* 3 9
   - Overview
   - Principles of budgeting
   - 1Definition
4. *GFRs* 3 8
   - Conditions governing expenditure, Canons of Financial Propriety
   - Guidelines for Finalisation of Contracts
   - Sanctions—communication, date of effect and validity
   - General conditions governing advances to Government Servants
5. *Delegation of Financial Power* Rules, 1978 3 8
   - Definition
   - Powers to create posts; to re-appropriate funds, to incur contingent/miscellaneous expenditure, to write off losses.
6. *General Provident Fund Rules* 3 5
   - Eligibility and conditions, nominations, subscriptions, advances, withdrawals and final payment

| | | | |
|---|---|---|---|
| 7. | *Travelling Allowances*<br>- TA on Tour<br>- TA on Transfer<br>- TA Advance | 4 | 10 |
| 8. | *Pay Fixation*<br>- Introduction and Definition<br>- Pay fixation of pay on initial appointment<br>- Pay fixation on higher post<br>- Pay fixation on appointment not involving higher duties and responsibilities<br>- Treatment of special pay<br>- Protection under Proviso<br>- Duty and increment | 6 | 15 |
| 9. | *Pension Rules*<br>- Qualifying service<br>- Emoluments and average emoluments<br>- Calculation of Pension<br>- Provisions regarding Retirement, Gratuity, Death Gratuity, Residual Gratuity<br>- Provisions regarding grant of family pension<br>- Commutation of pension | 6 | 15 |
| 10. | *Role and functions of DDO/HOO and Role of internal audit* | 2 | 5 |
| 11. | *Income Tax* | 3 | 5 |
| V. | GENERAL ASSESSMENT | 116 | 100 |
| | - Role & Function of Assistants | 2 | - |
| | - Computers—Introduction and Practice | 18 | 10 |
| | - Typewriting—Introduction and practice | 18 | 10 |
| | - Study Tours and Local Visits (25+5) | 30 | 20 |
| | - Book Review | 8 | 20 |
| | - Syndicate discussion | 10 | 20 |
| | - Punctuality, Attendance and Conduct | - | 20 |
| | - Course Administration | 30 | - |
| | TOTAL | 140 | 400 |

| S. No. | Topic | No. of Sessions | Marks | Faculty Back-up |
|---|---|---|---|---|
| | **MODULE–I** | | | |
| 1. | Course Administration | | | |
| | - Introduction and Course familiarisation | 2 | - | |
| | - Collection of books | 1 | - | |
| | - Examination, Valediction etc. | 10 | - | |
| | | 13 | | |
| 2. | Behavioural Science topics | 4 | - | |
| 3. | General Administration topics | | | |
| | - Government Machinery | 5 | 20 | |
| | - Office Procedure | 11 | 30 | |
| | - Departmental Security Instructions | 2 | 5 | |
| | | 18 | 55 | |
| 4. | Personal Administration Topics | | | |
| | - Constitution of India | 4 | 10 | |
| | - Conduct Rules | 4 | 10 | |
| | - Establishment Rules | 7 | 15 | |
| | - FRs/SRs | 4 | 10 | |
| | - Leave Rules | 4 | 10 | |
| | - LTC | 2 | 5 | |
| | - CSS Rules | 2 | 5 | |
| | - JCM | 1 | 2 | |
| | | 28 | 67 | |
| 5. | Financial Administration Topics | | | |
| | - Economic Development and Planning | 5 | 10 | |
| | - Project Planning | 4 | 10 | |
| | - Budget | 3 | 9 | |
| | - GFRs | 3 | 8 | |
| | - DFPRs | 3 | 8 | |
| | - General Provident Fund Rules | 3 | 5 | |
| | - Travelling Allowance | 4 | 10 | |
| | | 25 | 60 | |
| 6. | General Assessment | | | |
| | - Role and Functions of Assistants | 2 | - | |
| | - Typewriting—Introduction and Practice | 18 | 10 | |
| | - Book Review | 8 | 20 | |
| | - Course Administration | 4 | - | |
| | Total | 32 | 30 | |
| | TOTAL | 120 | 212 | |

| S.No. | Topic | No. of Sessions | Marks | Faculty Back-up |
|---|---|---|---|---|
| | **MODULE–II** | | | |
| 1. | General Administration topics | | | |
| | - Noting and Drafting | 8 | 25 | |
| | - Records Management | 4 | 10 | |
| | - Parliamentary Procedures | 4 | 10 | |
| | | 16 | 45 | |
| 2. | Personal Administration Topics | | | |
| | - CCS (CCA) Rules | 4 | 10 | |
| | - Reservation in Services | 6 | 10 | |
| | - Official Language Policy | 2 | 5 | |
| | - Central Administrative Tribunal | 2 | 4 | |
| | - How to handle court cases | 2 | 4 | |
| | | 16 | 33 | |
| 3. | Financial Administration Topics | | | |
| | - Pay Fixation Rules | 6 | 15 | |
| | - Pension Rules | 6 | 15 | |
| | - Role and functions of DDO/HOO and Role of Internal Audit | 2 | 5 | |
| | - Income Tax | 3 | 5 | |
| | | 17 | 40 | |
| 4. | General Assessment | | | |
| | - Computers—Introduction and Practice | 18 | 10 | |
| | - Study Tours and Local Visits (25+5) | 30 | 20 | |
| | - Syndicate Discussion | 10 | 20 | |
| | - Examination, and Valediction | 10 | - | |
| | - Punctuality, Attendance and Conduct | - | 20 | |
| | - Course Administration | 3 | - | |
| | | 71 | 70 | |
| | TOTAL | 120 | 188 | |

APPENDIX 4.4.b

## SESSION PLAN FOR ASSISTANT (REFRESHER) COURSE

### A. GENERAL MANAGEMENT AND OFFICE ADMINISTRATION

| | *Subject* | *No. of Sessions* |
|---|---|---|
| 1. | Duties and Responsibilities of Assistants/Sharing of Responsibilities | 2 |
| 2. | Constitution of India<br>Provisions relating to:<br>- The President<br>- The Vice-President<br>- Parliament<br>- Legislative Procedure<br>- Role and Functions of Executive Judiciary and the Legislation<br>- Appointment of President, Prime Minister and Council of Ministers | 2 |
| 3. | Machinery of Government<br>- Allocation of Business Rules and Transaction of Business Rules References to Cabinet<br>- Organizational Structure of the Executive machinery and their functions<br>- Important Constitutional authorities<br>- Other autonomous and independent organizations viz. Planning Commission, National Development Council, Cabinet and Cabinet Committees | 2 |
| 4. | Office Procedure<br>- Dak Receipt and Diarisation<br>- Filing System including functional Filing System<br>- Action on receipts and aids to processing of receipts<br>- Various forms of communications<br>- Checks on delays and inspection | 4 |
| 5. | Noting/Drafting | 6 |

| *Subject* | *No. of Sessions* |
|---|---|
| 6. Parliamentary Procedure<br>- Parliamentary questions<br>- Types/Notice period/Admissibility/<br>- Procedure for reply in Parliament<br>- Assurances in Parliament<br>- Parliamentary debates, Half an hour Discussion, Calling Attention, Adjournment Motion, Others<br>- Parliamentary Committees<br>Introduction<br>Composition/Functions<br>Meetings/Quorum/Venue/Report<br>Powers and Privileges | 4 |
| 7. Records Management<br>- What is information and why is it necessary?<br>- Nature and definition of records<br>- Records as a source of information<br>- Factors responsible for creation of records<br>- Public records—utility and value<br>- Stages and position for custody of records<br>- Necessity for creating and retaining<br>- Sound principles of effective records management<br>- Principal activities in records management<br>- Cost factors in records management<br>- Retrieval system | 4 |
| 8. Desk Officer System | 1 |
| 9. Departmental Security Instructions | 1 |
| B. PERSONNEL ADMINISTRATION | |
| 1. FR/SR (Other than pay fixation)<br>- General conditions of service<br>- Fee and Honorarium<br>- Joining time<br>- Maintenance of Service Book | 4 |

| Subject | | No. of Sessions |
|---|---|---|
| 2. Establishment Rules<br>- DPC Procedure<br>- Seniority Rules<br>- Probation/confirmation<br>- Recruitment Rules | | 6 |
| 3. Conduct Rules<br>- Fundamental Rights and Conduct Rules<br>- Relevance of Conduct Rules<br>- Various provisions of Conduct Rules<br>- Controls on Government Servants through Conduct Rules. | KMD | 4 |
| 4. Reservation in Services for SC/ST<br>- Constitutional Provisions<br>- Verification of Claim<br>- Scope and Applicability<br>- Exemption and Exclusion<br>- Rosters, Maintenance of Rosters etc.<br>- Carry Forward/Exchange | IJM | 4 |
| 5. CCS(CCA) Rules<br>- Penalties (Minor/Major)<br>- Procedure for Imposing Penalty<br>- Review, Appeal, etc. | SKR | 4 |
| 6. Leave Rules<br>- General conditions<br>- EL,HPL, Commuted Leave, LND, EOL, Maternity Leave, Study Leave | | 3 |
| 7. LTC<br>- General Conditions<br>- Block Years | | 2 |
| 8. Official Language Policy<br>- Constitutional Provisions<br>- Govt. of India Resolution 1968<br>- Official Languages used for the Official Purposes of Union, Rules, 1976. | | 2 |
| 9. Central Administrative Tribunal Rules/Procedure<br>- CAT Rules<br>- CAT Procedure | | 2 |

| *Subject* | | *No. of Sessions* |
|---|---|---|
| C. FINANCIAL ADMINISTRATION AND MANAGEMENT | | |
| 1. (Pay Fixation) | 3 | |
| - Duty | | |
| - Increment | | |
| - Pay fixation under normal rules | | |
| 2. Budget, Financial controls | | |
| - Budgeting | | 2 |
| - DFPRs | | 3 |
| - GFRs | | 2 |
| - Advances | | 3 |
| 3. TA Rules | | |
| - TA on Tour | | 3 |
| - TA on Transfer | | |
| 4. Pension Rules | 6 | |
| - Qualifying Service | | |
| - Emoluments and Average Emoluments | | |
| - Calculation of Pension | | |
| - Gratuities | | |
| - Family Pension | | |
| - Commutation of Pension | | |
| 5. GPF Rules | | 2 |
| - Rules | | |
| - Advances | | |
| - Withdrawals | | |
| 6. Income Tax | | 2 |
| D. BEHAVIOURAL SCIENCES | | |
| - Communication | | 4 |
| - Inter-personal effectiveness | | |
| - Trust and Collaboration | | |
| E. LOCAL VISITS | | 5 |
| - To Parliament | | |
| - To National Archives | | |
| F. Introduction and Registration | | 1 |
| - Valediction | | 2 |

APPENDIX 4.4.c

## SESSION PLAN FOR SECTION OFFICERS (PROBATIONERS) COURSE

### MODULE–I

Duration 5 weeks (including one week for Hindi Training)

| | *Topics* | *No. of Sessions* | *Faculty* |
|---|---|---|---|
| 1. | Public Administration | 7 | Guest |
| 2. | Machinery of Govt. and Transaction of Business Rules | 2 | YS |
| 3. | Basic Economics and Statistics | 8 | PRR |
| 4. | Constitution of India | 5 | SKR |
| 5. | Anti-Corruption Law | 8 | SKR/Guest |
| 6. | Office Procedure | 10 | PSS/KCG |
| 7. | CSS Rules | 2 | AC/SMG |
| 8. | Conduct Rules | 5 | KMD |
| 9. | Anti-poverty Programme | 4 | PRR |
| 10. | Official Language Policy | 2 | IJM |
| 11. | Typing | 20 | VKN |
| 12. | History and Culture | 4 | Guest |
| 13. | Role of Voluntary Agencies | 2 | Guest |
| 14. | Hindi Training (17-21 July, 1995) | 5 days | CHI |

### VILLAGE VISIT

(One Week)

### MODULE–II

Duration 5 weeks

| | *Topics* | *No. of Sessions* | *Faculty* |
|---|---|---|---|
| 1. | Office Procedure | 10 | PSS/KCG |
| 2. | Parliamentary Procedure | 10 | PSS/Guest |
| 3. | Deptt. Security Instructions | 2 | PSS/Guest |
| 4. | Establishment Rules | 8 | KMD/BS |
| 5. | Organizational Behaviour | 12 | SN/SS |
| 6. | Effective Speaking/Book Review | 5 | MPS/IJM |

| | Topics | No. of Sessions | Faculty |
|---|---|---|---|
| 7. | Inventory Management, Stores/Purchase Procedures, DGS&D Purchases | 8 | YS/MPS |
| 8. | CCA Rules | 8 | SKR |
| 9. | Reservation in Services | 4 | IJM/ES |
| 10. | Economic Planning and Development | 10 | PRR |
| 11. | Village Visit Seminar | 6 | MPS/IJM/ Guest |
| 12. | Visit to Parliament and BPST | 3 | IJM |
| 13. | Hands on experience on Computer | 15 | MPS/KMD/ IJM/VKN/KKP |
| 14. | Desk Officer System | 2 | PSS |

## STUDY TOUR

(Two weeks)

## MODULE–III

Duration 4 weeks

| | Topics | No. of Sessions | Faculty |
|---|---|---|---|
| 1. | Leave Rules | 4 | IJM |
| 2. | Records Management | 5 | PSS |
| 3. | Economic Planning and Development | 5 | PRR |
| 4. | FRs/SRs | 11 | VJ |
| 5. | Noting and Drafting | 16 | PSS |
| 6. | Organizational Behaviour | 12 | SN |
| 7. | TA/LTC Rules | 4 | PKS/IJM |
| 8. | Financial Management | 6 | PRR/PKS |
| 9. | GFR/DFPR | 6 | VJ |
| 10. | Pension Rules | 4 | PKS |
| 11. | GPF | 2 | BS |

## ON-THE-JOB-TRAINING

(30.10.95 to 01.12.95)

## MODULE–IV

Duration 2 weeks (04.12.95 to 15.12.95).

| | *Topics* | *No. of Sessions* | *Faculty* |
|---|---|---|---|
| 1. | Syndicate Discussion and OJT Term Paper Presentation | 18 | MPS/IJM |
| 2. | Personnel Management (PM) | 6 | Guest/KMD |
| 3. | Management Techniques, Effective Listening and Counselling | 5 | SMS/YS |
| 4. | Exaction Game | 10 | MPS/Guest |
| 5. | Arranging Meetings, Participation, Preparation of Minutes | 4 | IJM/Guest |
| 6. | Report Writing | 4 | Guest |

**APPENDIX 4.4.d**

## SESSION PLAN FOR SECTION OFFICERS (REFRESHERS) COURSE

STATEMENT OF OBJECTIVES

At the end of the training course, the participants will be able to:

1. Identify the role of a Section Officer in the Central Secretariat and apply supervisory skills.
2. Explain Organization theory.
3. Participate in the decision-making process.
4. Explain the procedure for preparing a Cabinet note, handling parliamentary matters and for purchase of stores.
5. Describe the norms of departmental security.
6. Explain the provisions of establishment rules.
7. Examine issues towards work-simplification.
8. Prepare briefs on agenda items and minutes of a meeting.
9. Identify changes consequent to economic liberalisation.
10. Prepare Budget.
11. Narrate how to deal with grievances of employees.
12. Make performance appraisal.
13. Explain provisions of orders on Reservation in Services for SC/ ST/OBCs, for verification of claims and maintenance of rosters.
14. Explain provisions of Project planning—formulation, implementation and evaluation.
15. Describe provisions of JCM and OL Policy.
16. Deal with Audit Objections and Audit paras.
17. Apply human relations skills in a given situation.
18. Work on Computers.
19. Identify causes of communication problems arising in a Section.
20. Describe the procedure for dealing with CAT and Court cases.
21. Streamline record keeping.
22. Identify problems of and suggest solutions for Wastelands and Watershed Development.
23. Describe salient features of Administrative Vigilance, Desk Officer System and rest of the topics covered.

## Week-wise Session Schedule and Session Plan

| *S. No.* | *Subject* | *No. of Sessions* |
|---|---|---|
| | 1st Week | |
| 1. | Agenda and Minutes of meetings | 3 |
| 2. | Department Security Instructions | 2 |
| 3. | Establishment Rules | 6 |
| 4. | Motivation | 2 |
| 5. | Communication | 3 |
| 6. | Management of Stress | 1 |
| 7. | Organization Theory | 2 |
| 8. | JCM | 1 |
| 9. | Court and CAT cases/procedure | 2 |
| | 2nd Week | |
| 10. | Decision Making | 2 |
| 11. | Leadership Styles | 3 |
| 12. | Wasteland and Watershed Management | 2 |
| 13. | Performance Appraisal | 2 |
| 14. | Parliament Questions, Assurances, etc. | 3 |
| 15. | Note for the Cabinet | 2 |
| 16. | Records Management | 2 |
| 17. | Desk Officer System | 2 |
| 18. | Reservation in Services | 4 |
| 19. | Project Planning | 3 |
| | 3rd Week | |
| 20. | Official Language Policy | 1 |
| 21. | Economic Liberalisation | 2 |
| 22. | Effective Supervision | 2 |
| 23. | Grievance Handling | 2 |
| 24. | Computers: DOS and DBase IIIplus | 18 |

| S. No. | Subject | No. of Sessions |
|---|---|---|
| | 4th Week | |
| 25. | Management of Change | 2 |
| 26. | Role and Function of S.O. | 2 |
| 27. | Store Purchase Procedure | 2 |
| 28. | Audit Objections | 2 |
| 29. | Administrative Vigilance | 2 |
| 30. | Budget | 3 |
| 31. | GFR/DFPRs | 2 |
| 32. | Work Simplification (Workshop) | 5 |
| 33. | Time Management | 1 |
| 34. | Learning Review /Action Plan | 1 |
| | Total | 94 |

**APPENDIX 4.4.e**

## SESSION PLAN FOR PROFESSIONAL DEVELOPMENT PROGRAMME FOR UNDER SECRETARIES OF CSS

| Subject | No. of Sessions |
|---|---|
| 1. Financial Management | |
| (a) Current Economic Environment | 2 |
| (b) Investment Decisions | 3 |
| (c) Public Sector Enterprises—Current Issues | 2 |
| (d) Management Accounting and Auditing | 3 |
| (e) Wasteland/Watershed Development Programme | 2 |
| Sub-total | 12 |
| 2. Organizational Behaviour | |
| (a) Human Values | 3 |
| (b) Communication | 2 |
| (c) Motivating Self and Subordinates | 2 |
| (d) Leadership Styles | 3 |
| (e) Conflict Management | 2 |
| (f) Team Building | 2 |
| (g) Organizational Creativity and Change | 2 |
| (h) Management of Stress | 1 |
| Sub-total | 17 |
| 3. Office Management and Procedure | |
| (a) Role of Branch Officer | 2 |
| (b) Administrative Vigilance—Overview | 2 |
| (c) Reservation in Services | 2 |
| (d) Grievance Handling | 2 |
| (e) Skill Development Work-shop | 5 |
| - Work Simplification | |
| - Records Management | |
| 4. Syndicate Work | 7 |
| 5. Exaction Game | 10 |

| | |
|---|---|
| 6. Management Techniques | |
| (a) Management Objectives | 2 |
| (b) Management Information System | 2 |
| (c) Time Management | 1 |
| (d) Decision-making Process in Govt. | 2 |
| 7. Public Administration—Role | 4 |
| 8. Computer | 15 |
| 9. Field Visits | 25 |
| - PSU, Rural Development Projects and a subordinate office of the Central Govt. | |
| 10. Course Administration | 3 |

**APPENDIX 4.4.f**

## WORK SCHEDULE OF THE TWENTIETH MANAGEMENT DEVELOPMENT PROGRAMME FOR EMPANELLED DEPUTY SECRETARIES OF C.S.S CONDUCTED AT IIPA, NEW DELHI FROM 28 MARCH TO 22 APRIL 1994

| *Day/Date* | *Time* | *Topic* | *Speaker* |
|---|---|---|---|
| | | **1st Week** | |
| Monday 28.3.94 | | Registration | |
| | I | Inauguration | Prof. S.P. Verma |
| | II | Introduction and Orientation of the Programme | K.N. Kabra |
| | III and IV | Accountibility and Autonomy in Administration - Panel Discussion | Arvind K Sharma<br>Kamal Mitra Chenoy<br>N.S. Sisodia |
| Tuesday 29.3.94 | I | Communalism in Contemporary India | Achin Vanaik |
| | II | Recent Development in Tax Policy | V. Upadhyay |
| | III and IV | Understanding the Economics and the Budget | Pranab Banerji |
| Wednesday 30.3.94 | I | Education Policy Today | Suresh Shukla |
| | II | Vigilance in Government | Tapati Neogi |
| | III and IV | Structural Changes in Indian Economic Implication | K.N. Kabra |
| Thursday 31.3.94 | I and II | Management of Conflict | Rajesh Singh |
| | III and IV | Internal Liberalisation - Panel Discussion | B.B. Bhattacharya<br>K.N. Kabra |
| | | **2nd Week** | |
| Monday 04.04.94 | I and II | Inter-personal Relations and Group Dynamics | R.P. Puri |
| | III | Formation of Syndicate Group | |
| | IV | Library | |
| Tuesday 05.04.94 | I and II | Quality Management for Public Services | Y.K. Chaudhury |
| | III and IV | Computer Application | R.K.Sachdeva<br>N.C. Ganguli<br>Charu Ashish Kapil |

| Day/Date | Time | Topic | Speaker |
|---|---|---|---|
| Wednesday 06.04.94 | I and II | Challenge of Development Administration Then and Now | Sujata Singh |
| | III and IV | Computer Application | N.C. Ganguli<br>Charu Ashish Kapil |
| Thursday 07.04.94 | I | Liberalisation and Public Administration | J.Guha Roy |
| | II | Basic Micro Economic Concepts Application | Asha Kapur Mehta |
| | III and IV | Computer Application | N.C. Ganguli<br>Charu Ashish Kapil |
| Friday 08.04.94 | I and II | Project Management | A.V. Chaturvedi |
| | III and IV | Computer Application | N.C. Ganguli<br>Charu Ashish Kapil |
| | | **3rd Week** | |
| Monday 11.04.94 | I | Financial Statement Analysis | Nanc Dhameja |
| | II | Costing for Management Decision | Nanc Dhameja |
| | III and IV | Experience Sharing | |
| Tuesday 12.04.94 | I | Privatisation | Nand Dhameja |
| | II | Management of Change | O.P. Minocha |
| | III and IV | Environment and Development<br>-Panel Discussion | S.Mudgil<br>A.K. Roy<br>Ashish Kothari<br>Shekhar Singh |
| Wednesday 13.04.94 | I and II | Network Analysis | A.V. Chaturvedi |
| | III and IV | External Liberalisation - Panel Discussion | Rajiv Kumar<br>Asha Kapur Mehta<br>Balraj Mehta |
| Thursday 14.04.94 | I and II | Administrative Law | S.S.Singh |
| | III | Management of CPR | Dolly Arora |
| | IV | Film | |
| Friday 15.04.94 | I and II | Investment Decision | N.C. Ganguli |
| | III and IV | Syndicate Group Exercise | |
| | | **4th Week** | |
| Monday to Friday 18.04.94 to 22.04.94 | | Attachment Programme at Academy of Administration, M.P., Bhopal. | |

**APPENDIX 4.4.g**
(Para 4.18)

## RESTRUCTURED EXECUTIVE TRAINING PROGRAMME FOR CSS OFFICERS

| *Item* | *Curriculum* | *Period* |
|---|---|---|
| 1. | Orientation programme at ISTM (Constitutional features of a federal policy, Centre-State relationship) | 1 week |
| 2. | Revenue Administration | |
| | 2.1. Village Revenue Officer | 1 week |
| | 2.2. Tehsil Officer | 1 week |
| | 2.3. Sub-divisional Officer | 1 week |
| | 2.4. Survey and settlement officer ( to study the system of maintenance of land records and to observe actual settlement operations, if possible) | 1 week |
| | 2.5. Attachment with Collector | 1 week |
| | Total = | 5 weeks |

During attachment in the Tehsil Office, SDOs office and Collectorate, the trainees should acquaint himself with the work of various sections in these offices. He should, in particular, observe the work of the SDO and the Collector, he should also accompany these officers on tour, whenever possible.

| | | |
|---|---|---|
| 3. | Police and Judicial Administrations | |
| | 3.1. Attachment with one or more police stations including a rural police station | 1 week |
| | 3.2. Attachment with the SP's office | 1 week |
| | 3.3. Attachment with Court of Judicial Magistrate | 1 week |
| | Total = | 3 weeks |

During two weeks attachment with the Police, the trainee will also study the functioning of the Special Branch, the

| *Item* | *Curriculum* | *Period* |
|---|---|---|

District Reserve Lines, Armed Police and the Prosecution Branch. He should accompany the SP (or DSP) on tour, particularly if the tour relates to a Law-and-Order situation and/or inspection of a Police Station.

4. DEVELOPMENT ADMINISTRATION (One week each)

4.1 Attachment with the District Agriculture Officer (study of agricultural extension/TV system, supply of inputs, coordination with other agencies concerned with agriculture development, e.g. agricultural credit, improved seeds, fertilisers, pesticides, irrigation, animal husbandry, etc.)

4.2 Attachment with Assistant/Deputy Registrar of Cooperative Societies (study of single and multi-purpose cooperative societies,cooperative credit, promotion of cooperatives, legal frame-work of cooperative bodies, etc.

4.3 Attachment with the Irrigation Department (study of Minor Irrigation, Lift Irrigation, Command Area Development, etc.)

4.4 Attachment with Animal Husbandry Officer (special emphasis on study of dairy development through Operation Flood)

4.5 Divisional Forest Officer (emphasis on study of social forestry programme)

4.6 District Labour Officer (study of problems related to bonded labour and enforcement of Minimum Wages Act in the agricultural sector)

4.7 Attachment with the District Health Officer (study of health care and family welfare programme)

4.8 Attachment with the District Education Officer (study of elementary education and non-formal education programmes)

4.9 Attachment with District Industry Centre (emphasis on the study of village and cottage industries, rural industrialisation and promotion of industry)

4.10 Attachment with the Panchayat Bodies (Zila Panchayat/ Mandal Panchayat/ Gram Panchayat)

| Item | Curriculum | Period |
|---|---|---|
| 4.11 | Attachment with DRDA, and Block Officer | |
| 4.12 | Attachment with a selected voluntary agency | |
| | During attachment with the BDO the trainee should concentrate in understanding the pivotal role of the block agency in rural development and its relationship with the DRDA on the one hand and Panchayat Raj Bodies on the other. | |
| | During the attachment with the voluntary agency, the trainee should try and understand the importance attached by the Government to such organizations in the development process. He should write a special report on the functioning of the agency to which he is attached. | |
| | BLOCK ATTACHMENT | |
| 5. | The training should be rounded off with the trainee being placed in independent charge as BDO | 4 weeks |
| 6. | Specialised attachment depending on Ministries where the participant works to give an indepth exposure to the problems faced by the State in order to develop better understanding of the State's problem in his area of work. | 3 weeks |
| 7. | Project work/specific assignment to be allotted by the State Project Report to be evaluated subsequently by the authority incharge of training in the State. | 8 weeks |

**APPENDIX 4.5**
(Para 4.46)

## MODEL CADRE TRAINING PLAN FOR THE CSS ASSISTANTS' GRADE

### Phase-I

*Direct Recruits:* All candidates selected for appointment as Direct Recruit Assistants will join the allotted Ministry on first working day of January, April, July or October every year. Any candidate who fails to join on the appointed day e.g. January 1, will join only on next fixed dated i.e., April 1, and so on. On appointment in the Ministry, no Assistant will be posted to any functional Section until he completes the Foundational and Induction (Phase I) Course as per the Schedule given below:

| | |
|---|---|
| First week | Attachment to Training Manager of the Ministry. Complete Instructional Module No. 1 |
| Second to tenth week | Institutional Training at ISTM |
| Eleventh and twelfth week | On-the-job training and reporting at ISTM |

*Promotees:* All promotee Assistants, within the first year of their induction to CSS on ad hoc or regular basis, will complete Phase-I Induction Course for Assistants at ISTM.

In respect of all Assistants, the first increment in the grade will be allowed only on completion of the Phase-I Course.

### Phase-II

Every Assistant, after completion of Foundational or Induction Course, as the case may be, shall complete at the earliest opportunity at least one of the specialised courses as may be recommended by the Cadre authority, before he completes his probationary period.

### Phase-III

During fifth year of his service in the grade of Assistant he will undergo a compulsory management course at ISTM.

## SECTION OFFICER'S GRADE

### Phase-I

*Section Officer (Direct Recruits):* All Direct Recruit Section Officers to CSS on being allocated to different Ministries will join the Ministry on July 1, every year, and will be deputed for Foundational Course as per the Schedule given below:

| | |
|---|---|
| First week | Attachment to Training Manager of the Ministry |
| 2nd to 8th | Foundational Module-I at ISTM |
| 9th to 12th | On-the-Job Training (A) |
| 13th to 21st | Executive Development Module-II |
| 22nd to 24th | On-the-Job Training (B) |

*Promotee Section Officers:* All promotee Section Officers within one year of their promotion will complete Executive Development Course for Section Officers at ISTM.

The first increment in the Section Officers' grade will be granted only after successful completion of the Phase-I Course.

### Phase-II

Every Section Officer after completion of his Phase-I Course shall complete at the earliest opportunity before completion of his probationary period one of the specialised courses recommended by the cadre authority.

### Phase-III

After completion of five years service in the grade every Section Officer will have to undergo either State Executive Training at any of the State of his choice, or a course (distance learning) on Public Policy and Administration conducted by IGNOU or such other body. Only such Section Officers who have completed either of these courses will be eligible for empanelment in Grade I of CSS.

## GRADE I OR UNDER SECRETARY

### Phase-I

All empanelled Grade I (Under Secretary) of CSS complete the Professional Development Course at ISTM during first year of their empanelment. The first increment in the Grade will be allowed only after completion of such training unless any officer has been exempted from such training with the approval of the Department of Personnel and Training.

**Phase-II**

During the second year of his appointment a Grade I officer shall be required to undergo one of the short Professional Development Courses on the area of his specialisation conducted by one of the Central Training Institutes.

## SELECTION GRADE (DEPUTY SECRETARY)

All empanelled officers in the Selection Grade shall be required to attend Management Development Course at IIPA (or ISTM). During the course, each officer will be required to prepare a dissertation paper on the assigned subject relating his area of work in the Ministry. A performance report will be prepared by the trainee officer himself which will be evaluated by an expert committee.

**APPENDIX 4.6**

(Para 4.30)

**A.K. Chaudhuri**
**Director, ISTM**
**(Joint Secretary to the GOI)**
Phones: 686 5589-93, 686 4182-83

D.O.No.A33040/1/94-ISTM(Trg.)

Dear

As you are aware, the Institute of Secretariat Training and Management (ISTM) is primarily responsible for imparting Foundational and In-service Training to the officers of the Central Secretariat Service, besides conducting other professional courses in Management and Training of Trainers etc.

2. The Training Research Unit of ISTM has undertaken a research project to study the efficacy of the training imparted by ISTM in the context of the functional need of the officers of the Central Secretariat Service. One of the aspects of this project is to study the role of the Ministries/ Department, as client organizations, in management of systematic training of their officers, in identifying their training needs and in the post-training follow-up of such officers. In this connection, your objective and unbiased views, as the in-charge of personnel administration of your department, will be of great value to this study. We shall be grateful to have your response in the enclosed questionnaire.

3. The information furnished by you will neither be used for any other purpose nor shall be quoted in any other context than for the data-analyses purposes of the study mentioned above.

4. Should you require any clarification/ information, Shri A.N. Chakravarty, Deputy Director, who is handling this project, may be contacted on any of the numbers mentioned above. The questionnaire, duly filled in, may kindly be returned to him (by name) by **28 February, 1995**.

Yours sincerely,

(A.K. CHAUDHURI)

**APPENDIX 4.6**

# MANAGEMENT OF TRAINING QUESTIONNAIRE

[To be filled in by or on behalf of the Head (JS-in-charge) of Administration Wing.]

1. Name and Address of the Min./Deptt./Office:______________

______________________________________________

2. No. of Employees →

| Group A | Group B | Group C | Group D | Total |
|---|---|---|---|---|
| | | | | |

3. No. of CSS Officers in the Deptt. →

| Dy. Secy. | Under Secy. | SO/DO | Asstt/ D.Attache | Total |
|---|---|---|---|---|
| | | | | |

4. The Cadre Training Plan for CSS provides that—

"... all directly recruited and promotee officers appointed to various Grades, shall be required to undergo the Foundational, Refreshers and Professional Development Training Courses prescribed therein, <u>within one year of their regular appointment</u> failing which their next increment shall be withheld ."

Has the above provision been implemented in your Department? (Pl. put a "**x**" for your answer)    Yes [ ]    No [ ]

If 'No', the reasons briefly______________________________

______________________________________________

5. No. of CSS Officers appointed and completed their Foundational and Induction Training Courses during the last three years:

| | | DS (CSS) | US (CSS) | SO (DR) | SO (P) | Asstt (DR) | Asstt (P) |
|---|---|---|---|---|---|---|---|
| 1993-94 | No. Appointed | | | | | | |
| | No. Trained | | | | | | |
| 1992-93 | No. Appointed | | | | | | |
| | No. Trained | | | | | | |
| 1991-92 | No. Appointed | | | | | | |
| | No. Trained | | | | | | |

6. Reasons for not attending the compulsory training courses in time by the above officers: (Pl. put an "**x**" in the appropriate column)

| | *Yes* | *Sometimes* | *No* |
|---|---|---|---|
| (i) Eligible officers are nominated, but not accepted by ISTM | [ ] | [ ] | [ ] |
| (ii) Eligible officers are nominated, but their bosses do not relieve them | [ ] | [ ] | [ ] |
| (iii) All eligible officers cannot be relieved due to exigencies of work | [ ] | [ ] | [ ] |
| (iv) Officers are not willing | [ ] | [ ] | [ ] |

7. As a general practice, how are the officers in your Department nominated for various training courses ? Please put an "x" in the appropriate columns applicable to your Department:

| | *Mostly* | *Sometimes* | *Never* |
|---|---|---|---|
| (i) On the basis of seniority | [ ] | [ ] | [ ] |
| (ii) On the basis of the performance and need of the existing job | [ ] | [ ] | [ ] |
| (iii) Keeping in view the future promotion and posting of the individual | [ ] | [ ] | [ ] |
| (iv) Recommending the officer as a reward for his good work | [ ] | [ ] | [ ] |
| (v) On identification of specific weakness which could be rectified through a particular course | [ ] | [ ] | [ ] |
| (vi) To learn new systems and procedure in the Organisation | [ ] | [ ] | [ ] |

| | Yes | Sometimes | No |
|---|---|---|---|
| (vii) For personal development without specific need in mind | [ ] | [ ] | [ ] |
| (viii) At the initiative of the individual officers | [ ] | [ ] | [ ] |
| (ix) The officers who could be easily spared | [ ] | [ ] | [ ] |
| (x) Any other (please specify) | [ ] | [ ] | [ ] |

8. Who are the people having a decisive role in identifying the training requirements of the officers in your department?

| | *Yes* | *Sometimes* | *No* |
|---|---|---|---|
| (i) The officer himself | [ ] | [ ] | [ ] |
| (ii) Training Unit/Admn. | [ ] | [ ] | [ ] |
| (iii) Immediate superior | [ ] | [ ] | [ ] |
| (iv) Highest level | [ ] | [ ] | [ ] |

9. As a matter of policy, do the superiors or any other training official discuss the training objectives and training needs of the individual or the organization with trainee officers before he is deputed for training ? *Yes* *Sometimes* *No*

[ ] [ ] [ ]

10. (a) Has any officer been designated as "Training Manager/ Training Coordinator" in your Deptt? *Yes* *No*

[ ] [ ]

If yes, his name and designation please,________________

________________________________________

(b) Is there a separate Training Management Unit in your Deptt.? *Yes* *No*

[ ] [ ]

(c) If yes, the name of the Unit/Section and the functions performed by it:

________________________________________

________________________________________

________________________________________

11. (i) Do you have a separate Training Budget for your Department? *Yes* [ ] *No* [ ]

(ii) If yes, is it

(a) based on the specific training requirements [ ]

(b) based on in-house training courses planned [ ]

(c) ad hoc assessment based on previous provision [ ]

12. Is there any practice of post-training follow up of the results in your Department? *Yes* [ ] *No* [ ]

If yes, what procedure is followed ? Please tick (✓) in appropriate columns.

| | *Yes* | *Sometimes* | *No* |
|---|---|---|---|
| (i) Hold a discussion with the trained officer about the application of his learning in the job situation. | [ ] | [ ] | [ ] |
| (ii) Officer submits a report on his training along with an Action Plan for changes/ improvements to be introduced | [ ] | [ ] | [ ] |
| (iii) Watch the follow up at the Action Plans | [ ] | [ ] | [ ] |
| (iv) Ask for a report from the supervisor about the improvements, if any, in the performance after training | [ ] | [ ] | [ ] |
| (iv) Analysis and evaluation of such reports by the Training Unit at the Deptt. in consultation with training institution | [ ] | [ ] | [ ] |

13. Who is normally responsible for monitoring the follow up of training?

| | *Yes* | *Sometimes* | *No* |
|---|---|---|---|
| (i) Training Manager/ Unit | [ ] | [ ] | [ ] |

| | Always | Mostly | Never |
|---|---|---|---|
| (ii) The boss under whom the officer is working | [ ] | [ ] | [ ] |
| (iii) Estt./Admn. Unit | [ ] | [ ] | [ ] |
| (iv) The Wing Head | [ ] | [ ] | [ ] |
| (v) Any other (please specify) ________________ | [ ] | [ ] | [ ] |

| | Always | Mostly | Never |
|---|---|---|---|
| 14. Is the placement of the trained officer in your Department made in accordance with the training that he has received? | [ ] | [ ] | [ ] |

15. Do the "policy/decision making" levels in your Department generally attach importance to the following aspects of training ?

| | Yes | Sometimes | No |
|---|---|---|---|
| (i) Periodical in-service training to all officers` | [ ] | [ ] | [ ] |
| (ii) Identifying training needs of individuals | [ ] | [ ] | [ ] |
| (iii) Nominating officers for training according to need | [ ] | [ ] | [ ] |
| (iv) Role of a Training Manager in the Deptt. | [ ] | [ ] | [ ] |
| (v) Allocation of separate Training Budget | [ ] | [ ] | [ ] |
| (vi) Arranging in-house training courses | [ ] | [ ] | [ ] |
| (vii) Follow-up of training | [ ] | [ ] | [ ] |

16. Do you agree that performance of the individuals at the operational levels of Asstt./SO/US can be improved by regularly nominating officer for appropriate training courses?

| Yes | Sometimes | No |
|---|---|---|
| [ ] | [ ] | [ ] |

If no, what according to you could be the reasons: (Please tick (✓) in against the applicable ones )

(i) Officers are not serious about training [ ]

(ii) No systematic method adopted by the Deptt. for nominating right officers for the right course [ ]

(iii) Appraisal system not being streamlined for identifying training needs of the officer [ ]

(iv) Lack of interaction in the Deptt. between training manager, person to be trained, his boss and senior officer [ ]

(v) Lack of guidance by the boss [ ]

(vi) Lack of interaction between the training institution and the organization [ ]

(vii) Lack of "direction from the top" or "policy on training". [ ]

17. Will it be possible for your Department/Office to arrange for interaction between your officers, training manager and training faculty of ISTM? *Yes* [ ] *No* [ ]

If yes, could you identify the purpose(s) of interaction from those given below (Please put an "x" in the box):

(i) For drawing up details of the course [ ]

(ii) For identifying specific performance problem of individuals [ ]

(iii) Drawing up the plan of identification of training needs [ ]

(iv) For setting Competence Standards* on job/tasks [ ]

(v) For selection/nomination of participants [ ]

(vi) Any other, please specify [ ]

_______________________________

If 'no', indicate the possible reasons.

(i) Time constraints [ ]

(ii) Constraint on expenditure [ ]

(iii) Lack of initiative from officer/staff of the Deptt. [ ]

(iv) No purpose is likely to be served by such an exercise [ ]

(v) Any other, please specify _______________________________

*Competence Standard = Standard of Performance based on required output (rather than desirable inputs) which reflect the actual expectation of performance in work role.

18. Kindly give your suggestion as to how the Ministries/Deptt. as client organization can help the training institutions in making training of their officers more purposeful?

Date: ______________________ Name and Designation

**Thanks for completing the questionnaire!**

**APPENDIX 4.7**
(Para 4.39)

**INSTITUTE OF SECRETARIAT TRAINING AND MANAGEMENT**
Old JNU Campus, New Mehrauli Road, New Delhi-110067

Dear

An exercise has been undertaken to assess and analyse the training needs of the officers of various grades of CSS in the context of evaluating the efficacy of the training imparted to them. To make this exercise meaningful it is important that we have your objective and unbiased feedback on the enclosed questionnaire.

This is an opinion survey. Therefore, the objective and considered views of the responders will be of value and not the names of the individuals, which in no case will be disclosed.

Kindly fill in the questionnaire and return it to the undersigned.

(A.N. CHAKRAVARTY)

## SURVEY OF TRAINING NEEDS QUESTIONNAIRE

(To be filled in by all officers of CSS)

### PART–A: Personal Data

1. NAME:
2. POST (encircle):Dir./DS/US(DF)/US(BO)/DO/SO/Desk Attache/ Asstt.
3. DATE OF APPOINTMENT(to the above post):
4. MINISTRY/DEPARTMENT/OFFICE:
5. QUALIFICATIONS: <u>Subject</u>

   Graduate [ ] ____________________

   Post Graduate [ ] ____________________

   Doctoral [ ] ____________________

   Others [ ] Specify____________________
6. TRAINING (specify courses attended in the last five years):

| S.No. | Title | Institute | Dates | | Usefulness to work Direct=2 Indirect=1 Remotely=0 |
|---|---|---|---|---|---|
| | | | From | To | |
| | | | | | |

7. NAME OF THE DIVISION/BRANCH/SECTION (Please give brief description of the responsibilities/charge also):

   ____________________
8. YOUR CURRENT AREAS OF WORK (Please tick (✓) the appropriate box(es):

   General Administration [ ]

   Personnel/Establishment [ ]

   Finance [ ]

   Accounts [ ]

   Budget [ ]

   Vigilance [ ]

Policy* Formulation [ ] *In the substantive
Policy* Implementation [ ] areas of your Min./Deptt.
Parliamentary matters [ ]
O&M and Work-Study [ ]
Research and Development [ ]
Others specify____________ [ ]

9. PERSONS WHOSE WORK YOU ARE DIRECTLY SUPERVISING: No.______ Designation ________________

**PART–B: Training Needs**

Please answer the questions by putting an "**x**" in the appropriate box:

| | *Yes* | *No* | *Sometimes* |
|---|---|---|---|
| 1. Do you think, training is a must for improving performance on the job? | [ ] | [ ] | [ ] |
| 2. Do you think that officers at higher/highest level in your Deptt. believe in the need of training for improving performance? | [ ] | [ ] | [ ] |
| 3. Do you think Induction/Orientation Training is essential on promotion to the next grade? | [ ] | [ ] | [ ] |

If no, state why ________________________________________

4. Do you think officers are nominated for training courses on the basis of—
Decision exclusively by the Admn. [ ]
Initiative taken by the supervisor [ ]
Initiative taken exclusively by the officer [ ]

| | *Yes* | *No* | *Sometimes* |
|---|---|---|---|
| 5. Do you think that a Foundational Training is must for newly recruited officers in CSS ( Asstt. and SO level) | [ ] | [ ] | [ ] |

If yes, the dur ation of such course should be:
2 weeks [ ] 4 weeks [ ] 3 months [ ] 6 months [ ] more [ ]
Specify ________

6. In your opinion, officers in the various levels require training on specific rules/procedure skills and managerial/behavioural skills in different degrees. Please indicate by putting an "**x**" in appropriate box.

| *Level* | *Degree of training needed in rules and procedure skills* | | | *Degree of training needed in managerial/ behaviour skills* | | |
|---|---|---|---|---|---|---|
| | *High* | *Mode-rate* | *Negli-gible* | *High* | *Mode-rate* | *Negli-gible* |
| Deputy Secy. | [ ] | [ ] | [ ] | [ ] | [ ] | [ ] |
| Under Secretary | [ ] | [ ] | [ ] | [ ] | [ ] | [ ] |
| Section Officer | [ ] | [ ] | [ ] | [ ] | [ ] | [ ] |
| Assistant | [ ] | [ ] | [ ] | [ ] | [ ] | [ ] |

7. Given below is the indicative list of subject areas of training. Please choose 5 (five) most important ones which you think (i) would be useful to your current role and responsibilities and (ii) you would recommend for your immediate subordinates*:

**Please go through the entire list before you record**

| | For you | For your subordinate* |
|---|---|---|
| General Management concepts | [ ] | [ ] |
| Secretariat Procedure | [ ] | [ ] |
| Noting and Drafting | [ ] | [ ] |
| Records Management | [ ] | [ ] |
| Personnel Management | [ ] | [ ] |
| Establishment Rules | [ ] | [ ] |
| Financial Management | [ ] | [ ] |
| Financial Rules | [ ] | [ ] |
| Economic Policy | [ ] | [ ] |

*Assistants may ignore this column

Management Accounting [ ] [ ]
Budgeting [ ] [ ]
Constitutional Laws [ ] [ ]
Industrial and Labour Laws [ ] [ ]
Anti-Corruption Laws [ ] [ ]
Disciplinary Procedure [ ] [ ]
Handling Court Cases [ ] [ ]
Computer Application [ ] [ ]
Management Information System [ ] [ ]
Career Management and Training [ ] [ ]
Decision Making [ ] [ ]
Time Management [ ] [ ]
Quantitative Techniques [ ] [ ]
Leadership Styles [ ] [ ]
Managing Innovation and Creativity [ ] [ ]
Interpersonal Communication [ ] [ ]
Self-analysis and Motivating Self [ ] [ ]
Management of Conflict [ ] [ ]
Understanding Group and
Team Building [ ] [ ]
Managing Change [ ] [ ]
(new technology or procedure)
Materials Management [ ] [ ]
Managing Stress in Organization [ ] [ ]
Project Management [ ] [ ]
Improving Communication Skills [ ] [ ]
Public Relations [ ] [ ]
Grievance Handling [ ] [ ]
Any other you may like to recommend
______________________________ [ ] [ ]
______________________________ [ ] [ ]

**APPENDIX 5.1**
(Para 5.02)

## TRAINING VALIDATION QUESTIONNAIRE
Assistants (Direct Recruits) Course

Name of the participant______________________________________

Ministry/Department__________________________________________

### Objectives of the Course

(a) To increase professional competence by imparting training in Office Procedure and in writing of notes and drafts.

(b) To expose the participants to modern techniques of Office Management.

(c) To familiarise them with the various rules and procedures which they are required to operate in their day to day work.

(d) To provide attitudinal approaches to the work environment and to superiors, colleagues and subordinates.

1 (a) How far has the course enabled you to acquire the necessary competence/skill in

| | *Subject* | *Fully* | *Considerably* | *Partly* | *Vaguely* |
|---|---|---|---|---|---|
| 1. | Office Procedure | [ ] | [ ] | [ ] | [ ] |
| 2. | Noting and Drafting | [ ] | [ ] | [ ] | [ ] |
| 3. | Financial Rules | [ ] | [ ] | [ ] | [ ] |

(b) How far has the course added to your knowledge of the following:

| | | *To a great extent* | *To a considerable extent* | *To some extent* | *Not at all* |
|---|---|---|---|---|---|
| 1. | Machinery of Govt. | [ ] | [ ] | [ ] | [ ] |
| 2. | Office Procedure | [ ] | [ ] | [ ] | [ ] |
| 3. | Noting and Drafting | [ ] | [ ] | [ ] | [ ] |
| 4. | Official Language Policy | [ ] | [ ] | [ ] | [ ] |
| 5. | Security of Inf. | [ ] | [ ] | [ ] | [ ] |
| 6. | Records Management | [ ] | [ ] | [ ] | [ ] |

| | | | | | |
|---|---|---|---|---|---|
| 7. | Disciplinary Rules | [ ] | [ ] | [ ] | [ ] |
| 8. | Conduct Rules | [ ] | [ ] | [ ] | [ ] |
| 9. | Parliamentary Procedure | [ ] | [ ] | [ ] | [ ] |
| 10. | Establishment Rules | [ ] | [ ] | [ ] | [ ] |
| 11. | Reservation in Services | [ ] | [ ] | [ ] | [ ] |
| 12. | Fin. Control and Budget | [ ] | [ ] | [ ] | [ ] |
| 13. | Fundamental Rules | [ ] | [ ] | [ ] | [ ] |
| 14. | TA and LTC Rules | [ ] | [ ] | [ ] | [ ] |
| 15. | Leave Rules | [ ] | [ ] | [ ] | [ ] |
| 16. | Pension Rules | [ ] | [ ] | [ ] | [ ] |
| 17. | Provident Fund Rules | [ ] | [ ] | [ ] | [ ] |
| 18. | Public Administration | [ ] | [ ] | [ ] | [ ] |
| 19. | Constitution of India | [ ] | [ ] | [ ] | [ ] |
| 20. | Eco. Dev. and Planning | [ ] | [ ] | [ ] | [ ] |
| 21. | Indian Culture | [ ] | [ ] | [ ] | [ ] |
| 22. | Behavioural Sciences | [ ] | [ ] | [ ] | [ ] |

2. Were your expectation from the course any different from those cited in the objective?

Yes [ ] No [ ]

If yes, in what manner?

3. Was the duration of the course adequate [ ]
too long [ ]
too short [ ]

What should be covered during that duration ?

Subjects to be deleted/reduced :

Subjects to be introduced/increased:

4. Was the time allowed for individual sessions adequate?

Yes [ ] No [ ]

If 'no', please give reasons

5. Were the course topics sequenced logically?

Yes [ ] No [ ]

If 'no', give specific instance

6. Which of the following methods/tools were employed in the programme ( they may be tick marked ) and give your ratings on their effectiveness ?

| | *Very Effective* | *Effective* | *Not Effective* |
|---|---|---|---|
| Lecture | [ ] | [ ] | [ ] |
| Syndicate | [ ] | [ ] | [ ] |
| Exercises | [ ] | [ ] | [ ] |
| Case Studies | [ ] | [ ] | [ ] |
| Films | [ ] | [ ] | [ ] |
| Any other (specify) | [ ] | [ ] | [ ] |

7. Did you find the course material supplied to you relevant ?

   Mostly [ ] Considerably [ ] Partly [ ]

   Was it also adequate ? Yes [ ] No [ ]

   If 'no', what else should have been provided ?

8. Any other remarks or suggestions to improve the course effectiveness.

9. How far has the study tour enabled you to achieve its objectives

   To a great extent [ ] To a considerable extent [ ]

   To some extent [ ] Not at all [ ]

   Was the duration of the study tour Adequate [ ]

   Too long [ ]

   Too short [ ]

   Have you been able to establish a better report with other members of the group—

   Yes [ ] No [ ]

10. How would you rate the following physical facilities provided during the training ?

| | Good | Satisfactory | Not satisfactory |
|---|---|---|---|
| - Classroom | [ ] | [ ] | [ ] |
| - Library | [ ] | [ ] | [ ] |
| - Working Lunch | [ ] | [ ] | [ ] |
| - Dining Hall | [ ] | [ ] | [ ] |
| - Residential accommodation | [ ] | [ ] | [ ] |

**APPENDIX 5.2**
(Para 5.12)

## PRE-TRAINING QUESTIONNAIRE
(Participant)

Name of the Course: ____ Assistant (Direct Recruits)

1. Name :
2. Ministry/Department:
3. Section in which last posted:
4. Year of qualifying
   Asstt's Grade Exam/rank:
5. Date of Appointment as Assistant:
6. Service : CSS/AFHQCS/RBSS
7. Educational Qualifications:
8. Brief Description of work done as Assistant:

---

Please go through the objectives of the course and syllabus given in the Annexure.

1. Do the objectives stated in the Annexure meet your

| | *Fully* | *Partially* | *No* |
|---|---|---|---|
| (a) Individual need for your work and professional development | [ ] | [ ] | [ ] |
| (b) Organizational needs | [ ] | [ ] | [ ] |

2. (a) Who was involved in the decision to nominate you for this course? Tick against appropriate column:
   (i) Initiative taken exclusively by you [ ]
   (ii) Initiative taken by your supervisor [ ]
   (iii) Decision left exclusively to admn. [ ]

   (b) If the answer to (a) above is other than (i), had you been given the option, would you have opted yourself for this training ? If yes, why ?

3. Right at the time of joining this course whether, in your opinion:
   (i) You knew nothing about your job [ ]

(ii) You were trying to learn the work [ ]

(iii) You were already performing your job, by and large, to the satisfaction of your supervisor [ ]

| | | *To a great extent* | *To some extent* | *Not at all* |
|---|---|---|---|---|
| 4. (a) | Were you receiving necessary training on your job from your Supervisor (SO) | [ ] | [ ] | [ ] |
| (b) | Did you get opportunity to learn about your job | | | |
| (i) | Through observation/immitation of others in the Section | [ ] | [ ] | [ ] |
| (ii) | Through guidance from your peers | [ ] | [ ] | [ ] |

5. Do you think that there is need of this Foundational Training Programme to enable you to have the basic knowledge of your work and to learn the necessary skill ?

| *Yes* | *To some extent* | *No* |
|---|---|---|
| [ ] | [ ] | [ ] |

6. Do you think you have been nominated for this course ?

(i) at the right time [ ]

(ii) too early [ ]

(iii) too late [ ]

7. What do you think your objectives and expectations are from this course in terms of your ?

(a) individual need [ ]

(b) organizational need [ ]

8. Do you think the subjects included in the syllabus would adequately cover the nature and subjects of your job back in the Ministry ?

| *Yes* | *To some extent* | *No* |
|---|---|---|
| [ ] | [ ] | [ ] |

9. Do you think you have already some/adequate knowledge about some of the subjects included in the course ? Name them, if any.

**APPENDIX 5.3.a**
(Para 5.14)

## PRE-TRAINING QUESTIONNAIRE
(Participant)

Name of the Course: _____ Section Officers (Refreshers)

[ To be filled in by all Section Officers of CSS attending SO (ref) Course at ISTM]

1. Name :
2. Ministry/Department :
3. Section in which last posted :
4. Year of Selection :
5. Date of Appointment as SO :
7. Educational qualification :
8. Brief description of work :

_______________________________________________

_______________________________________________

_______________________________________________

**Please go through the objectives of the course and syllabus supplied to you**

1. Do the objectives stated for the course meet your

| | *Fully* | *Partially* | *No* |
|---|---|---|---|
| (a) Individual need and professional development | [ ] | [ ] | [ ] |
| (b) Organizational needs | [ ] | [ ] | [ ] |

2. Right at the time of joining this course whether, in your opinion :

| | |
|---|---|
| (i) You knew nothing about your job | [ ] |
| (ii) You were trying to learn the work | [ ] |
| (iii) You were already performing your job, by and large, to the satisfaction of your Supervisor | [ ] |

3. Do you think that there is need of this training programme to enable you to have the basic knowledge of your work and to learn the necessary skill

| *Yes* | *To some extent* | *No* |
|---|---|---|
| [ ] | [ ] | [ ] |

4. Do you think you have been nominated for this course
   (i) at the right time [ ]
   (ii) too early [ ]
   (iii) too late [ ]
5. Please indicate as to what extent the following topics included in this course would relate to your present/future work in the Ministry:

| *Topic* | *Relates to my work* | | |
|---|---|---|---|
| | *Directly* | *Indirectly* | *Remotely* |
| 1. Role and Function of SO | | | |
| 2. Organization Theory | | | |
| 3. Decision Making | | | |
| 4. Cabinet Note | | | |
| 5. Agenda and Minutes of Meetings | | | |
| 6. Parliament Questions/ Assurance Committees | | | |
| 7. Deptl. Security Instructions | | | |
| 8. Computers: DBase IIIPlus | | | |
| 9. Economic Liberalisation | | | |
| 10. Budget | | | |
| 11. Project Planning | | | |
| 12. Audit Paras/Objections | | | |
| 13. Store Purchases | | | |
| 14. Effective Supervision | | | |
| 15. Performance Appraisal | | | |
| 16. Grievance Handling | | | |
| 17. JCM | | | |
| 18. Reservation in Services for SC/ST/OBC | | | |
| 19. Establishment Rules | | | |
| - Rectt. Rules | | | |
| - Confirmation | | | |
| - Seniority | | | |
| - DPC Procedure | | | |
| - Consultation with UPSC | | | |
| 20. Official Language Policy | | | |
| 21. Leadership Styles | | | |
| 22. Motivation | | | |
| 23. Communication | | | |
| 24. Inter-personal Relations | | | |
| 25. Management of Stress | | | |
| 26. Management of Change | | | |
| 27. Records Management | | | |
| 28. Problem Solving | | | |

6. Do you think you have already some/adequate knowledge about some of the subjects included in the course? Yes/No

   Name them, if any:

7. Do you think some more topics, which has direct relevance to your work, could be added? Yes/No. Name them, if any

## PRE-TRAINING DATA FOR SO (REF) COURSE

1. The objectives stated for the Course met the trainees'

| | *Fully* | *Partially* | *No* |
|---|---|---|---|
| (a) individual need and professional development | 50% | 50% | — |
| (b) organizational need | 50% | 50% | — |

2. Right at the time of joining this course the trainers :

| | |
|---|---|
| (i) knew nothing about the job | — |
| (ii) were trying to learn the work | 50% |
| (iii) were already performing their job, by and large, to the satisfaction of your Supervisor | 50% |

3. Trainees think that there is need of this training programme to enable them to have basic knowledge of their work and to learn the necessary skill

| *Yes* | *To some extent* | *No* |
|---|---|---|
| 80% | 20% | — |

4. Trainees think they have been nominated for this course

| | |
|---|---|
| (i) at the right time | 90% |
| (ii) too early | — |
| (iii) too late | 10% |

5. Trainees indicated (percentage) as to what extent the following topics included in this course would relate to their present/future work in the Ministry:

| | *Topic* | *Relates to my work* | | |
|---|---|---|---|---|
| | | *Directly* | *Indirectly* | *Remotely* |
| 1. | Role and function of SO | 95 | 05 | - |
| 2. | Organization Theory | 45 | 45 | 10 |
| 3. | Decision Making | 50 | 40 | 10 |
| 4. | Cabinet Note | 50 | 25 | 25 |
| 5. | Agenda and Minutes of Meetings | 50 | 30 | 20 |
| 6. | Parliament Questions/Assurance Committees | 75 | — | 25 |
| 7. | Departmental Security Instructions | 50 | 35 | 15 |

| | | | | |
|---|---|---|---|---|
| 8. | Computers: DBase IIIPlus | 50 | 20 | 30 |
| 9. | Economic Liberalisation | 20 | 35 | 45 |
| 10. | Budget | 30 | 40 | 30 |
| 11. | Project Planning | 10 | 45 | 45 |
| 12. | Audit Paras/Objections | 45 | 15 | 40 |
| 13. | Store Purchases | 25 | - | 75 |
| 14. | Effective Supervision | 90 | - | 10 |
| 15. | Performance Appraisal | 50 | 20 | 30 |
| 16. | Grievance Handling | 50 | 05 | 45 |
| 17. | JCM | 20 | 20 | 60 |
| 18. | Reservation in Services for SC/ST | 20 | 20 | 60 |
| 19. | Establishment Rules | | | |
| | - Rectt. Rules | 50 | 25 | 25 |
| | - Confirmation | 50 | 25 | 25 |
| | - Seniority | 50 | 25 | 25 |
| | - DPC Procedure | 50 | 25 | 25 |
| | - Consultation with UPSC | 50 | 10 | 40 |
| 20. | Official Language Policy | 60 | 40 | - |
| 21. | Leadership Styles | 75 | 15 | 10 |
| 22. | Motivation | 80 | 15 | 05 |
| 23. | Communication | 75 | 25 | - |
| 24. | Inter-personal Relations | 90 | 10 | - |
| 25. | Management of Stress | 75 | 15 | 10 |
| 26. | Management of Change | 60 | 20 | 20 |
| 27. | Records Management | 75 | 25 | - |
| 28. | Problem Solving | 90 | 10 | - |

6. Trainees think they have already some/adequate knowledge about some of the subjects included in the course.

7. Trainees have not indicated any significant topics to be added to the course.

**APPENDIX 5.3**
(Para 5.14)

## PRE-TRAINING QUESTIONNAIRE
(Participants)

Name of the Course: Professional Development Programme for CSS Grade I (Under Secretaries)

1. Name of the participant :
2. Ministry/Department :
3. Date of appointment as US : / /
4. Date of appointment to CSS : / / as Asstt.(DR)/SO (Prob)
5. Brief description of your present work :

___

___

___

6. As Under Secretary, are you presently working as:
   (a) Conventional Branch Officer [ ]
   or (b) Desk Functionary under Desk Officer System [ ]
7. Kindly give the name and designation of your immediate superior:

___

___

___

**Please go through the objectives of the course**

1. Do the objectives of the course meet your:

| | *Fully* | *Partially* | *Remotely* |
|---|---|---|---|
| (a) individual need and professional development | [ ] | [ ] | [ ] |
| (b) organizational needs | [ ] | [ ] | [ ] |

2. Do you think that there is need of this training programme to enable you to have the basic knowledge of your work and to learn the necessary skills
   Yes 50% To some extent 35% No 15%
3. Do you think you have been nominated for this course
   (i) at the right time 25
   (ii) too early None
   (iii) too late 75

4. Please indicate as to what extent the following topics included in this course would relate to your present/future work in the Ministry : (Please tick / in the appropriate box)

| *Topic* | *Relate to my work* | | |
|---|---|---|---|
| | *Directly* | *Indirectly* | *Remotely* |
| 1. Current Economic Environment | [ ] | [ ] | [ ] |
| 2. Investment Decisions | [ ] | [ ] | [ ] |
| 3. Management Accounting and Audit | [ ] | [ ] | [ ] |
| 4. Role of I.F.A. | [ ] | [ ] | [ ] |
| 5. Project Planning and Appraisal | [ ] | [ ] | [ ] |
| 6. Wasteland/Watershed Development | [ ] | [ ] | [ ] |
| 7. Leadership Styles | [ ] | [ ] | [ ] |
| 8. Motivating Self and Subordinate | [ ] | [ ] | [ ] |
| 9. Effective Communication | [ ] | [ ] | [ ] |
| 10. Team Building | [ ] | [ ] | [ ] |
| 11. Management of Stress | [ ] | [ ] | [ ] |
| 12. Organization Creativity and Change | [ ] | [ ] | [ ] |
| 13. Role of Branch Officers | [ ] | [ ] | [ ] |
| 14. Administrative Vigilance | [ ] | [ ] | [ ] |
| 15. Performance Appraisal | [ ] | [ ] | [ ] |
| 16. Reservation in Services of SC/ST | [ ] | [ ] | [ ] |
| 17. Joint Consultative Machinery | [ ] | [ ] | [ ] |
| 18. Administrative Tribunal | [ ] | [ ] | [ ] |
| 19. Grievance Handling | [ ] | [ ] | [ ] |
| 20. Records Management | [ ] | [ ] | [ ] |
| 21. Management by Objective | [ ] | [ ] | [ ] |
| 22. Management Information System | [ ] | [ ] | [ ] |
| 23. Time Management | [ ] | [ ] | [ ] |
| 24. Network Techniques | [ ] | [ ] | [ ] |
| 25. Decision-Making Process in Govt. | [ ] | [ ] | [ ] |
| 26. Public Administration | [ ] | [ ] | [ ] |
| 27. Computer Application | [ ] | [ ] | [ ] |

5. Do you think you have already some/adequate knowledge/skill on some of the topics mentioned above? Yes/No
   Name them, if any:

6. Do you think some more topics, which has direct relevance to your work, could be added? Yes/No.
   Name them, if any:

## PRE-TRAINING DATA FOR PDP
(Participants)

1. Do the objectives of the Course meet your:

| | *Fully* | *Partially* | *Remotely* |
|---|---|---|---|
| (a) individual need and professional development | 60% | 55% | — |
| (b) organizational needs | 55% | 30% | 10% |

2. Do you think that there is need of this training programme to enable you to have the basic knowledge of your work and to learn the necessary skills?

| *Yes* | *To some extent* | *No* |
|---|---|---|
| 50% | 35% | 15% |

3. Do you think you have been nominated for this course?

| | |
|---|---|
| (i) at the right time | 25% |
| (ii) too early | — |
| (iii) too late | 75% |

4. Please indicate as to what extent the following topics included in this course would relate to your present/future work in the Ministry : (Please tick **'x'** in the appropriate box)

| | *Topic* | *Relate to my work* | | |
|---|---|---|---|---|
| | | *Directly* | *Indirectly* | *Remotely* |
| 1. | Current Economic Environment | 25 | 60 | 15 |
| 2. | Investment Decisions | 30 | 40 | 30 |
| 3. | Management Accounting and Audit | 35 | 20 | 45 |
| 4. | Role of IFA | 35 | 10 | 55 |
| 5. | Project Planning and Appraisal | 35 | 35 | 30 |
| 6. | Wasteland/Watershed Development | 05 | 40 | 55 |
| 7. | Leadership Styles | 90 | 05 | 05 |
| 8. | Motivating Self and Subordinate | 80 | 10 | 10 |
| 9. | Effective Communication | 80 | 20 | - |
| 10. | Team Building | 75 | 25 | - |
| 11. | Management of Stress | 80 | 20 | - |
| 12. | Organization Creativity and Change | 50 | 25 | 25 |
| 13. | Role of Branch Officers | 80 | 20 | |

| | | | | |
|---|---|---|---|---|
| 14. | Administrative Vigilance | 60 | 25 | 15 |
| 15. | Performance Appraisal | 65 | 20 | 15 |
| 16. | Reservation in Services of SC/ST | 50 | 25 | 25 |
| 17. | Joint Consultative Machinery | 50 | 25 | 25 |
| 18. | Administrative Tribunal | 50 | 25 | 25 |
| 19. | Grievance Handling | 70 | 10 | 20 |
| 20. | Records Management | 60 | 30 | 10 |
| 21. | Management Objective | 65 | 20 | 15 |
| 22. | Management Information System | 60 | 40 | - |
| 23. | Time Management | 75 | 25 | - |
| 24. | Network Techniques | 25 | 30 | 45 |
| 25. | Decision-Making Process in Govt. | 75 | 20 | 05 |
| 26. | Public Administration | 75 | 05 | 20 |
| 27. | Computer Application | 70 | 25 | 05 |

5. Trainees think they have already some/adequate knowledge about some of the subjects included in the course.

6. Trainees think the following topics have direct relevance to their work, could be added:

   - Management of PSU, its role relationship with admv. Ministry, Foreign Trade Policy, direct and indirect Tax Policy; UNDP/World Bank/IMF/Foreign Aided Projects; Banking/Customs/Foreign Exchange etc. Privatisation.
   - Welfare Officer; Responsive admn.
   - Space Management—Modernisation.
   - Centre-State relationship—Constitution.

**APPENDIX 5.4**
(Para 6.15)

## INSTITUTE OF SECRETARIAT TRAINING AND MANAGEMENT

Course Validation Questionnaire

NAME OF THE COURSE :

DURATION : From: / / To: / /

NO. OF PARTICIPANTS :

**COURSE OBJECTIVE**

| | *Fully* | *Consi-derably* | *Partly* | *Vaguely* | *If partly or Vaguely, specify with reasons* |
|---|---|---|---|---|---|
| 1. Were the objectives of Course made clear to you in the beginning? | | | | | |
| 2. Have these objectives been achieved? | | | | | |
| 3. Have the objectives of the course matched with your expectations from the course? | | | | | |

**COURSE INPUT**

1. Do you think the course input topics were relevant and adequate for achieving the objectives of the course? Yes/No

   If no, please specify (i) additions ____________
   (ii) deletions ____________

2 Were the various sessions/topics logically sequenced? Yes/No

   If no, please specify ____________________

3. Medium of instructions: Do you think the Sessions would have been more effective if the medium was (a) Hindi only
   (b) Hindi-English
   (c) English only

## PHYSICAL FACILITIES

| | *Good* | *Just Ade-quate* | *Needs Improv-ments* | *If needs Improvement How?* |
|---|---|---|---|---|
| **CLASSROOM** | | | | |
| Seating | | | | |
| Lighting | | | | |
| Audibility | | | | |
| Visual Aids | | | | |
| Toilets | | | | |
| Drinking Water | | | | |
| **LIBRARY** | | | | |
| Reading Room | | | | |
| Reference Facility | | | | |
| **HOSTEL** | | | | |
| Lodging: Furnitures | | | | |
| Linen | | | | |
| Water & Sanitation | | | | |
| Services | | | | |
| Boarding: Food | | | | |
| Dining Hall | | | | |
| Services | | | | |
| Recreation: Reading Room | | | | |
| TV Room | | | | |
| Sports/Games | | | | |
| Room | | | | |
| CANTEEN (for non-residents): | | | | |
| Tea | | | | |
| Food | | | | |
| Services | | | | |
| Cleanliness of the Institute premises | | | | |

# Instant Feedback Form

| Instructions: Please put a cross [X] in the appropriate box to indicate your choice of option under each column against each topic. The views should be indicated by each individual participant objectively and independently keeping in view his own training needs. Where any of the question is not applicable, may be indicated as N.A. in that column. You need not disclose your identity here. | | | Objective | | | Learning Content | | | Methodology | | | | | | | | | Reading Material | | | Presentation | | | | | | Duration | | | Job Relation | | | Knowledge Skill Gain | | | Remarks |
|---|---|---|---|---|---|---|---|---|---|---|---|---|---|---|---|---|---|---|---|---|---|---|---|---|---|---|---|---|---|---|---|---|---|---|---|---|
| | | | Was the learning objectives of them topic lade clear at the beginning | | | Matching with the objective was the content relevant | | | Was the training methods used | | | Has the Exercise at the end (if any) been able to cover the learning points | | | How were questions handled during the sessions | | | Has the reading material supplied been useful in under-standing the topic | | | How do you rate the presenta-tion of the topic | | | If needs improve-ment is it in regard to | | | Whether the time allowed to the topic was | | | Was the topic relevant to your present job | | | Has the learning added to your previous knowl-edge/skill | | | Any other comment, you may like to make |
| Name of the topic/ Learning Unit | No. of ses-ssion | Fac-ulty (use code) | Fully | Adequately | Vaguely | Fully | Mostly | Vaguely | Very Effective | Effective | Not effective | Fully | Mostly | Vaguely | Excellent | Satisfactory | Unsatisfactory | Fully | Mostly | Vaguely | Excellent | Good | Needs Improvement | Clearity | Sequence | Examples | Long | Just Right | Short | Directly | Likely | Remotely | Fully | Considerably | Not quite | |
| | | | | | | | | | | | | | | | | | | | | | | | | | | | | | | | | | | | | |
| | | | | | | | | | | | | | | | | | | | | | | | | | | | | | | | | | | | | |
| | | | | | | | | | | | | | | | | | | | | | | | | | | | | | | | | | | | | |
| | | | | | | | | | | | | | | | | | | | | | | | | | | | | | | | | | | | | |
| | | | | | | | | | | | | | | | | | | | | | | | | | | | | | | | | | | | | |
| | | | | | | | | | | | | | | | | | | | | | | | | | | | | | | | | | | | | |
| | | | | | | | | | | | | | | | | | | | | | | | | | | | | | | | | | | | | |
| | | | | | | | | | | | | | | | | | | | | | | | | | | | | | | | | | | | | |
| | | | | | | | | | | | | | | | | | | | | | | | | | | | | | | | | | | | | |
| | | | | | | | | | | | | | | | | | | | | | | | | | | | | | | | | | | | | |
| | | | | | | | | | | | | | | | | | | | | | | | | | | | | | | | | | | | | |
| | | | | | | | | | | | | | | | | | | | | | | | | | | | | | | | | | | | | |
| | | | | | | | | | | | | | | | | | | | | | | | | | | | | | | | | | | | | |
| | | | | | | | | | | | | | | | | | | | | | | | | | | | | | | | | | | | | |
| | | | | | | | | | | | | | | | | | | | | | | | | | | | | | | | | | | | | |
| | | | | | | | | | | | | | | | | | | | | | | | | | | | | | | | | | | | | |
| | | | | | | | | | | | | | | | | | | | | | | | | | | | | | | | | | | | | |
| | | | | | | | | | | | | | | | | | | | | | | | | | | | | | | | | | | | | |
| | | | | | | | | | | | | | | | | | | | | | | | | | | | | | | | | | | | | |
| | | | | | | | | | | | | | | | | | | | | | | | | | | | | | | | | | | | | |
| | | | | | | | | | | | | | | | | | | | | | | | | | | | | | | | | | | | | |

**APPENDIX 5.5.a**

## FOLLOW-UP QUESTIONNAIRE (PARTICIPANT)

Assistants (Direct Recruits) Course

1. Name:
2. Ministry/Department/Office:
3. No. and date of the Asstt(DR) course attended:
4. Section in which posted:
5. Name and Designation of immediate boss:

______________________________

6. Brief description of duties:

______________________________

**Part I**

I. Various topics were covered in the Foundational Course you attended at ISTM. Kindly indicate against the space provided for each whether the inputs covered under these topics helped you in better performance in your job, and if not, the reasons thereof, by putting an "**x**" in the appropriate column:

| *Topic covered in the course* | *Did it, anyway contribute to better performance in your job* | | *If 'no', indicate the reason by putting an 'x' in the appropriate box from column 3,4,5 and 6* | | | |
|---|---|---|---|---|---|---|
| | | | *Function does not relate to the job* | *Training inputs insufficient or not related to the work situation* | *Organi-zational cons-traints* | *Indivi-dual cons-traints* |
| | *Yes* | *No* | | | | |
| 1 | 2 | | 3 | 4 | 5 | 6 |
| 1. Office procedure (filing, referencing and handling papers) | [ ] | [ ] | [ ] | [ ] | [ ] | [ ] |
| 2. Noting and Drafting | [ ] | [ ] | [ ] | [ ] | [ ] | [ ] |

| | | | | | | |
|---|---|---|---|---|---|---|
| 3. Records Management | [ ] | [ ] | [ ] | [ ] | [ ] | [ ] |
| 4. Handling classified information/ papers | [ ] | [ ] | [ ] | [ ] | [ ] | [ ] |
| 5. Disciplinary/ Vigilance matters | [ ] | [ ] | [ ] | [ ] | [ ] | [ ] |
| 6. Dealing with Parliamentary papers/ questions | [ ] | [ ] | [ ] | [ ] | [ ] | [ ] |
| 7. Dealing with established matters regarding: | | | | | | |
| (i) Recruitment/ Promotion/ | [ ] | [ ] | [ ] | [ ] | [ ] | [ ] |
| (ii) Pay fixa-tion/leave | [ ] | [ ] | [ ] | [ ] | [ ] | [ ] |
| (iii) Pension cases | [ ] | [ ] | [ ] | [ ] | [ ] | [ ] |
| (iv) TA/LTC | [ ] | [ ] | [ ] | [ ] | [ ] | [ ] |
| (v) GPF | [ ] | [ ] | [ ] | [ ] | [ ] | [ ] |
| 8. Preparation of Budget | [ ] | [ ] | [ ] | [ ] | [ ] | [ ] |

## Part II

I. Based on specific work/cases assigned after attending the Foundational Programme what do you think is the degree of relevance of rules/procedures and skill discussed at the programme to your work situation:

| | |
|---|---|
| Has the direct relevance | [ ] |
| has indirect relevance | [ ] |
| only some of the things has relevance | [ ] |
| has no relevance | [ ] |

II. Comparing to your pre-training work-performance with that after-training please indicate:

| | Increased | Same as before | Undecided | Decreased |
|---|---|---|---|---|
| 1. Your overall feeling of satisfaction in your work | [ ] | [ ] | [ ] | [ ] |
| 2. Your efficiency to examining cases/problems and apply correct rules | [ ] | [ ] | [ ] | [ ] |
| 3. Your ability to record notes/drafts on cases | [ ] | [ ] | [ ] | [ ] |
| 4. Your efficiency in dealing with your boss and peers | [ ] | [ ] | [ ] | [ ] |
| 5. Number of cases examined and submitted to higher officers which received approval without major change | [ ] | [ ] | [ ] | [ ] |
| 6. Amount of work assigned to you by your boss | [ ] | [ ] | [ ] | [ ] |
| 7. Seeking your opinion/views by your boss before taking a decision on a case other than submitted by you | [ ] | [ ] | [ ] | [ ] |

III. Please indicate your choice for each of the statement listed

| | Agree | Undecided | Disagree |
|---|---|---|---|
| 1. Asstt(DR) course has improved my skill/efficiency in my job | [ ] | [ ] | [ ] |
| 2. The programme placed too much emphasis on such rules/procedures as were of little practical value to me | [ ] | [ ] | [ ] |
| 3. The programme did not cater to what my Department/Section expected to get out of it | [ ] | [ ] | [ ] |

| | | | | |
|---|---|---|---|---|
| 4. | I feel more confident and better equipped for various cases/ problems on my desk | [ ] | [ ] | [ ] |
| 5. | My attending the programme has improved my status in the Section | [ ] | [ ] | [ ] |
| 6. | The programme has raised my personal goals and aspirations | [ ] | [ ] | [ ] |
| 7. | I do not find any change in my personal develop-ment | [ ] | [ ] | [ ] |
| 8. | The programme has infused lot of self-confidence in me | [ ] | [ ] | [ ] |
| 9. | The programme offered me an opportunity to be more open minded | [ ] | [ ] | [ ] |
| 10. | The programme created an interest for individual learning | [ ] | [ ] | [ ] |
| 11. | I derived lot of benefit through my interaction with other Assistants from various Ministries/Deptts. | [ ] | [ ] | [ ] |
| 12. | What I learnt at ISTM is sufficiently similar to my job characteris-tic in my Deptt. | [ ] | [ ] | [ ] |
| 13. | I feel restricted by the convention/procedure prevalent in my Section | [ ] | [ ] | [ ] |
| 14. | The office atmosphere does not favour innovations | [ ] | [ ] | [ ] |

| | | | |
|---|---|---|---|
| 15. Assistants learn more by working on the desk and training makes little difference | [ ] | [ ] | [ ] |
| 16. My officers stimulates and approve innovations | [ ] | [ ] | [ ] |
| 17. I could learn more from books and self-study than from attending training course | [ ] | [ ] | [ ] |

IV. Does any particular strength or weakness in the programme stand out in your mind? Please specify.

V. What is your general reaction to the training programme you attended.

Signature

Date:

**APPENDIX 5.5.b**

## FOLLOW-UP QUESTIONNAIRE (SUPERVISOR)

Name of the Assistant

Name of Section (Present)

Date of posting in the Section

### Part I

I Can you identify any specific way in which the Assistant has tried out his knowledge and skill subsequent to attending the Assistant (DR) Course at ISTM with reference to the following functions covered in the programme:
(Please tick appropriate column)

| *Function* | *Definite improvement seen and attributed to the training* | *If no improvement was made please tick the most appropriate answer from column 3,4,5 and 6* | | | |
|---|---|---|---|---|---|
| | | *Function does not relate to the job* | *Training inputs insufficient or not related to the work situation* | *Organi-zational cons-traints* | *Indivi-dual cons-traints* |
| 1 | 2 | 3 | 4 | 5 | 6 |
| 1. Office Procedure (filing, referencing and handling papers) | [ ] | [ ] | [ ] | [ ] | [ ] |
| 2. Noting and Drafting | [ ] | [ ] | [ ] | [ ] | [ ] |
| 3. Records Management | [ ] | [ ] | [ ] | [ ] | [ ] |
| 4. Handling classified information/ papers | [ ] | [ ] | [ ] | [ ] | [ ] |

| | | | | | |
|---|---|---|---|---|---|
| 5. Disciplinary/ Vigilance matters | [ ] | [ ] | [ ] | [ ] | [ ] |
| 6. Dealing with Parliamentary papers/ questions | [ ] | [ ] | [ ] | [ ] | [ ] |
| 7. Dealing with established matters regarding: | | | | | |
| (i) Recruitment/ Promotion/ | [ ] | [ ] | [ ] | [ ] | [ ] |
| (ii) Pay fixation/leave | [ ] | [ ] | [ ] | [ ] | [ ] |
| (iii) Pension cases | [ ] | [ ] | [ ] | [ ] | [ ] |
| (iv) TA/LTC | [ ] | [ ] | [ ] | [ ] | [ ] |
| (v) GPF | [ ] | [ ] | [ ] | [ ] | [ ] |
| 8. Preparation of Budget | [ ] | [ ] | [ ] | [ ] | [ ] |

II. Please indicate your choice for each of the statements given below with reference to the Assistant subsequent to his attending Assistant (DR) Course:

| | *Agree* | *Undecided* | *Disagree* |
|---|---|---|---|
| 1. The training has improved his skill/ efficiency in his job | [ ] | [ ] | [ ] |
| 2. The programme placed too much emphasis on such rules/procedures as were of little practical value to him | [ ] | [ ] | [ ] |
| 3. The programme did not cater to what the Department/Section expected him to get out of it | [ ] | [ ] | [ ] |
| 4. He feels more confident and better equipped for various csses/problems on his desk | [ ] | [ ] | [ ] |

| | | | |
|---|---|---|---|
| 5. His attending the programme has improved his status in the Section | [ ] | [ ] | [ ] |
| 6. His working relationship with his colleagues has improved | [ ] | [ ] | [ ] |
| 7. He handles problems in a more systematic and analytical manner | [ ] | [ ] | [ ] |
| 8. I feel the programme contributed little to his development | [ ] | [ ] | [ ] |
| 9. He has shown good performance in handling challenging tasks | [ ] | [ ] | [ ] |
| 10. After attending the programme he has not demonstrated any innovative skills | [ ] | [ ] | [ ] |
| 11. Assistants learn more by working on the desk and training makes little difference | [ ] | [ ] | [ ] |
| 12. His present job performance is significantly better than his earlier performance | [ ] | [ ] | [ ] |
| 13. Assistant can learn more from books and self-study than from attending training course | [ ] | [ ] | [ ] |

III. Any suggestion you have in terms of the individual and organizational needs which can help us improve the future training courses.

Signature:

Name:

Date:

**APPENDIX 5.5.c**

## FOLLOW-UP QUESTIONNAIRE (PARTICIPANT)

Assistants (Refresher) Course

1. Name:
2. Ministry/Department/Office:
3. No. and date of the Asstt(Ref) Course attended:
4. Section in which posted:
5. Name and Designation of immediate boss:

   ______________________________

6. Brief description of duties:

   ______________________________

### Part I

I. Various topics were covered in the Foundational Course you attended at ISTM. Kindly indicate against the space provided for each whether the inputs covered under these topics helped you in better performance in your job, and if not, the reasons therefore, by putting an "**x**" in the appropriate column:

| *Topic covered in the course* | *Did it, anyway contribute to better performance in your job* | | *If 'no', indicate the reason by putting an 'x' in the appropriate box from column 3,4,5 and 6* | | | |
|---|---|---|---|---|---|---|
| | *Yes* | *No* | *Function does not relate to the job* | *Training inputs insufficient or not related to the work situation* | *Organi-zational cons-traints* | *Indivi-dual cons-traints* |
| 1 | 2 | | 3 | 4 | 5 | 6 |
| 1. Office Procedure (filing, referencing and handling papers) | [ ] | [ ] | [ ] | [ ] | [ ] | [ ] |
| 2. Noting and Drafting | [ ] | [ ] | [ ] | [ ] | [ ] | [ ] |

| | | | | | | |
|---|---|---|---|---|---|---|
| 3. Records Management | [ ] | [ ] | [ ] | [ ] | [ ] | [ ] |
| 4. Handling classified information/ papers | [ ] | [ ] | [ ] | [ ] | [ ] | [ ] |
| 5. Disciplinary/ Vigilance matters | [ ] | [ ] | [ ] | [ ] | [ ] | [ ] |
| 6. Dealing with Parliamentary papers/ questions | [ ] | [ ] | [ ] | [ ] | [ ] | [ ] |
| 7. Dealing with established matters regarding: | | | | | | |
| (i) Recruitment/ Promotion/ | [ ] | [ ] | [ ] | [ ] | [ ] | [ ] |
| (ii) Pay fixation/leave | [ ] | [ ] | [ ] | [ ] | [ ] | [ ] |
| (iii) Pension cases | [ ] | [ ] | [ ] | [ ] | [ ] | [ ] |
| (iv) TA/LTC | [ ] | [ ] | [ ] | [ ] | [ ] | [ ] |
| (v) GPF | [ ] | [ ] | [ ] | [ ] | [ ] | [ ] |
| 8. Preparation of Budget | [ ] | [ ] | [ ] | [ ] | [ ] | [ ] |

## Part II

I. Based on specific work/cases assigned after attending the Foundational Programme what do you think the degree of relevance of rules/procedures and skill discussed at the programme to your work situations:

| | |
|---|---|
| Has direct relevance | [ ] |
| has indirect relevance | [ ] |
| only some of the things have relevance | [ ] |
| has no relevance | [ ] |

II. Comparing to your pre-training work-performance with that after training, please indicate:

| | Increased | Same as before | Undecided | Decreased |
|---|---|---|---|---|
| 1. Your overall feeling of satisfaction in your work | [ ] | [ ] | [ ] | [ ] |
| 2. Your efficiency in examining cases/problems and applying correct rules | [ ] | [ ] | [ ] | [ ] |
| 3. Your ability to record Notes/Drafts on cases | [ ] | [ ] | [ ] | [ ] |
| 4. Your efficiency in dealing with your boss and peers | [ ] | [ ] | [ ] | [ ] |
| 5. Number of cases examined and submitted to higher officers which received approval without major change | [ ] | [ ] | [ ] | [ ] |
| 6. Amount of work assigned to you by your boss | [ ] | [ ] | [ ] | [ ] |
| 7. Seeking your opinion/views by your boss before taking a decision on a case other than submitted by you | [ ] | [ ] | [ ] | [ ] |

III. Please indicate your choice for each of the statement listed

| | Agree | Undecided | Disagree |
|---|---|---|---|
| 1. Asstt (DR) Course has improved my skill/efficiency in my job | [ ] | [ ] | [ ] |
| 2. The programme placed too much emphasis on such rules/procedures as were of little practical value to me | [ ] | [ ] | [ ] |
| 3. The programme did not cater to what my Department/Section expected to get out of it | [ ] | [ ] | [ ] |

| | | | |
|---|---|---|---|
| 4. I feel more confident and better equipped for various cases/ problems on my desk | [ ] | [ ] | [ ] |
| 5. My attending the programme has improved my status in the Section | [ ] | [ ] | [ ] |
| 6. The programme has raised my personal goals and aspirations | [ ] | [ ] | [ ] |
| 7. I do not find any change in my personal development | [ ] | [ ] | [ ] |
| 8. The programme has infused a lot of self-confidence in me | [ ] | [ ] | [ ] |
| 9. The programme offered me an opportunity to be more open minded | [ ] | [ ] | [ ] |
| 10. The programme created an interest for individual learning | [ ] | [ ] | [ ] |
| 11. I derived lot of benefit through my interaction with other Assistants from various Ministries/Deptts. | [ ] | [ ] | [ ] |
| 12. What I learnt at ISTM is sufficiently similar to my job characteristic in my Deptt. | [ ] | [ ] | [ ] |
| 13. I feel restricted by the convention/procedure prevalent in my Section | [ ] | [ ] | [ ] |
| 14. The office atmosphere does not favour innovations | [ ] | [ ] | [ ] |

| | | | |
|---|---|---|---|
| 15. Assistants learn more by working on the desk and training makes little difference | [ ] | [ ] | [ ] |
| 16. My officers stimulate and approve innovations | [ ] | [ ] | [ ] |
| 17. I could learn more from books and self-study than from attending training course | [ ] | [ ] | [ ] |

IV. Does any particular strength or weakness in the programme stand out in your mind? Please specify

V. What is your general reaction to the training programme you attended?

Signature

Date:

## FOLLOW-UP QUESTIONNAIRE (SUPERVISOR)

Name of the Assistant

Name of Section (Present)

Date of posting in the Section

### Part I

I. Can you identify any specific way in which the Assistant has tried out his knowledge and skill subsequent to attending the Assistant (Refresher) Course at ISTM with reference to the following functions covered in the programme:
(Please tick appropriate column)

| *Function* | *Definite improvement seen and attributed to the training* | *If 'no', improvement was made, please tick the most appropriate answer from column 3,4,5 and 6* | | | |
|---|---|---|---|---|---|
| | | *Function does not relate to the job* | *Training inputs insufficient or not related to the work situation* | *Organi-zational cons-traints* | *Indivi-dual cons-traints* |
| 1 | 2 | 3 | 4 | 5 | 6 |
| 1. Office Procedure (filing, referencing and handling papers) | [ ] | [ ] | [ ] | [ ] | [ ] |
| 2. Noting and Drafting | [ ] | [ ] | [ ] | [ ] | [ ] |
| 3. Records Management | [ ] | [ ] | [ ] | [ ] | [ ] |
| 4. Handling classified information/ papers | [ ] | [ ] | [ ] | [ ] | [ ] |
| 5. Disciplinary/ Vigilance Matters | [ ] | [ ] | [ ] | [ ] | [ ] |

| | | | | | |
|---|---|---|---|---|---|
| 6. Dealing with Parliamentary papers/ questions | [ ] | [ ] | [ ] | [ ] | [ ] |
| 7. Dealing with established matters regarding: | | | | | |
| (i) Recruitment/ Promotion/ | [ ] | [ ] | [ ] | [ ] | [ ] |
| (ii) Pay fixa-tion/leave | [ ] | [ ] | [ ] | [ ] | [ ] |
| (iii) Pension cases | [ ] | [ ] | [ ] | [ ] | [ ] |
| (iv) TA/LTC | [ ] | [ ] | [ ] | [ ] | [ ] |
| (v) GPF | [ ] | [ ] | [ ] | [ ] | [ ] |
| 8. Preparation of Budget | [ ] | [ ] | [ ] | [ ] | [ ] |

II. Please indicate your choice for each of the statements given below with reference to the Assistant subsequent to his attending Assistant (DR) Course:

| | *Agree* | *Undecided* | *Disagree* |
|---|---|---|---|
| 1. The training has improved his skill/ efficiency in his job | [ ] | [ ] | [ ] |
| 2. The programme placed too much emphasis on such rules/procedures as were of little practical value to him | [ ] | [ ] | [ ] |
| 3. The programme did not cater to what the Department/Section expected him to get out of it | [ ] | [ ] | [ ] |
| 4. He feels more confident and better equipped for various cases/problems on his desk | [ ] | [ ] | [ ] |

| | | | |
|---|---|---|---|
| 5. His attending the programme has improved his status in the Section | [ ] | [ ] | [ ] |
| 6. Working relationship with his colleagues has improved | [ ] | [ ] | [ ] |
| 7. He handles problems in a more systematic and analytical manner | [ ] | [ ] | [ ] |
| 8. I feel the programme contributed little to his development | [ ] | [ ] | [ ] |
| 9. He has shown good performance in handling challenging tasks | [ ] | [ ] | [ ] |
| 10. After attending the programme he has not demonstrated any innovative skills | [ ] | [ ] | [ ] |
| 11. Assistants learn more by working on the desk and training makes little difference | [ ] | [ ] | [ ] |
| 12. His present job performance is significantly better than his earlier performance | [ ] | [ ] | [ ] |
| 13. Assistant can learn more from books and self-study than from attending training course | [ ] | [ ] | [ ] |

III. Any suggestion you have in terms of the individua and organizational needs which can help us improve the future training courses.

Signature:

Name:

Date:

**APPENDIX 5.5.d**

## FOLLOW-UP QUESTIONNAIRE (PARTICIPANT)

Section Officers (Probationer's) Course

1. Name:
2. Ministry/Department/Office:
3. Date of Appointment as SO:
4. No. and date of the SO(Prob) Course attended:
5. Section in which posted:
6. Name & Designation of immediate boss:

---

7. Brief description of duties:

---

### Part I

I. Various topics were covered in the Foundational Course you attended at ISTM. Kindly indicate against the space provided for each whether the inputs covered under these topics helped you in better performance in your job, and if not, the reasons thereof, by putting an "**x**" in the appropriate column:

| *Broad topics covered in the course* | *Did it, anyway contribute to performance in your job* | | *If 'no', indicate the reason by putting an 'x' in the appropriate box from column 3,4,5 and 6* | | | |
|---|---|---|---|---|---|---|
| | | | *Function does not relate to the job* | *Training inputs insufficient or not related to the work situation* | *Organi-zational cons-traints* | *Indivi-dual cons-traints* |
| | *Yes* | *No* | | | | |
| 1 | 2 | | 3 | 4 | 5 | 6 |
| 1. Office Procedure (filing, referencing and handling papers) | [ ] | [ ] | [ ] | [ ] | [ ] | [ ] |
| 2. Noting and Drafting | [ ] | [ ] | [ ] | [ ] | [ ] | [ ] |

| | | | | | | |
|---|---|---|---|---|---|---|
| 3. Records Management | [ ] | [ ] | [ ] | [ ] | [ ] | [ ] |
| 4. Handling classified information/ papers | [ ] | [ ] | [ ] | [ ] | [ ] | [ ] |
| 5. Disciplinary/ Vigilance matters | [ ] | [ ] | [ ] | [ ] | [ ] | [ ] |
| 6. Dealing with Parliamentary papers/ questions | [ ] | [ ] | [ ] | [ ] | [ ] | [ ] |
| 7. Dealing with established matters regarding: | | | | | | |
| (i) Recruitment/ Promotion | [ ] | [ ] | [ ] | [ ] | [ ] | [ ] |
| (ii) Reservation in Services | [ ] | [ ] | [ ] | [ ] | [ ] | [ ] |
| (iii) Pay fixa- tion/leave | [ ] | [ ] | [ ] | [ ] | [ ] | [ ] |
| (iv) Pension cases | [ ] | [ ] | [ ] | [ ] | [ ] | [ ] |
| (v) TA/LTC | [ ] | [ ] | [ ] | [ ] | [ ] | [ ] |
| (vi) GPF | [ ] | [ ] | [ ] | [ ] | [ ] | [ ] |
| 8. Preparation of Budget | [ ] | [ ] | [ ] | [ ] | [ ] | [ ] |
| 9. House Keeping | [ ] | [ ] | [ ] | [ ] | [ ] | [ ] |
| 10. Store Pur- chase and Inventory Mgt. | [ ] | [ ] | [ ] | [ ] | [ ] | [ ] |
| 11. Implementation of Official Language | [ ] | [ ] | [ ] | [ ] | [ ] | [ ] |
| 12. Arranging Meetings, Participation and Preparation of Minutes | [ ] | [ ] | [ ] | [ ] | [ ] | [ ] |

| | | | | | | |
|---|---|---|---|---|---|---|
| 13. Report Writing | [ ] | [ ] | [ ] | [ ] | [ ] | [ ] |
| 14. Management Techniques (O&M and Work-Study) | [ ] | [ ] | [ ] | [ ] | [ ] | [ ] |
| 15. Computer Usage | [ ] | [ ] | [ ] | [ ] | [ ] | [ ] |

## Part II

I. Based on specific work/cases assigned after attending the Foundational programme what do you think the degree of relevance of rules/procedures and skill discussed at the programme to your work situation:

| | |
|---|---|
| Has the direct relevance | [ ] |
| has indirect relevance | [ ] |
| only some of the things have relevance | [ ] |
| has no relevance | [ ] |

II. Please answer the following questions by indicating your choice in the appropriate columns:

| | *Yes* | *No* | *Undecided* |
|---|---|---|---|
| 1. Has the course, generally, provided required knowledge/ skill for your job | [ ] | [ ] | [ ] |
| 2. Do you feel confident and well-equipped to handle various problems on your desk | [ ] | [ ] | [ ] |
| 3. Has the course placed too much emphasis on such rules/ procedures as were of little practical value to you. | [ ] | [ ] | [ ] |
| 4. Did the course cater to what your Department/Section expected out of it | [ ] | [ ] | [ ] |
| 5. Did the course create an interest for individual learning | [ ] | [ ] | [ ] |

| | | | |
|---|---|---|---|
| 6. Did you derive benefits through your interaction with other participants from various Ministries | [ ] | [ ] | [ ] |
| 7. Did you feel restricted by the convention/procedures already prevalent in your Section | [ ] | [ ] | [ ] |
| 8. Do the office atmosphere favour innovations | [ ] | [ ] | [ ] |
| 9. Do your officers stimulate and approve innovations | [ ] | [ ] | [ ] |
| 10. Do you think, you could learn more by working on the job, and training makes little difference | [ ] | [ ] | [ ] |
| 11. Do you think, you could learn more from books and self-study than from attending training course | [ ] | [ ] | [ ] |

IV. Does any particular strength or weakness in the programme stand out in your mind? Please specify

V. Suggest how your training in ISTM could have been more useful to your organization.

Signature

Date:

**APPENDIX 5.5.e**

## FOLLOW-UP QUESTIONNAIRE (PARTICIPANT)

Section Officers (Refresher) Course

1. Name:
2. Ministry/Department/Office:
3. No. and date of the SO(Ref) Course attended:
4. Section in which posted:
5. Name & Designation of immediate boss:

6. Brief description of duties:

### Part I

I. Various topics were covered in the Refreshers' Course you attended at ISTM. Kindly indicate against the space provided for each whether the inputs covered under these topics helped you in better performance in your job, and if not, the reasons thereof, by putting an "**x**" in the appropriate column:

| *Topic covered in the course* | *Did it, anyway contribute to better performance in your job* | | *If 'no', indicate the reason by putting an 'x' in the appropriate box from column 3,4,5 and 6* | | | |
|---|---|---|---|---|---|---|
| | *Yes* | *No* | *Function does not relate to the job* | *Training inputs insufficient or not related to the work situation* | *Organizational cons-traints* | *Individual cons-traints* |
| 1 | 2 | | 3 | 4 | 5 | 6 |
| 1. Role and functions of S.O. | [ ] | [ ] | [ ] | [ ] | [ ] | [ ] |
| 2. Organization Theory | [ ] | [ ] | [ ] | [ ] | [ ] | [ ] |
| 3. Decision Making | [ ] | [ ] | [ ] | [ ] | [ ] | [ ] |
| 4. Cabinet Note | [ ] | [ ] | [ ] | [ ] | [ ] | [ ] |

| | | | | | | |
|---|---|---|---|---|---|---|
| 5. Agenda and Minutes of Meeting | [ ] | [ ] | [ ] | [ ] | [ ] | [ ] |
| 6. Parliament questions/ assurances | [ ] | [ ] | [ ] | [ ] | [ ] | [ ] |
| 7. Dealing with established matters regarding: | | | | | | |
| (i) Recruitment Rules | [ ] | [ ] | [ ] | [ ] | [ ] | [ ] |
| (ii) Confirma-tion | [ ] | [ ] | [ ] | [ ] | [ ] | [ ] |
| (iii) Seniority rules | [ ] | [ ] | [ ] | [ ] | [ ] | [ ] |
| (iv) Consult with UPSC | [ ] | [ ] | [ ] | [ ] | [ ] | [ ] |
| 8. Deptl. Security Instructions | [ ] | [ ] | [ ] | [ ] | [ ] | [ ] |
| 9. Economic Liberalisation | [ ] | [ ] | [ ] | [ ] | [ ] | [ ] |
| 10. Computer Application | [ ] | [ ] | [ ] | [ ] | [ ] | [ ] |
| 11. Budget | [ ] | [ ] | [ ] | [ ] | [ ] | [ ] |
| 12. Project Planning | [ ] | [ ] | [ ] | [ ] | [ ] | [ ] |
| 13. Audit Paras/ Objections | [ ] | [ ] | [ ] | [ ] | [ ] | [ ] |
| 14. Store Purchases | [ ] | [ ] | [ ] | [ ] | [ ] | [ ] |
| 15. Effective Supervision | [ ] | [ ] | [ ] | [ ] | [ ] | [ ] |
| 16. Performance appraisal | [ ] | [ ] | [ ] | [ ] | [ ] | [ ] |
| 17. Grievance Handling | [ ] | [ ] | [ ] | [ ] | [ ] | [ ] |
| 18. JCM | [ ] | [ ] | [ ] | [ ] | [ ] | [ ] |
| 19. Reservation in Services | [ ] | [ ] | [ ] | [ ] | [ ] | [ ] |

| | | | | | | |
|---|---|---|---|---|---|---|
| 20. Official Language Policy | [ ] | [ ] | [ ] | [ ] | [ ] | [ ] |
| 21. Records Management | [ ] | [ ] | [ ] | [ ] | [ ] | [ ] |

**Part II**

I. Based on specific work/cases assigned after attending the Refreshers' course what do you think the degree of relevance of rules/procedures and skill discussed at the programme to your work situation:

| | |
|---|---|
| Has direct relevance | [ ] |
| has indirect relevance | [ ] |
| only some of the things have relevance | [ ] |
| has no relevance | [ ] |

II. Comparing to your pre-training work-performance with that after training please indicate:

| | Increased | Same as before | Undecided | Decreased |
|---|---|---|---|---|
| 1. Your overall feeling of satisfaction in your work | [ ] | [ ] | [ ] | [ ] |
| 2. Your efficiency to examining cases/problems and apply correct rules | [ ] | [ ] | [ ] | [ ] |
| 3. Your ability to supervise the work of the Section | [ ] | [ ] | [ ] | [ ] |
| 4. Your efficiency in dealing with your boss and peers | [ ] | [ ] | [ ] | [ ] |
| 5. Number of cases examined and submitted to higher officers which received approval without major change | [ ] | [ ] | [ ] | [ ] |
| 6. Amount of work assigned to you by your boss | [ ] | [ ] | [ ] | [ ] |

| | | | | |
|---|---|---|---|---|
| 7. Seeking your opinion/ views by your boss before taking a decision on a case other than submitted by you | [ ] | [ ] | [ ] | [ ] |

III. Please indicate your choice for each of the statement listed

| | *Yes* | *Undecided* | *No* |
|---|---|---|---|
| 1. Has the SO(Ref) Course improved your skill/ efficiency in the job | [ ] | [ ] | [ ] |
| 2. The programme placed too much emphasis on such rules/procedures as were of little practical value to you | [ ] | [ ] | [ ] |
| 3. The programme did not cater to what your Department/Section expected to get out of it | [ ] | [ ] | [ ] |
| 4. Do you feel more confident and better equipped to deal with various cases/ problems on your desk | [ ] | [ ] | [ ] |
| 5. The course has raised your personal goals and aspirations | [ ] | [ ] | [ ] |
| 6. The programme has infused lot of self-confidence in you | [ ] | [ ] | [ ] |
| 7. Did the course offer you opportunities to be more open minded | [ ] | [ ] | [ ] |
| 8. The programme created an interest for individual learning | [ ] | [ ] | [ ] |
| 9. Did you derive any benefits through your interaction with | [ ] | [ ] | [ ] |

| | | | |
|---|---|---|---|
| other Section Officers from various Ministries/Deptts. | | | |
| 10. What you learnt at ISTM, is it sufficiently similar to your job characteristic in your Deptt. | [ ] | [ ] | [ ] |
| 11. Do you feel restricted by the convention/procedure prevalent in your Section | [ ] | [ ] | [ ] |
| 12. Does the office atmosphere favour innovations | [ ] | [ ] | [ ] |
| 13. Officers learn more by working on the desk and training makes little difference | [ ] | [ ] | [ ] |

IV. Does any particular strength or weakness in the programme stand out in your mind? Please specify.

V. What is your general reaction to the training programme you attended?

**APPENDIX 5.5.f**

## FOLLOW-UP QUESTIONNAIRE (PARTICIPANT)
## Professional Development Course for Under Secretaries

1. Name:
2. Ministry/Department/Office:
3. No. and date of the PDP Course attended:
4. Division in which posted:
5. Name & Designation of immediate boss:

______________________________

6. Brief description of duties:

______________________________

### Part I

I. Various topics were covered in the PDP Course you attended at ISTM. Kindly indicate against the space provided for each whether the inputs covered under these topics helped you in better performance in your job, and if not, the reasons thereof, by putting an "**x**" in the appropriate column:

| *Topic covered in the course* | *Did it, anyway contribute to better performance in your job* | | *If 'no', indicate the reason by putting an 'x' in the appropriate box from column 3,4,5 and 6* | | | |
|---|---|---|---|---|---|---|
| | *Yes* | *No* | *Function does not relate to the job* | *Training inputs insufficient or not related to the work situation* | *Organi-zational cons-traints* | *Indivi-dual cons-traints* |
| 1, | 2 | | 3 | 4 | 5 | 6 |
| 1. Role and Functions of Branch Officers | [ ] | [ ] | [ ] | [ ] | [ ] | [ ] |
| 2. Administrative Vigilance | [ ] | [ ] | [ ] | [ ] | [ ] | [ ] |
| 3. Performance Appraisal | [ ] | [ ] | [ ] | [ ] | [ ] | [ ] |
| 4. Reservation in Services | [ ] | [ ] | [ ] | [ ] | [ ] | [ ] |
| 5. Joint Consultative Machinery | [ ] | [ ] | [ ] | [ ] | [ ] | [ ] |

| | | | | | | |
|---|---|---|---|---|---|---|
| 6. Grievance Handling | [ ] | [ ] | [ ] | [ ] | [ ] | [ ] |
| 7. Records Management | [ ] | [ ] | [ ] | [ ] | [ ] | [ ] |
| 8. Management by Objectives | [ ] | [ ] | [ ] | [ ] | [ ] | [ ] |
| 9. Time Management | [ ] | [ ] | [ ] | [ ] | [ ] | [ ] |
| 10. Decision Making | [ ] | [ ] | [ ] | [ ] | [ ] | [ ] |
| 11. Role of Public Administration | [ ] | [ ] | [ ] | [ ] | [ ] | [ ] |
| 12. Leadership Styles | [ ] | [ ] | [ ] | [ ] | [ ] | [ ] |
| 13. Motivating self and Subordinates | [ ] | [ ] | [ ] | [ ] | [ ] | [ ] |
| 14. Effective Commu-nication | [ ] | [ ] | [ ] | [ ] | [ ] | [ ] |
| 15. Team Building | [ ] | [ ] | [ ] | [ ] | [ ] | [ ] |
| 16. Management of Stress | [ ] | [ ] | [ ] | [ ] | [ ] | [ ] |
| 17. Organizational Creativity and Changes | [ ] | [ ] | [ ] | [ ] | [ ] | [ ] |
| 18. Current Economic Environment | [ ] | [ ] | [ ] | [ ] | [ ] | [ ] |
| 19. Investment Decisions | [ ] | [ ] | [ ] | [ ] | [ ] | [ ] |
| 20. Management Accounting and Audit | [ ] | [ ] | [ ] | [ ] | [ ] | [ ] |
| 21. Role of Internal Finance Adviser | [ ] | [ ] | [ ] | [ ] | [ ] | [ ] |

| | | | | | | |
|---|---|---|---|---|---|---|
| 22. Project Planning and Appraisal | [ ] | [ ] | [ ] | [ ] | [ ] | [ ] |
| 23. Wasteland/ Watershed Development Programme | [ ] | [ ] | [ ] | [ ] | [ ] | [ ] |
| 24. Computer Application | [ ] | [ ] | [ ] | [ ] | [ ] | [ ] |

## Part II

I. Based on specific work/cases assigned after attending the Professional Development Programme what do you think the degree of relevance of rules/procedures and skill discussed at the programme to your work situation:

| | |
|---|---|
| Has the direct relevance | [ ] |
| has indirect relevance | [ ] |
| only some of the things have relevance | [ ] |
| has no relevance | [ ] |

II. Comparing to your pre-training work-performance with that after training please indicate:

| | Increased | Same as before | Undeci-ded | Decrea-sed |
|---|---|---|---|---|
| 1. Your overall feeling of satisfaction in your work | [ ] | [ ] | [ ] | [ ] |
| 2. Your efficiency to examining cases/problems and apply correct rules | [ ] | [ ] | [ ] | [ ] |
| 3. Your ability to take decisions on cases/problems | [ ] | [ ] | [ ] | [ ] |
| 4. Your efficiency in dealing with your boss and peers | [ ] | [ ] | [ ] | [ ] |
| 5. Number of cases examined and submitted to higher officers which received approval without major change | [ ] | [ ] | [ ] | [ ] |

| | | | | | |
|---|---|---|---|---|---|
| 6. | Amount of work assigned to you by your boss | [ ] | [ ] | [ ] | [ ] |
| 7. | Seeking your opinion/ views by your boss before taking a decision on a case other than submitted by you | [ ] | [ ] | [ ] | [ ] |

III. Please indicate your choice for each of the statement listed

| | | *Yes* | *Undecided* | *No* |
|---|---|---|---|---|
| 1. | Has the PDP Course improved your skill/ efficiency in the job | [ ] | [ ] | [ ] |
| 2. | The programme placed too much emphasis on such rules/procedures as were of little practical value to you | [ ] | [ ] | [ ] |
| 3. | The programme did not cater to what your Department/Section expected to get out of it | [ ] | [ ] | [ ] |
| 4. | Do you feel more confident and better equipped to deal with various cases/ problems on your desk | [ ] | [ ] | [ ] |
| 5. | Has your attending the programme improved your status in the Division | [ ] | [ ] | [ ] |
| 6. | The course has raised your personal goals and aspirations | [ ] | [ ] | [ ] |
| 7. | Do you find any change in your personal development | [ ] | [ ] | [ ] |
| 8. | The programme has infused a lot of self-confidence in you | [ ] | [ ] | [ ] |
| 9. | Did the course after your opportunities to be more open minded | [ ] | [ ] | [ ] |

| | | | |
|---|---|---|---|
| 10. The programme created an interest for individual learning | [ ] | [ ] | [ ] |
| 11. Did you derive any benefits through your interaction with other Under Secretaries from various Ministries/Deptts. | [ ] | [ ] | [ ] |
| 12. What you learnt at ISTM, is it sufficiently similar to your job characteristic in your Deptt. | [ ] | [ ] | [ ] |
| 13. Do you feel restricted by the convention/procedure prevalent in your Deptt. | [ ] | [ ] | [ ] |
| 14. Does the office atmosphere favour innovations | [ ] | [ ] | [ ] |
| 15. Officers learn more by working on the desk and training makes little difference | [ ] | [ ] | [ ] |
| 16. Officers could learn more from books and self-study than from attending training courses | [ ] | [ ] | [ ] |

IV. Does any particular strength or weakness in the programme stand out in your mind? Please specify.

V. What is your general reaction to the training programme you attended.

Signature

Date:

# BIBLIOGRAPHY


A-Shaleh, Abdel-Fata. *Training Administration in India*, Jaipur: Arihant Publishing House, 1994.

Bennett, Roger. *Improving Trainer Effectiveness.* UK, Gower Publishing Company, 1988.

Bhatnagar O.P. *Evaluation Methodology for Training: Theory and Practice.* New Delhi: Oxford and IBH, 1987.

Boydell ,T.M. *Guide to the Identification of Training Needs.* London, BACIA, 1971.

Buckley, Roger and Jim Caple. *The Theory and Practice of Training.* London: Kogan Page Ltd., 1992.

Byers, Kenneth T.(Ed.) *Employee Training and Development in Public Service.* Toronto: Institute of Public Administration, 1958.

Callard, Keith B. *Employees Training and Development in the Public Service.* Toronto: Toronto Institute of Public Administration,1958.

Chakravarty, A.N. *Evaluation of Training Programme—a Study (Training Monograph).* New Delhi: Institute of Secretariat Training and Management, 1989.

Chaturvedi, T.N. *Training in Public Administration: The Changing Perspectives.* New Delhi: IIPA, 1969.

———— *Training in Public Administration.* New Delhi IIPA,1989.

Commonwealth Secretariat, *Effective Use of Training Methodologies :Report and Recommendations.* London: Commonwealth Secretariat, Marlborough House, 1979.

Craig, Bittel. *Training & Development Handbook (ASTD).*

Dayal, Iswar. *New Perspectives for Public Administration in India.* New Delhi: Training Division, Government of India, 1975.

——— *"Methodology of Civil Service Training in India"*. IJPA: XXXIV, 1988.

Denvova, Charles. *Test Construction for Training Evaluation. 1979.*

Dey, Bata K., *Personnel Administration in India,*

Goldstein, I.L. *Training Programme Development and Evaluation.* California: Cole Publishing, 1874.

Goyal, Rajni. *State Civil Service Training in India.* Jaipur: RBSA Publishers, 1988.

Hamblin, A.C. *Evaluation and Control of Training.* London: Mc Graw Hill, 1974.

*Home Affairs Ministry of, Administrative Reforms Commission on Training,* 1969.

ILO. *An Introductory Course in Teaching and Training.* International Labour Organisation (ILO), 1981.

ILO. *Introductory Courses in Teaching and Training.* Methods for Management Development, Geneva: ILO, 1977.

Joneja, G.C.L. *Training of Public Services in Developing Society.* Mussoorie: LBS National Academy of Administration, 1979.

Kenny, John and Margaret A. Reid. *Training Interventions.* IPM, 1987.

Kumar, Ramesh and Jagdish C. Kukar. *Training and Administrative Development.* Jaipur: HCM State Institute of Public Administration, 1979.

Lynton, R.L. and Udai Pareek, *Training for Development.* Bombay: B. Taraporewala Sons & Co., 1973.

Mathur, H.M. *Training of Civil Servants in India.*

Anisuzzaman, Md. *Training for Public Services.* Dacca: National Institute of Public Administration, 1969.

Michalak, Donald and Edwin G. Yager. *Making the Training Process Work.* London: Harper & Row Publishers, 1979.

Miller , Vincent A. *The Guidebook for International Trainers,*

Misra , B.B. *Government and Bureaucracy in India 1947-1976.* Delhi: Oxford University Press, 1986.

Paul, Chowdhry D. *Training Methodology and Management,*

Rae, Leslie, *The Skills of Training,*

Ramaswami, N. *A Handbook of Training and Development.* New Delhi: T.R. Publications, 1992.

Reilly, Wyn. *Training Administrators for Development: An Introduction to Public Service,*

Rhodes, Raw, *Training in Civil Service.* London: Joint University Council for Social and Public Administration, 1977.

Richter, L. *Training Needs: Assessment and Monitoring.* I.L.O., 1986.

Saxena, A.P. *"Accountibility in Training of Administration". Indian Journal of Public Administration,* July-Sept. 1983.

Saxena, A.P. "Training and Development in Government". New Delhi: IIPA, 1974.

————"Training in Government—Objectives & Opportunities". New Delhi: IIPA, 1985.

————"Some Issues in Post-training Evaluation." *Prashasanika,* July-Dec., 1973.

Schaffer, Bernard. *Administrative Training and Development—A Comparative Study.* Washington: Praeger Publishers, 1974.

Singh, Jaideep, *"Case Studies for Training in Public Administration: A Report.* New Delhi, IIPA, 1982.

Sinker, Paul. "Problems of Recruitment and Training of Civil Servants in the UK". New Delhi: IIPA, 1955.

Swaroop, S.N. *"Identifying Training Needs in Central Ministries*—Management in Government, New Delhi, Deptt. of Administrative Reforms, Government of India, 1986.

Tickner, F.J. *Modern Staff Training: A Survey of Training Needs and Methods of Today.* London: University of London Press, 1952.

Tracey W.R. *Designing Training and Development System.* Bombay Taraporevala Publishing Industries (P) Ltd., 1977.

United Nations, *Handbook of Training in the Public Service.* New York: United Nations Publication, 1966.

Virmani, B.R. and Pramilla Seth. *Evaluating Management Training and Development.* Hyderabad: Vision Books, 1985.

Whitelaw, M. *"Evaluation of Management Training—A Review."* London: Institute of Personnel Management, 1972.

# Index